2002

Caring for Kids in Communities

STUDIES IN THE
POSTMODERN THEORY OF EDUCATION

Joe L. Kincheloe and Shirley R. Steinberg
General Editors

Vol. 12

PETER LANG
New York • Washington, D.C./Baltimore • Bern
Frankfurt am Main • Berlin • Brussels • Vienna • Oxford

Julia Ellis, Jan Small-McGinley,
& Lucy De Fabrizio

Caring for Kids
in Communities

Using Mentorship, Peer Support, & Student
Leadership Programs in Schools

PETER LANG
New York • Washington, D.C./Baltimore • Bern
Frankfurt am Main • Berlin • Brussels • Vienna • Oxford

LIBRARY OF CONGRESS CATALOGING-IN-PUBLICATION DATA

Ellis, Julia.
Caring for kids in communities: using mentorship, peer support, and student leadership
programs in schools / Julia Ellis, Jan Small-McGinley, Lucy De Fabrizio.
p. cm. — (Counterpoints; vol. 12)
Includes bibliographical references.
1. Group work in education. 2. Peer-group tutoring of students. 3. Mentoring
in education. 4. Student participation in administration. 5. Educational
leadership. I. Small-McGinley, Jan. II. De Fabrizio, Lucy.
III. Title. IV. Counterpoints (New York, N.Y.); vol. 12.
LB1032 .E43   371.102–dc21   00-049729
ISBN 0-8204-1834-X
ISSN 1058-1634

DIE DEUTSCHE BIBLIOTHEK-CIP-EINHEITSAUFNAHME

Ellis, Julia:
Caring for kids in communities: using mentorship, peer support, and student leadership
programs in schools / Julia Ellis; Jan Small-McGinley; Lucy De Fabrizio.
–New York; Washington, D.C./Baltimore; Bern;
Frankfurt am Main; Berlin; Brussels; Vienna; Oxford: Lang.
(Counterpoints; Vol. 12)
ISBN 0-8204-1834-X

Cover art by jan jagodzinski, University of Alberta
Cover design by Lisa Dillon

The paper in this book meets the guidelines for permanence and durability
of the Committee on Production Guidelines for Book Longevity
of the Council of Library Resources.

Printed in the United States of America

ॐ

For
Corinna, Craig and Mark
Patrick and Janelle
Doug and Alex

ॐ

❧ Contents ☙

❧ Tables ☙

ಬಾ Acknowledgments ೀ

I t is difficult to properly acknowledge our debts for the research represented in this text. We owe so much to so many—students, mentors, parents, teachers, program coordinators, and school administrators—who participated in our research by sharing their experiences with us or working collaboratively with us to develop new programs.

We were fortunate to find several programs that had been in operation for five or seven years. Coordinators, participants, and "graduates" of such programs were able to clearly identify the benefits and useful practices developed over time.

Similarly, coordinators of newer programs who were still reflecting on the trial and error of the first two years contributed fresh insights about how to enable activities to work well for all participants and the school as a whole.

Very importantly, schools that worked with us to develop new programs afforded us the opportunity to learn with them at each step of the way. Through the support of these schools we were able to involve all program participants in our research and to "take up residence" in the schools while completing intensive case studies of selected participants.

We are very grateful to each person who shared their experience in our research. Each one helped us understand the ways that mentorship, peer support, and student leadership programs in schools work to support students in forming important relationships and developing new competencies and predispositions.

We also wish to express our thanks to series editors Shirley Steinberg and Joe Kincheloe who have generously provided mentorship and peer support to so many.

Chapters 2, 3, and 5 were originally presented at the National Canadian Childhood Conference, November 4, 1997, held in Edmonton, Alberta. An earlier version of these chapters and the Appendices were first published in *Volunteer Mentorship Programs K–12*, by the Alberta Teachers' Association, Edmonton, Alberta in 1998 and in *Volunteer Mentorship Programs: A Practical Handbook*, also published by the Alberta Teachers' Association, Edmonton, Alberta in 1999. An earlier version of Chapter 3 was first published in *Reaching Today's Youth: The Community Circle of Caring Journal, August 1999.*

Chapter 4 was originally presented at the Literacy in the 21ˢᵗ Century Conference at the University of Alberta, October 24, 1997. The paper was first published in the *Alberta Journal of Educational Research, 44*(2).

Chapters 6, 7, 8, and 9 were presented at the Canadian Society for Studies in Education (CSSE), in Edmonton, Alberta, May 23, 2000.

Chapters 10, 11, 12, 13, and 14 were presented at the Canadian Society for Studies in Education (CSSE), Edmonton, Alberta, May 24, 2000.

Chapters 15, 16, and 17 were presented at the North Central Teachers' Convention in Edmonton, Alberta, on February 9, 1999. An earlier draft of these chapters appeared in *Peer Support and Student Leadership Programs*, published by the Alberta Teachers' Association in Edmonton, Alberta, in 1998. An earlier version of Chapter 17 was published in *The Canadian Association of Principals' Journal, 8*(2).

❧ Chapter One ☙

INTRODUCTION AND OVERVIEW

Caring for children and youth more collectively in communities requires many and varied interlocking initiatives. In the large work that is to be done, schools can play a major role by both supporting caring school climates and providing students with more relationships with adults. While schools may understand student learning to be their mandate, it is undeniable that children learn better when they feel cared for and, like most people, behave better when they care for those around them and wish to preserve relationships with these others. Many kinds of mentorship, peer support, and student leadership programs can be used by schools to systematically ensure a number of sources of support for the growth of all students generally and for targeted students in particular.

The Importance of Belonging and Attachment

In an examination of what communities need to do to raise caring and responsible children and adolescents, Benson (1997) has mapped a framework of developmental assets that he calls building blocks of human development. He identifies *external assets* as support, empowerment, boundaries and expectations, and constructive use of time, and *internal assets* as commitment to learning, positive values, social competencies, and positive identity. He notes that the *external asset* of support—opportunities to experience love, affirmation, and acceptance—appears to be instrumental in a number of developmental outcomes, including internalization of boundaries and values, taking action to help others, and development of empathy and self-esteem.

Many psychologists and educational reformers such as Pestalozzi (Green, 1913), Adler (1939), Bandura (1977), Bowlby (1973), Glasser (1986), and Maslow (1971) have recognized love, belonging, or secure attachments as the keystone of a solid foundation for a child's development. In Native American tribal wisdom, the Circle of Courage includes the four quadrants or principles of *belonging, mastery, independence,* and *generosity* (Brokenleg, 1998). Brendtro and Long (1995), who have worked with violent youth for over 30 years, have come to understand these principles as basic developmental needs for children and have referred to them as the needs for *attachment, achievement, autonomy*, and *altruism*. Attachments are relationships that grow out of consistent love, encouragement, comfort, affirmation and mutually gratifying interaction. Given that attachment entails mutuality and provides the affirmation and encouragement for the child to try new tasks and gain confidence, its role in contributing to achievement, autonomy and altruism seems obvious. Ample research has also given evidence of the converse—that in the absence of secure attachments or healthy relationships with caregivers, learning, problem-solving, self-esteem, social skills, self-control, and empathy are impaired. Research literature is replete with painful stories of the rage, despair, delinquency, and violence of young people who experienced abandonment, rejection, abuse, or other forms of broken belongings rather than connection with and nurturance from caregivers.

Perhaps especially within the last quarter century, Western culture has tended to view parents alone as primarily responsible for the love and nurturance of their children and for providing them with secure attachment. Clearly, by itself, this is not a realistic expectation. Some parents, or some parents at some times, may lack the skills and resources for effective caregiving or may be overwhelmed at times with life's complexities. Even when parents do a fine job, they alone may not be enough. Children also need significant attachments with adults who are not their parents, such as extended family members, interactive neighbors, coaches, or other adults who consistently show interest in them. Because children must be in school for a large portion of the day, and because feeling cared for will support their academic achievement, it makes sense for schools to coordinate programs that will facilitate caring relationships with peers and adults.

K–12 and Sensitive Periods

In reviewing the directions communities need to take to care for kids, Benson (1997) identified a number of culture shifts that need to occur. A few of these suggestions were:

- move from talking about children and youth in terms of *deficits* to talking about them in terms of what is being promoted vis-à-vis positive attributes and community connections
- move from a focus on troubled and troubling youth to a focus on all children and adolescents
- move from a focus on ages 0 to 5 to a focus on ages 0 to 18
- move from age segregation to an intergenerational community

These are key ideas that can usefully inform discussions and plans for ensuring a caring climate in schools and providing students with more attachments for support.

In the past, remedial programs or other interventions have mainly been offered to students after their learning and/or behavioral difficulties have been clearly demonstrated and identified. This has usually occurred after grade 3 (Flaxman & Ascher, 1992). Very often these programs were too late to be significantly effective. Researchers have come to recognize the unique importance of the early school years as a sensitive period in establishing the developmental infrastructure on which later experience will build. Pianta and Walsh (1996) have explained this phenomenon as follows.

> Minor adjustments to the child's trajectory of adaptation in the early years of school can have major effects on the child's later path through school and life.... [During sensitive periods in development] certain capacities [skills, knowledge, and attitudes critical for school success] are formed that feed forward (Ford & Ford, 1987) into later competencies developed by the child. That is, the effect of developing (or not) these capacities is not necessarily evident within the sensitive period, but becomes increasingly evident later, as demands for performance that builds on these early capacities increase. (pp. 29–30)

Awareness of the importance of the early school years in children's development gives good reason to consider providing exceptional support for all students during these years. Smith (1996) has referred to this early establishment of the child's trajectory of adaptation to school as the "unborn curriculum." Research has shown that how students relate to school tasks, the school environment, and to themselves as learners is well established by grade 3 (Alexander & Entwistle, 1988, as cited in Pianta & Walsh, 1996). One can speculate that other sets of years may also be sensitive periods for the development of different kinds of capacities. For example, secondary school counselors have found that those students who are able and inclined to work in peer support programs are young people who have fulfilled similar responsibilities in earlier years. Thus it could be suggested that the middle school or junior high years may be a sensitive period for the development of various kinds of leadership and organizational capacities such as interpersonal communication, group problem solving, self-confidence, planning, commitment and persistence, community-mindedness, and altruism.

If students do not experience adequate support during sensitive periods, how effective can later interventions be? Flaxman and Ascher (1992) noted that by the 1980s, most compensatory education and youth employment programs were viewed as only marginally successful in forestalling academic failure or dropping out of school, or in making youth employable for anything but low-skill jobs. They critiqued previous intervention programs for having focused solely on imparting skills or manipulating the youth's motivations, attitudes, or behaviors, rather than working with the young people as "complex, physical, psychological and social beings in environments and institutions over which they had little control" (p. 2). Any caring and help that was provided to recipients in these programs was fortuitous and unplanned and not considered part of the programs' effects. Mentoring, by contrast, is conceptualized as a more whole way to respond to the whole child or youth.

The Notion of Mentoring

> Unlike traditional teaching where everyone is supposed to learn the same curriculum, often at the same pace—despite personal interests, abilities, or conflicts—mentoring asks that these very interests and conflicts be the heart of the relationship between the adult and the youth. Thus, personalized care and attention to individual needs lie at the core of mentoring. (Flaxman & Ascher, 1992, p. 11)

Brodkin and Coleman (1996) have defined "mentor" as "one who provides one-to-one support and attention, is a friend and a role model, boosts a child's self-esteem, enhances a student's educational experience" (p. 21). "Mentoring" is described as "meeting regularly over an extended period of time with the goal of enabling a special bond of mutual commitment based on the development of respect, communication and personal growth" (p. 21). In this conception of mentoring, the expected outcomes are both enhanced self-esteem and educational experience. It is expected that the mentor will be experienced as a friend and not just a tutor. It is also expected that the mentor will enhance the young person's educational experience in ways that go beyond recreational pursuits.

Flaxman and Ascher (1992) state that the heart of natural or spontaneous mentoring has always been to provide assistance during a period of transition, such as that from childhood to adolescence or from novice to expert, and that the goal of mentoring is to help the child or youth gain social learning and command over tasks of their everyday life in school, work, or society. This occurs through jointly carried-out activities in which the mentor alternately models, teaches, manages, questions, and structures a task for the child/youth.

These definitions work well to show how the concept of mentoring in fact entails addressing the needs of the child or youth for *attachment, achievement, autonomy,* and *altruism.* As Brendtro and Long (1995) have argued, any program developed for a child or youth should begin with a holistic appreciation of the child's life circumstances and the particular support needs for attachment, achievement, autonomy, or altruism. As mentors cultivate friendly, conversational relationships with their mentees, they become increasingly aware of what is already in place and what would constitute the highest priority contributions to the mentee's growth.

An understanding of mentorship can also be usefully informed by Fromm's (1956) model of the four elements that are common to positive relationships: caring, responsibility, respect, and knowledge. Caring entails concern for the life and growth of the person in the relationship. Responsibility means being ready to act to meet the needs, expressed or unexpressed, of another human being. Respect entails having the ability to see an individual as s/he is and allowing that person to develop without exploitation. Knowledge includes not a superficial awareness but genuine understanding of the other's feelings, even if they are not readily apparent. Mentors begin with a willingness to care for the life and growth of the younger person. As will be illustrated in later chapters, once mentors acquire knowledge of the child, that knowledge gives focus and direction for caring and responsibility and enables the exercise of respect, which requires recognition of the child's limits, feelings, and responses.

Finally, a discussion of the notion of mentoring would not be complete without acknowledging the deep reciprocity at work in mentorship relationships. Fromm (1956; as cited in Yamamoto, 1988, p. 188) has articulated the nature of giving that takes place in mentoring relationships, explaining that as the mentor gives of what is alive in him or her, s/he enhances the other's sense of aliveness, which in turn reflects back to the mentor and enhances his or her sense of aliveness.

> He gives of himself, of the most precious he has, he gives of his life,…he gives him of that which is alive in him; he gives him of his joy, of his interest, of his understanding, of his knowledge, of his humor, of his sadness—of all expressions and manifestations of that which is alive in him. In thus giving of his life, he enriches the other person, he enhances the other's sense of aliveness. He does not give in order to receive; giving is in itself exquisite joy. But in giving he cannot help bringing something to life in the other person, and this which is brought to life reflects back to him; in truly giving, he cannot help receiving that which is given back to him;…in the act of giving something is born, and both persons involved are grateful for the life that is born for both of them.

We have observed and heard this dynamic in the reports of many mentors. Below are just two examples of how mentors express this phenomenon.

> And just to be able to see that when I walk into the room he knows that it's our time, and he has a big smile on his face and he's very excited. That just gives me a good feeling all over.
> She sees me and she's all happy and smiles.

If there is a magic in mentorship relationships that moves them beyond tutoring, coaching, or supervision, it is perhaps the way in which the aliveness of both parties is enriched as the child or youth reflects back what the mentor has brought to life in him or her.

The Potency of Peer Support and Student Leadership Programs

Peer support and student leadership programs can serve in many ways to support the life and growth needs of both the students participating in a program and the student population of the school. The students who are members of such programs obtain training and experience that supports their own belonging, achievement, autonomy, and altruism. Writing on the topic of "a rightful place," Bettelheim (1994) has argued that belonging, or a rightful place, cannot be granted but only earned through a person's own efforts to make a contribution to the welfare of others.

Members of peer support and student leadership programs provide direct service or assistance of many kinds to the student body and wider community. They also organize activities that enable the entire student body to be helpful to others. Some of the events they organize are simply enjoyable activities that lift spirits for the day and create opportunities for students and staff to interact with each other in good-humored ways. Some of the events are specifically intended to facilitate positive attention to individual members of the student body by the whole school, or to enable students to individually express positive sentiments to other students. As a complex package of services, events, and activities, the work of such programs can provide direct support to individual students, increase school spirit, enhance belonging, and facilitate altruism and commitment to community-minded projects.

Support for All Students and for Targeted Students

When considering a focus on all students, rather than only on students with difficulties, and a focus on grades K–12, it can be useful to think about multiple programs and multiple facets within programs. Table 1 shows how mentorship programs can be employed to provide support for all students and for targeted students. Table 2 gives examples of how the multiple strands or aspects of peer support and student leadership programs can provide support both for all students and for targeted students. These examples are drawn from programs we have researched and reported on in later chapters in this text. In those chapters we endeavor to clarify the benefits of these programs and the practicalities of operating them successfully.

Table 1: Mentorship Programs for All Students or Targeted Students

For All Students

- All students in grades 1 and 2 are assigned a mentor. The program has a literacy emphasis, but lunch hours are used for the sessions and mentors are encouraged to use part of the time for visiting and building a relationship with the child.

- Mentors in a literacy support program are assigned to all children in kindergarten and grade 1 in an inner-city school serving high-needs students.

For Targeted Students in Elementary School

- Mentors in a literacy/math support program are assigned to high-needs students in all grades.

- Grade 4 and 5 boys who come from single-mom homes and who are frequently sent to the vice principal's office for discipline become members of the Good Guys Program. Each week, two of eight men serving as mentors in this program take their turn to do an after-school recreational activity with these boys.

For Targeted Students in Secondary School

- At a secondary school, incoming grade 10 students with a history of poor attendance or isolation at school are matched with mentors (teachers and classified staff who volunteer).

Table 2: Peer Support and Student Leadership Programs Supporting All Students and Targeted Students

Supporting All Students

- In a K–6 school, as part of their health class, all grade 6 students receive the training and invitation to be members of peer support. Thus the growth of all grade 6 students is supported in the areas of communication, self-esteem, leadership and organizational abilities, and altruism.

- The activities or events organized by a peer support program (e.g., retreats, special days, fun contests, fund-raising and drives, love-a-grams, etc.) provide opportunities for relationship building and bonding among all students in the school. In this way, all students have a better opportunity to experience a feeling of belonging in the school.

- Community service activities organized and promoted by a peer support program increase the opportunities for all students in the school to engage in altruistic projects.

- In a junior high where incoming grade 7 students are from a number of feeder schools, the grade 9 peer support members serve as counselors to facilitate bonding among all the grade 7 students at a one-week fun camp in September.

Table continued on next page.

Table continued from previous page.

Supporting Targeted Students in Junior and Senior High

- Services organized or provided by a peer support program can include one-on-one help to other students with organizational and study skills or tutoring for exams.

- New, isolated, or withdrawn students can be assigned a "buddy" from the peer support program.

- One of the responsibilities of peer support program members can be to seek out and support students who are upset or need to talk.

Supporting Targeted Students in Elementary School

- In an elementary school, grade 6 peer support members facilitate positive play among younger students who are otherwise inclined to fight during recess time.

- New, isolated, or withdrawn students can be assigned a "buddy" from the peer support program.

- Grade 6 peer support members serve as cross-age tutors for younger students who struggle academically.

- In a multilingual, inner-city school, same-language/culture grade 1 children serve as "play buddies" for matched kindergarten children three half-days per week.

Overview of Research Conducted

In this text we wish to share our research on a number of school-based programs that provided students with adult attachments, contributed to a climate of caring, or empowered students to care. These took the forms of mentorship programs, peer support programs, and student leadership programs. Over a two-year period (1996–1998) we endeavored to:

- work with schools to collaboratively develop and research mentorship programs for students in the early school years
- locate and study other existing mentorship programs spanning the years of K–12
- locate and study peer support programs spanning the years of K–12
- locate and study student leadership programs

Our intent was not to develop a comprehensive list of existing programs in any specific geographical area, but rather to conduct case studies of a wide range of programs with a view to learning how they work and what their benefits are.

We collected data on each of the programs through whatever means were feasible, including audiotaped and videotaped interviews with program coordinators, students, mentors, parents; students' written narrative reports; and program documents and records. The programs were located in schools in Edmonton, Sherwood Park, Fultonvale, Clive, Lacombe, and Red Deer, Alberta.

We also chose to report on two peer support programs that we found in Ontario and learned about through film or program documents and interviews with program coordinators. Because most of the programs we found and studied had been in operation for five to seven years, the program coordinators were well informed about program benefits and the practicalities of operating such programs successfully.

In the mentorship programs that we helped to develop, we conducted three intensive studies over 18 months on the following questions:

- In a short-term mentorship program (8–10 weeks) with minimal training and structure for mentors, do the mentors and children achieve mutually satisfying relationships and are the mentors effective in providing academic support to the children?
- How does the mentor's pedagogy work? What informs or guides the mentor's instructional planning and decision making? To what extent is the mentor's pedagogy shaped by the child or the child's responses?
- How do the mentors and children develop their relationships? What are the dynamics or key components of nonrelated adults cultivating relationships with young children in one-hour-per-week mentorship sessions over an 8-to-10-week period?

These research questions were considered important given that the schedules of schools and available mentors make short-term programs most feasible. Further, there is little research available on mentorship programs for young children and little in-depth qualitative research on mentorship programs for older students. The findings from these three studies were expected to clarify the potential value of such programs and the processes for their successful implementation. An understanding of the dynamics of mentoring young children would be useful to program developers who must make many decisions about the structure, resources, and support for such programs.

Organization of the Text

This text is organized into two parts, with Part One focusing on mentorship programs and Part Two presenting our research on peer support and student leadership programs.

Part One: Mentorship Programs

In Part One we present our research on school-based programs using adults as volunteer mentors for students. In Section A of Part One we describe six mentorship programs spanning K–12, outlining their histories, organizational structures, and benefits. Evaluation reports for three of these programs are included as well as guidelines for starting literacy mentorship programs in elementary schools.

Chapter 2 outlines the operation and benefits of five mentorship programs in elementary schools. Two of these were programs we initiated collaboratively with the schools. Another two were programs operated by individual teachers for their own classrooms. Both of these programs engaged retirees or grandparents as mentors and used a single time block each week for the sessions. The fifth program, the Good Guys Program, was for grades 4 and 5 boys from single-mom homes. Grade 8 students who were graduates of this program advised us that such a program would also be welcomed by junior high students.

Chapter 3 presents our research on the mentorship program for grade 10 students who were considered at risk of dropping out before completing high school. Mentors were teachers and classified staff members at the school. The data for this study included seven-year longitudinal data collected by the program coordinator and our videotaped interviews with mentor pairs and the program coordinator. Sample standardized documents and support materials needed for operating this program are included in the Appendices.

During the first four months of our development work with mentorship programs in the early school years, we tried to learn whether such short-term programs with little training or structure for mentors could have value for participants. Most mentors had only one orientation session and a few handout materials, and they were asked to spend one hour a week with the child to visit, read and write together, and do art or games related to reading or math. In Chapter 4 we present our evaluation of the two literacy mentorship programs we helped to develop—one for grades 1 and 2 in a school with an early literacy emphasis and one for a kindergarten class in an inner-city school with a high-needs student population. This chapter also reviews issues related to both mentorship and early reading intervention.

Chapter 5 has been written to provide guidelines for beginning literacy mentorship programs in elementary schools. It is based on our research with the two programs we collaboratively developed and our interviews with other teachers who have been operating mentorship programs in their classrooms. Sample program documents and support materials are included in the Appendices.

In Sections B and C of Part One, we present research from the second and third terms of our literacy mentorship program for the early school years. In the first research segment with this program, our study focused on whether this model had promise. That is, if mentors came to the school for one hour a week for eight weeks to work with a child in kindergarten, grade 1 or grade 2, was it worth it? Did the mentor and child establish a mutually satisfying relationship? Was the child's self-esteem and academic growth supported? The answer to these questions was a clear "yes." In the next two segments of our research we wanted to learn about the nature of the mentors' pedagogy and the dynamics of the mentors' cultivation of relationships with young children. Findings from this research could help to inform the design and planning of such mentorship programs. Working collaboratively with the school staff to develop and operate these programs, we were very aware of pressures and predispositions to over-structure the activities of the mentors and children. It was tempting for teachers to give the mentors any worksheets the children hadn't finished in class that day. The principal had a strong background in literacy development and language arts, and at certain times she wondered about giving the mentors a booklet of structured activities to follow each week. She also felt that any craft activities used by mentors could have been replaced by ones that might more clearly qualify as "literature response" activities. Because most mentors were not certified teachers, could there be any certainty that the child's time was being well spent? This is a very important question for program planners, particularly when school time is used for mentorship sessions.

Section B presents findings from our research on the mentors' pedagogy. Chapter 6 is an illustrative case study of one mentor pair. Chapters 7 and 8 provide an analysis of the pedagogical experiences of a number of mentors at the school. Chapter 9 discusses program development issues related to the findings of the research on the mentors' pedagogy.

Section C of Part One presents research on the mentors' development of relationships with the children. Case studies of four mentor pairs are included as Chapters 10, 11, 12, and 13. Chapter 14 offers an analysis and interpretation of these case studies.

Part Two: Peer Support and Student Leadership Programs

In Part Two we present our research on a number of peer support and student leadership programs. Chapter 15 outlines the operation and benefits of five peer support programs spanning K–12: a K–1 program, an elementary school program, a junior high program, and two secondary school programs. Chapter 16 describes two student leadership programs. Both of these were operating in rural ECS–9 schools. (ECS or Early Childhood Services is a program for 4½- to 5½-year-old children.) One used the context of a complementary course and the other did not. We interviewed students in the junior high peer support program and asked for written reports from students in one of the student leadership programs. Our analyses of students' perspectives on these programs are presented in Chapter 17. Chapter 18 presents reflections on the significance and benefits of the programs studied.

It has been argued that a measure of the health of a society is the care it gives to its youngest members. By facilitating mentorship programs, schools can open the door for many more community members to participate in caring for young people in manageable and satisfying ways. By coordinating peer support and student leadership programs, schools can empower all students to care for each other and their communities. We hope that the program descriptions and analyses shared in this text can stimulate discussion about how schools can work with the opportunities and constraints of their own sites to offer more programs such as these.

> Social change will not come to us like an avalanche down the mountain. Social change will come through seeds growing in well-prepared soil—and it is we, like the earthworms, who prepare the soil....We realize there are no guarantees as to what will come up. Yet we do know that without the seeds and the prepared soil nothing will grow at all. (Franklin, 1990, p. 121)

❧ Part One ☙

MENTORSHIP PROGRAMS

᚛ Section A ᚜

PROGRAM DESCRIPTIONS
AND EVALUATIONS

❧ Chapter Two ❧

FIVE ELEMENTARY SCHOOL MENTORSHIP PROGRAMS

This chapter describes five mentorship programs in elementary schools, outlining their histories, organizational structures, and benefits. The first two programs presented, for kindergarten and for grades 1 and 2, were ones that we initiated and collaboratively developed with the schools. The next two programs, for grade 3 and for grade 5, were ones that individual teachers operated for their own classrooms using a single time block each week and engaging seniors, who had more flexibility to be available for the single time block. The fifth program was for grade 4 and 5 boys from single-mom homes. The limit for this program was eight boys, to make their transportation to recreational activities by two cars viable. Junior high students who were graduates of this program said that the program would be welcomed by students at any age. Descriptions are provided for the following programs:

- A Kindergarten Literacy Mentorship Program: Norwood School
- A Grades 1 and 2 Literacy Mentorship Program: High Park School
- A Grade 3 Reading Buddy Program: G. H. Dawe Community School
- A Grade 5 Writing Partners Program: Lacombe Upper Elementary School
- The Good Guys Program (Suggested as a useful model for grades 4 through 9): G. H. Dawe Community School

Following are some of the many good reasons for schools to consider facilitating mentorship programs for students in their schools.

- Volunteer mentorship programs provide the organizational structures for adults in the community to care more collectively for all children and youth.

- It has been argued that in today's society, all children are at risk of not having enough one-on-one attention from caring adults.
- Longitudinal research has shown that mentoring relationships contribute to the resiliency of at-risk youth.
- Researchers working with violent youth have concluded that the most powerful restraints on violent behavior are healthy human attachments. Children who are securely attached to adults learn trust, competence, self-management, and prosocial behavior.
- Mentoring relationships enhance students' self-esteem.
- Mentoring relationships can support achievement in powerful ways. A trusting relationship with a mentor can offer a student a base of support, safety, and encouragement for taking the risks required in new learning.
- When students like and admire their mentors, they wish to imitate them. Thus mentors can be effective role models for many complex behaviors, values, and attitudes.
- During periods of transition, people of any age benefit from mentoring. Some children or youth can "fall through the cracks" if they are not able to find their own informal mentors during the many transition periods from kindergarten through grade 12.

A Kindergarten Literacy Support Mentorship Program
Norwood School

In January 1997, Julia Ellis and Jan Small-McGinley worked with Norwood School in Edmonton to develop a literacy mentorship program for the kindergarten class. Sandra Woitas, principal at the school, continued the program and provided all students with mentors from kindergarten through grade 6. Norwood School is an inner-city school and was fourth on the list of high-needs schools in Edmonton Public Schools.

Mentors

Twelve mentors were recruited from university or college from education or early childhood education programs. One of the 12 mentors worked with each of two children. Mentors were assigned to the children with highest needs. Thirteen of the 17 kindergarten children had mentors.

Schedule

Mentors chose a one-hour time block from any afternoon except Thursdays. Because the children had music and physical education on Thursday afternoons, it was decided at the outset that that time would be protected.

Communication

The kindergarten teacher, Lisa Bacchus, was very committed to the program. She initiated communication booklets in which she and the mentors wrote back and forth to each other each week. She also provided the mentors with file folders in which they kept all of the children's work that was completed during the sessions.

Physical Space

At the first session each child gave his or her mentor a tour of the school. The children could choose to use any space they wished for the mentorship sessions. They typically chose to use the library on the second floor of the school. In the library there was a huge tepee. The children usually chose a table in the library for the literacy development games and paper and pencil activities, and the inside of the tepee itself for reading books together.

Children's Response to Mentors

Ms. Bacchus taught kindergarten in another school in the mornings. She noticed that the children in her Norwood kindergarten class were very quiet and not inclined to vocalize in class. She observed, however, that after the first 20 minutes with their mentors, they enjoyed talking to them nonstop in their one-on-one sessions. Children waited eagerly at the door with books under their arms when it was time for their mentors to arrive. As the program progressed, more of the children also started opening up in class, joining in songs, and putting up their hands to answer questions. In the following interview excerpt a mentor describes how a child came to respond very quickly to the one-on-one interaction: "When I first met him, he didn't want to really talk; he was very shy. And the teacher had mentioned to me that he really needed to work on his vocabulary and his language and talking about things, and when I came again, he just wouldn't stop talking." Mentors' comments highlighted both the quality of the relationships and the progress made with literacy development.

> He just, I think, really enjoyed having the extra attention and just getting a story read to him. And we laughed, and I joked about the story with him, and we just really clicked; we just really bonded together, I guess.
>
> We've been working a lot with stories right now, and he recognizes now that books have titles, they open, and you read left to right. And I've tried to get him to follow along with the print and stuff with me while I read and recognize certain letters....We are working on the letter S, and he really likes the sound of S, and he always says, "Snake." And he'll pick out the letter S in the text now.

Further Development

Six months after this program began, Norwood School was successful in an application to the United Way for funding that included support for a full-time program coordinator for the mentorship program. Following the first year of the program, the priority was to recruit literacy mentors for all of the grade 1 students. The long-term goal of the program was to provide mentors for all of the students in the school. The program coordinator, Roslyn Klak, was successful in recruiting over 148 mentors in less than two years. In 1999/2000, every student in the school had a mentor.

A Grades 1 and 2 Literacy Mentorship Program
High Park School

In January 1997, Julia Ellis and Jan Small-McGinley began working with High Park School in Edmonton to develop a literacy mentorship program for grades 1 and 2 students. Mary Michailides, principal at the school, welcomed the program concept given the literacy emphasis at the school and the awareness that every student can benefit from the one-on-one attention of another caring adult in their lives. The school was 40th on the list of high-needs schools and drew from a mixed socioeconomic neighborhood.

Finding Mentors

At the beginning of January 1997, we began recruitment efforts to find volunteer mentors for the program. The program began with six Faculty of Education students from the University of Alberta. The principal posted a sign in front of the school that read, "Be a mentor and make a difference. Phone 489–1145." The sign brought a number of parents and employees from local businesses into the program. School staff also persuaded relatives and friends to become mentors in the program. By the third week of January, there were mentors for all of the grade 1 students and almost all of the grade 2 students. Some mentors were also matched with a few of the high-needs children in grades 3 and 4.

Matching

The teachers considered the needs of children and the preferences and characteristics of the mentors as much as possible when matching. For example, children who already had a solid base of relationship support outside of school, but struggled academically, were matched with university students who were eager to try new instructional ideas that they had learned in teacher education classes. Children who appreciated a lot of personal attention and time to talk with adults were matched with people who offered maturity and a comforting presence. Mentors were also invited to indicate any preferences they had for the characteristics of a child they would like to work with. When possible, the hobbies and interests of the mentor were also considered in matching.

Program Structure and Supports

Orientation

All mentors had orientation sessions before beginning work with their children. This was usually at the supper hour and food was provided. At the sessions, mentors were apprised of program purpose, goals, and methods; school information; legal and ethical conduct requirements; support materials in their folders; weekly communication procedures; scheduling opportunities. Mentors were also invited to brainstorm ideas for activities or procedures they might like to use in their sessions.

Physical Space

A small room in the school was furnished to serve as the mentor room. Books for the program were kept there. "All About Me" posters from both children and mentors decorated the walls. Other spaces in the school were also used by mentors and children: the library, music room, gym, and hallway. When we noticed mentors working in a too-crowded mentor room, we learned that new mentors had to be reminded that they were welcome to use the other spaces.

Time Schedules

Mentors were encouraged to choose a lunch-hour time slot if possible, but were accommodated for whatever time schedule would work well for them. As the number of mentors increased, we realized that it might have been a good idea to plan for this possibility by allocating certain half days to one classroom and different half days to another. Our priority, however, had been to find mentors for all grade 1 students first, and we couldn't know how many mentors we would finally have.

Program Activities

Mentors and children spent their session time together building a relationship, sharing books, and doing literature response or math development activities. Both mentors and children brought books to the sessions.

Support for Mentors

All mentors were encouraged to bring materials to introduce themselves to children and to use the first session to help the child make an "All About Me" poster.

Mentors were given handouts listing:

- strategies for getting to know a child or building a relationship with a child;
- good practices to follow when sharing a book with a child;
- examples of literature response activities;
- examples of hands-on activities to support reading and writing.

Interested mentors were also provided with a workshop on paired reading. When mentors were community members who were not university students, we learned to keep handouts to a minimum. Too many pages of handouts created the impression that what we were asking them to do was beyond their expertise.

Whenever possible, school staff and researchers had debriefing sessions with small groups of mentors to learn how things were going and to share ideas and feedback.

The school offered a warm and consistent hospitality. Cookies were always put out for both children and mentors to enjoy during their sessions. Coffee for mentors was always prepared. A meal was kept warm on the stove in the staff room and mentors were invited to come there for a hot snack before or after their sessions.

To recognize mentors, the school held a tea, teachers supported the children in making thank-you crafts, the principal sent personal cards by mail, and the school gave certificates, letters, and gifts during Random Acts of Kindness Week.

Communication Procedures

Weekly communication with the mentors was, for the most part, conducted by teachers when the mentors came to the classroom door to meet the children. This could be somewhat disruptive. The teachers felt that they should have created a communication system in the mentor room so that each mentor could check his or her own file folder upon arrival at the school. The teachers could then have used these file folders to leave notes, notices, or new materials for the mentor.

Need for a Program Coordinator

Working with High Park School, we learned about many of the important tasks a program coordinator would complete: receiving and returning phone calls to new volunteers, helping with recruitment, scheduling, communicating, record keeping, preparing materials folders for orientation sessions, monitoring matches, debriefing with mentors, organizing refreshments, planning celebrations and thank-you gifts, and more. All of these tasks were undertaken by the school staff. Many had to be completed during particularly busy times of the year.

Program Benefits

In our research, the children's interview responses emphasized that:

- they liked their mentors.
- they liked talking to their mentors.
- their mentors made them feel proud and special.
- they would like to spend even more time with their mentors.
- some would like to play even more with their mentors (board games or gym activities).
- working with their mentors made reading fun.
- they perceived themselves to be getting better at reading and schoolwork because of their work with their mentors.

It was evident in interviews with mentors that:

- working with the children was gratifying.
- they perceived the children's appreciation of their sessions together.
- they used a variety of approaches to support reading comprehension and to keep the work at a challenging level for the children.
- they perceived their efforts to be supporting children's growth with reading.

School staff noticed how eagerly and proudly children shared work that they had completed with their mentors. Teachers observed that the children began to show more confidence in their behavior and their performance with assigned work in the classroom.

A Grade 3 Reading Buddy Program
G. H. Dawe Community School

Linda Plaxton, a teacher at G. H. Dawe Community School in Red Deer, had been operating a volunteer mentorship program for her grade 3 classes for over five years. She initiated her program one school year when she observed that 11 of her 29 students could benefit from extra help with reading. During her first five years of operating this program, she had 54 people in total serving as mentors. In the first year, one of the mentors brought in all of the other members of the art club he belonged to. This group provided a strong base of stability and cohesiveness for the group of mentors.

Goals

Linda Plaxton had two program goals. She wanted the students to strengthen their reading and comprehension abilities. She also wanted them to enjoy the benefits of working closely with involved and caring community members. All of the children enjoy spending time with their mentors. For some of the children, however, especially those who lack access to extended family, these relationships have a very special significance—they run rather than walk when they finally have their weekly opportunity to spend time with their mentor.

Schedule

Linda Plaxton has scheduled the weekly mentorship sessions for Friday mornings, 10:45 A.M. to 12:00 noon. She selected Fridays because the children are very excited for the rest of the day after their time with their mentors. Coffee is always ready half an hour before the mentorship sessions begin. The mentors enjoy coming early to have coffee and visit with the other mentors. A parent volunteer comes to the school each week to prepare the coffee and have it ready for their arrival.

Ms. Plaxton waits until the end of September each year to begin the program so that she has time to get to know each of the students' characteristics and needs first. The program then continues until close to Christmastime. The program begins again in February and runs until the end of May. January is omitted, as many of the mentors are retired people who travel during January. At the end of May, mentors want the time to work on their gardens.

Program Activities

During the mentorship sessions, the mentors help children to select appropriate library books. They read to the children and have the children read to them. They also play language arts games with the children.

Program Support

Fund-raising has been a major component of the program support that Linda Plaxton has provided for the reading buddy program. She needed additional reading books and language games for grade 3 children and even a trolley for storage and transportation of these. Funds were also required for a number of the celebrations, social activities, and thank-you gifts described in more detail in the next section.

Treating Mentors Like Gold. The most important support for mentors in this program is their ongoing conversation with the program coordinator and teacher, Linda Plaxton. During the mentorship sessions, Ms. Plaxton circulates around the room, stopping to have 10-minute conversations with as many mentors as possible each week. She said that it is important to remember what has been happening in the mentors' lives and to keep an ongoing conversation in progress. In this way, mentors feel respected and regarded as whole people themselves and their connection to the program is one of adult relationships as well.

Linda Plaxton uses a variety of methods to let mentors know that their work is greatly appreciated:

- Christmas cards and year-end thank-you cards (sent through the mail rather than passed through the children).
- A parent volunteer circulates to take photographs of mentors and children for the mentorship program album.
- A variety of celebrations throughout the year.
- At the end-of-year celebration, an outdoor picnic, the children give two-minute prepared public speeches using a microphone to thank their mentors.
- The children are supported in making a craft to give as a thank-you present to their mentors.

Some of the mentors were also very generous with gifts to the children. Linda Plaxton eventually found it beneficial to advise mentors that if they were giving gifts, to limit spending to five dollars. She also found it useful to let them know that suitable gifts might take the form of crayons, glue, felt pens, activity books, or chocolate.

Parent Involvement. Parents were encouraged to come to the school on one or two of the Friday mornings in order to meet their child's reading buddy. They were also encouraged to volunteer to help on some of the celebration days and, if possible, to occasionally send a treat on special occasions. Parents were also asked to help their children with bottle and can collections that were used for raising $500 a year to pay for the social activities.

A Grade 5 Writing Partners Program
Lacombe Upper Elementary School

Two teachers, Leanne Walton and Jodi Goodrick, initiated a volunteer mentorship program that engaged grandparents or seniors from the community as mentors working with grade 5 students to help them with their writing. The context for this writing project was an eight-week unit on the topic of "Canada—Past, Present, and Future." Jodi Goodrick, the Learning Assistance Center teacher in the school, worked together with Leanne Walton and her grade 5 class to operate this program. Jodi Goodrick prepared a written report on this project, and much of this material is excerpted or adapted from that report.

Rationale

As the Learning Assistance Center teacher, Jodi Goodrick was aware of the large number of students who were identified for special assistance due to learning disabilities and/or behavior disorders. She wanted these students to be able to have extra help from volunteers and to have a teacher present during their work sessions with volunteers. A whole class mentorship program would provide that opportunity.

Over the years, through her conversations with students, Ms. Goodrick had also become aware that many of them greatly valued their relationships with grandparents. Students often identified a grandparent as being a primary source of support, even though several of their grandparents lived quite a distance away. They said that they felt accepted by their grandparents, no matter what their faults were. This gave Jodi Goodrick the idea to plan to have seniors as the mentors in the program.

Recruitment

Recruitment began by having students in the grade 5 class identify their own grandparents as possible mentors. Four of the students had grandparents who lived locally and were available for the program. To extend recruitment, Ms. Goodrick learned the names of two seniors in the community who were well known and very involved in community activities. These people helped her to learn the names of other potential mentors. Jodi phoned these seniors as well, and even if they were not available, they often gave the names of one or two other people who would be suitable. After approximately 35 phone calls, Ms. Goodrick had 12 seniors who were interested and available. She decided that that would be enough to make 12 small groups in the classroom.

Matching

The four grandparents of students in the class were matched with their grandchildren and their grandchildren's class partners. There were three retired teachers among the mentors, and these people were matched with students who might have more difficulties with their work. The other students and mentors were matched randomly, as Ms. Goodrick did not have very much information about the backgrounds and interests of these seniors.

Orientation

Jodi Goodrick and Leanne Walton explained to the seniors that they wanted the students to learn firsthand about the past and to be able to identify changes by comparing the past with the present. They assured the mentors that the teachers would be responsible for all marking, editing, and deadlines. Once this was explained, many of the seniors were much more comfortable with the idea. The teachers had to make it very clear that the seniors were not required to be textbook history experts, grammar experts, or English-language experts.

To establish rapport between seniors and students, the program began with the students reading one-page autobiographies to their senior partners. In turn, the seniors shared personal information about themselves with the students. Having cookies and juice available supported a friendly relaxed atmosphere for this first session.

Program Activity

Each week the students and the seniors met for one hour in the library, each group at its own table. The students asked the seniors questions about pre-selected subtopics to do with the past. The students jotted down notes based on the information shared by the senior partners. Later they wrote up in full what they had learned in the interviews and read this back to the senior partners the following week. At this time the senior partners helped them to add or delete any information. Each of the weeks proceeded with this same routine.

Between mentorship sessions the students did additional work on the topic in class. Students were very eager to also read this material to their senior partners, not because they were required to, but because they began to see the seniors as their partners and wanted their input into their writing.

Finally, on the last week the students took the seniors to the computer lab to show them how the computer and various software programs worked. Many of the seniors did not have much experience with computers, so the students were able to be the "teachers." Both the students and seniors seemed to particularly enjoy this component.

At the completion of the program the students presented books of their writing to their senior partners at a luncheon held at the school just prior to Christmas. Seniors offered to bring artifacts from older days to show at this time. These were artifacts they had discussed with students, and the seniors were pleased to provide a display of this memorabilia from their lives at that concluding celebration.

Future Directions

Other teachers in the school also expressed interest in working on class projects with seniors. Ms. Goodrick had these suggestions:

- Plan such projects for spring, since many seniors travel in fall and winter.
- Recruit parent volunteers to assist with telephone recruitment of seniors.
- Use advertisements in local newspapers.
- Find transportation support for interested seniors at the lodge (seniors' residence).

Mentor Recognition

Ms. Goodrick advised that it is very important to provide both private and public recognition for the mentors. In the Lacombe program, acknowledgment was provided at teas, in the school newsletters or newspapers, and through thank-you cards from students.

The Good Guys Program
G. H. Dawe Community School
(Suggested as a useful model for grades 4 through 9)

From 1992 to 1997, Marty Klipper, vice principal at G. H. Dawe Community School in Red Deer, coordinated the Good Guys Program. In this program, a team of eight men served as mentors for eight boys in grades 4 and 5. Each week, 2 of the men provided an after-school, family-like recreational activity for all eight of the boys. This program model appears very promising for older students and girls as well.

Program Rationale

Marty Klipper and the principal, Rob Goring, had noticed that a number of the boys who were repeatedly sent to their offices for disciplinary action came from single-parent families in which the parent was female. They felt that these boys could benefit from having more positive male contact in their lives. Mr. Klipper also noticed at bicycle spring tune-up time that these boys' bikes were in need of attention. This gave him the idea for a program that would entail family-like activities such as doing bicycle maintenance and then going for an ice cream, carving jack-o'-lanterns, kite-making, and so forth. He used the metaphor of a basketball team to explain his plan for taking a manageable contribution from each of a large number of men to provide the boys with a wonderful program.

Program Objectives

The program was intended to support the boys in developing:

- improved self-esteem
- improved in-school behavior
- improved school performance and achievement
- improved interpersonal relationships with peers and adults
- a sense of belonging within a group of positive men
- awareness of community resources available for independent activity
- an appreciation for positive, healthy developmental activities

Program Structure

Mentors. The mentors included three to five school staff members and other men who were friends of school staff or of the school. Mentors were asked to make a commitment to the program for only three months at a time. The mentors' commitment entailed:

- participation in a planning meeting
- participation in an orientation session
- working with another mentor to coplan and cofacilitate an after-school activity for all eight students once in each four-week period

Communication. At the end of each week, the boys in the program learned about the program activity planned for the following week (which day, what time, which mentors, what activity, what place, clothing or materials needed) through a Good Guys Club newsletter.

The program activities began with an orientation session in the form of a picnic which enabled the students and their mothers to meet all of the mentors in the program. To invite student participation in the program, the vice principal telephoned each of the mothers to describe the program and request her permission for her son's participation.

Transportation. The limit of eight boys for the program was set to facilitate transportation using the vehicles of only two mentors. As it turned out, the mentors had vans and were able to bring their own children of that age to the activities as well. Mentors picked up the boys either at school or at home, depending on the start time of the activity, and returned them to their homes.

Funding and Resources. Donations from various community and individual sources covered the expenses involved in activities (fishing equipment, pumpkins, treats, bowling, swimming, golf, skates and skating). The mentors often used their own garages for activities such as pumpkin carving or kite-making. The men used their own interest and skill areas to advantage in planning activities: bicycling, woodworking, canoeing, fishing, and so forth. "Guest" mentors, including women, sometimes participated by leading a session on pottery making or other specialized activities.

Family-like Approach. The mentors endeavored to approach activities in a way that was similar to the way they would do them with their own children. Thus, for fishing, the boys were brought to a store to select their own equipment as one week's activity, and then the fishing itself was scheduled as the next week's activity. For pumpkin carving, the boys were first brought to a grocery store to select their own pumpkins, then back home to a garage for carving and then out for an ice cream treat.

Advantages of the Program Model

Manageable Commitment. This program model makes it possible for the participating students to benefit from the attention and expertise of a number of adults without the program entailing an onerous commitment on the part of the mentors. In a 14-week cycle, each mentor participates in only one planning meeting, one orientation session, and three after-school activities, which are co-planned and cofacilitated with one other mentor.

Flexibility. The program permitted good flexibility for scheduling. Mentors chose their week of participation at the beginning of each four-week period. They could wait till the week before to choose the particular day of their activity. Activities were typically scheduled 6:30 P.M. to 9:30 P.M. on a weeknight. When guest mentors became available, they were easily incorporated into this planning.

Multiple Mentors as Models. During each week's outing, students had the opportunity to observe two men in a positive, healthy interaction over a prolonged period of time. They also had the opportunity to observe that all of the men, whether or not they were teachers, shared similar values and positive habits. When mentors brought their own sons on the outings, the students could see that the men set limits for their own children in the same way that they did with the boys in the program.

Benefits Reported by Students

Students in grades 8 and 6 who had been in the Good Guys Program in grades 4 and/or 5 have described their experience of the program and its benefits. They suggested that the program should be available to students from kindergarten through grade 12, with modifications to activities to make them age-appropriate.

Relieved Boredom. Students said that the activities were always fun. Everybody "loved the bowling!" Students explained that before the program started, it was boring to "just hang around the house all the time with nothing to do." When their mothers came home after working all day they were too tired to do things with the boys. The weekly outings with the Good Guys Program were a highlight in their lives. They began to coax their moms to do similar activities with them on weekends.

New Friendships. Once the program started, the students in the Good Guys Program started to hang out together in the school hallways to talk with anticipation about each upcoming outing. One of the students said that he also started to go over and play with the children of one of the mentors who lived near him. When one of the mentors was a firefighter, students got to know all of the firefighters at the station. Students said that the mentors seemed "not like teachers but like they're your best friends."

Learned to Use School and Community Resources. Students learned how to access a variety of resources within the school and larger community. Mentors intentionally chose facilities such as swimming pools that were further away so that the students would have the experience of accessing new places. Even within the school, a mentor helped the students learn that the computers were there for their use and how to access them. Prior to that, some students said that they had been "afraid to go in there." Mentors gave help with schoolwork personally and also coached students on how to request help from their teachers.

Developed Lasting Skills and Interests. One of the grade 8 students explained that when he was in the program he wanted to be a hockey player but he didn't know how to skate. Through the program he got skates and began skating. Now he's been playing hockey on a team for three years, and he is also on a lacrosse team and in a tennis league. Graduates of the program talked about skills and interests they acquired for golf and other pastimes.

Improved Grades. Students reported that their grades improved after the program started. Instead of Cs they began getting As and Bs. One of the students reported that he's consistently been on the Honor Roll ever since he was in the program. Students said that the program "gave them an extra push in pursuing their goals." Students often used the expression, "You were in Good Guys, you know what to do."

Improved Personalities. Students said that the program helped them with their personalities and that they learned to be friendly and show enthusiasm for whatever they were doing.

Inspired Altruism. The program experience also inspired altruistic behavior from students. One of the mothers observed that after the program started, her son became more attentive and nurturing toward younger nieces and nephews. In some instances, both the student and the student's mother began participating in volunteer work in the school and community.

Sample Timeline for a Good Guys Year

September/October	Identification & Selection of Boys Recruiting of Men
October	Organizational Meeting for Mentors Orientation Meeting for Mentors, Students and their Mothers
November-January	First Three Cycles of Four Weeks Each
February	Break for One Week
February-April	Second Three Cycles of Four Weeks Each
May	Closing Activity

Closing Discussion

The histories of these programs demonstrate the feasibility and benefits of mentorship programs of many different kinds in elementary schools. They can be short-term or ongoing, classroom-based or school-based, for targeted students or all students, and they may include an academic focus or emphasize recreational and social support. After our conference presentations on these programs, a number of schools began to initiate literacy-based mentorship programs. For an ongoing school-based mentorship program, a program coordinator is a necessity. At the time of writing, a needs assessment supported by a community consortium was in progress in the Edmonton area to clarify the rationale for mentorship programs and the funding required to support such programs in interested schools.

❦ Chapter Three ❧

A Secondary School Mentorship Program

It's so great to have an adult friend and to meet someone who really cares—someone who is a good listener, someone I can take my problems to but who allows me to make the final decision. And my mentor is fun! We're friends!!

—A student in the mentorship program

It was a sunny May morning in 1998 when we arrived at Bev Facey Composite High School to enjoy a pizza lunch with three students, their mentors, and Nina Hoffman, the school counselor who coordinated the mentoring program. The students and mentors had agreed to have lunch with us and participate in a videotaped interview.

Some 1,200 students attend this school in Sherwood Park, a city of 45,000 on the outskirts of Edmonton, the capital of Alberta. Nina had started the mentorship program six years earlier as one of the school's stay-in-school initiatives. Incoming at-risk students are matched with professional and classified school staff members who agree to meet with the students each week during the grade 10 year. Nina hoped the program would support students who were "falling through the cracks" or who were not able to develop their own informal mentoring contacts. The activities Nina completed to operate the program are shown in Table 3.

Table 3: Program Coordination Activities

STUDENT SELECTION	**Spring**
	• Consult with counselors and staff from feeder schools to learn which students might need additional support in making a smooth transition to the secondary school environment.

Table continued on next page.

Table continued from previous page.

	• In particular, check with professional staff who work with learning assistance or integrated occupational programs.
	Fall
	• Interview these students to tell them about the purpose of the program and the commitments involved.
	• If the students wish to participate in the program, they complete information forms to identify their interests and to clarify what they would appreciate in a mentorship program. The students also sign a contract regarding the commitment they are making to the program.
	• Letters are sent to parents/guardians to request their support for the students' participation.
STAFF SELECTION AND MATCHING	**Spring and Fall**
	• Conduct an awareness campaign using posters and pictures from previous cohorts to invite school staff to participate in this program.
	• Provide staff with specific information about the responsibilities and expectations associated with the program as well as evaluation results from prior years.
	• Interested staff complete an information sheet indicating their interests, hobbies, and preferences regarding the characteristics of a student to mentor (e.g., gender, in or not in one's own classes).
	• Once matches are made, provide mentors with the students' information sheets and class schedules.
COMMUNICATION WITH SCHOOL STAFF	• Provide all school staff with a list of the mentors and the students they are matched with.
	• Encourage school staff to communicate with the mentors about any important topics pertaining to the students (e.g., an upcoming exam, any unresolved problems).
SUPPORTING MENTOR PAIRS	• Provide mentors with the students' report card information at reporting periods (with student permission), study and organizational information for students, goal-setting worksheets, magazines related to issues of youth and staying in school.
	• Organize three whole-group social gatherings for

Table continued on next page.

Table continued from previous page.

mentors and students. The first one, called "Mentor mingle," is the occasion when mentors and students meet each other for the first time. This is a pizza party, and games and icebreakers are used to help all present get to know everyone else and their own mentorship partners. After this session, mentors and students begin having their weekly meetings. Also hold celebrations in the form of a luncheon in December and a barbecue at year's end.

- Throughout the year, use a number of opportunities to acknowledge each person's participation. Send notes, thank-you cards, and gift or goodie bags at occasions such as Thanksgiving and Valentine's Day.
- In general, work proactively to maintain the program, troubleshoot, and respond to problems that are beyond the scope of the mentor's work.

Six weeks earlier, we had interviewed Nina to begin learning about the program. This day, before the lunch, we interviewed her again with questions we had sent in advance. She was well prepared with facts, figures, and documents to share.

An impressive research base supports this mentoring program. Longitudinal research studies have indicated that mentoring relationships have contributed to the resiliency of at-risk youth (Werner & Smith, 1989). Economically disadvantaged youth have credited their success to the support of a caring adult in their lives (Lefkowitz, 1986). And further research has indicated that economically disadvantaged youth obtain academic, psychosocial, and career benefits from their participation in such programs (Blum & Jones, 1993; Slicker & Palmer, 1993).

All of these benefits have found expression in the Bev Facey program, a tribute to the consistent skill and care of its coordinators. Each spring, program staff identify at-risk students in incoming classes by consulting with counselors at feeder schools. Students who have a history of absenteeism or isolation, or who are otherwise deemed at risk, are invited to participate. As part of needs assessment, students who express interest are given a one-page questionnaire in the fall to assess how negatively they perceive school and themselves.

Mentors are chosen with similar care. All faculty and staff at Bev Facey are informed of the program. Interested respondents convene for an informational meeting. To aid in matching, each mentor also informs coordinators of their own background interests, which might form the basis for a new bond with a student. Each staff participant must commit to meet with their student for at least 15 minutes each week; for the students, this agreement is formalized in a written contract.

The program coordinators provide print materials to guide new mentors. These materials advise mentors, for instance, to maintain a light tone in the first weeks and to inquire about academics only after the relationship has strengthened. Throughout, they are supplied with support materials, such as goal-setting worksheets and study guides. With the students' permission, mentors can also receive a copy of each report card.

The participants in our May luncheon interview included Bob and his mentor, an English teacher we'll call Ms. A. Sharon was paired with Ms. B, a classified staff member who works in the school library. And Marg's mentor was Ms. C, a science teacher in the school. We used the following questions as simple prompts to invite the participants to tell us about the program:

1. When did you tend to meet each week for your 15-minute session?
2. What did you like about the program?
3. Could you share a special memory from your mentorship sessions?
4. What would you say to other high schools about why they should think about starting this kind of a program?

Each pair took turns offering answers to each question. All gave lengthy responses, using the questions as points of departure to describe the mentorship relationship.

Bob and Ms. A

Bob and Ms. A shared a love of reading and a zany sense of humor. Bob clearly enjoyed surprising Ms. A with the "obscure" pieces he found to read. Both said they spent most of their time together laughing and giggling. Ms. A said she enjoyed Bob's "wacky sense of humor, unique views on life, and his observations." Bob clearly enjoyed hearing her describe his views as "unique" and repeated the phrase with a chortle.

They met on Mondays at lunch hours and usually lost track of the time when they were together. Ms. A said that if Bob didn't show up, she went looking for him later in the week. Bob took great pleasure in emphasizing that Ms. A "would al-l-l-l-ways come looking" for him if he missed a Monday. In fact, Bob generally appreciated the way Ms. A would "nag" him about things he needed to do.

Bob came from a rural area and was not well acquainted with Sherwood Park. He said that through Ms. A's help it was "really good to know community resources and figure out what happens in the school as well."

Ms. A outlined their developing relationship, as they moved from discussing what they read to discussing other aspects of school and life:

> You start with a common topic or commonality and then the report cards would come. We [mentors] get a special copy and we'd get a chance to discuss those things. If something was happening in another class, we'd talk on a different level about "What's your problem? How are you feeling? Would you like me to talk to the teacher? Are you fine by yourself?" And afterward I would never have to talk to the other teacher, we'd simply speak through the problem together. So it went beyond literature to pretty well all aspects of his life.

Bob said that by knowing Ms. A and the other mentors in the program, he learned that teachers are also human beings, not just authority figures, and he began to find all teachers a little more approachable. Even so, because he "could be shy and intimidated by some teachers," he said "it was good to know that [he] had that liaison available."

Bob liked being able to talk to Ms. A about problems or decisions. He said that "it feels safer discussing your problems with a teacher because they're not as emotionally involved as your parents."

After the mentorship relationship was well established, Bob became a student in Ms. A's English class. In spite of her apprehensions about this, Ms. A said it worked well because she already knew his reading interests, and their kibitzing just became part of the classroom climate. Bob said, "If you know the teacher, you tend to learn better from her." Asked for his special memory of the mentorship relationship, he said, "She always made me laugh."

Sharon and Ms. B

Ms. B worked in the library, so Sharon was able to visit her at any time. In the second semester of the mentorship, Ms. B made arrangements for Sharon to complete a work experience for course credit in the library. Thereafter, she said, the other two women working in the library also became Sharon's "mothers."

Sharon said that she and Ms. B "hit it off pretty great, too, right from the start. We'd sit there and talk about both our families and everything." Ms. B said that she cared a lot for Sharon and that knowing her helped her to realize that many students have personal problems.

Ms. B described her advocacy role for Sharon:

> I was able, with Sharon's permission, to approach other teachers and say, "You know, can we work through this? Is there some way we can meet Sharon's aca-

demic needs but take a few things into consideration?" And I think teachers who weren't in the program appreciated that as well, because there's always things you don't know about.

There were also several occasions when Ms. B sought out Nina Hoffman and her resources to address a crisis or to avert one.

In goal-setting discussions, Ms. B and Sharon focused not just on school-work but also on personal issues, such as romantic relationships. Ms. B thought it helpful that she could share stories of troubles in the lives of some of her relatives. Sharon concurred, saying that it helped "to get a different perspective." Through the group social events for all mentors and students, Sharon met others in the program. She said that a number of them became "more people to talk to and to get ideas from."

When asked about a special memory, Sharon said that she would "always remember every time we were together," that it was "great," and that it was "like having a lifetime friend."

Marg and Ms. C

Marg was fairly quiet during the interview, but she smiled frequently in response to many of Ms. C's comments and stories. Marg lived on a farm, and Ms. C. spoke with delight of all the things she learned about the activities and responsibilities in Marg's life. Marg described the beginning of their relationship: "Well, I don't know, I just liked her personality, and we just hit it right off. And one thing, she said she had a sister that was a lot like me, so I just found it easier to get to know her." During the first semester, Marg was in Ms. C's science class, and they chatted before and after class. Then, as Ms. C put it, they "just started enjoying having lunches together." They celebrated many firsts in Marg's life—her first job, her first car, and "getting asked out." Ms. C said she enjoyed seeing Marg grow from a shy little tenth-grade student who wouldn't take her nose out of a book to a confident eleventh-grade student. Ms. C explained how their personal relationship made it easy for her to move into a coaching or advocacy role:

> It's safe ground because if you have a student in your class, and you want to know how they're doing in other classes, it's hard to approach them. This way, we always have this little communication going, so when it's time for report cards, I didn't feel like I was being nosy. I'd been given the opportunity to sit down and say, "Hey, Marg, this is real cool," or "Science is pretty scary stuff." And it gave you that chance to go one step further without feeling like you were butting in, because we'd already discussed far more personal things than report cards.

The nature of their relationship actually made it easier to discuss personal issues. Ms. C said, "Sometimes it's hard to talk to your mom because it's judgmental. Sometimes it's safer to talk to the teacher because you know we're not going to be horrified." When Ms. C prompted Marg to share her special memory, Marg replied, "That you actually listened to me talk about horses, 'cause I couldn't find nobody else who would." They had both read *The Horse Whisperer* and were planning to see and discuss the movie.

Mentors' Reflections and Observations

As shown by the statements above, mentors were well aware that once they had established friendly, personal relationships with students, they could safely and comfortably offer coaching or advocacy support with school and life problems. This appeared to be the key, powerful dynamic of the mentoring relationships. The mentors saw real benefits resulting from their support. One noted that sometimes second or third chances can make all the difference for a student.

The mentors also observed that membership in the program led all teachers to appreciate these students as "real people," since all staff were informed about student-mentor pairs and were invited to consult with mentors about any unresolved issues related to these students. Students in this program could definitely not "fall between the cracks" unnoticed.

While students said they found teachers "less intimidating" because of the program, mentors observed that this in fact resulted in more respect, rather than less. Consequently, it was not a problem to have the student one mentored in one's own class. Each mentor found it satisfying to have a special bond with a student. Ms. C said that she enjoyed watching Marg's growth, as if Marg were her own child. Ms. B said that the mentoring experience helped her to respond to all students in a more understanding way. Ms. A said that rather than being a burden, it was a pleasure to get to know at least one student personally.

Other Indicators of Program Benefits

Nina Hoffman analyzed the previous year's attendance records for the 17 tenth-grade students who were then in the program. In the first semester, the average number of class periods missed by these students was 27, whereas in the second semester it was 14. A final examination was waived for six students because of perfect attendance. Seven students were recipients on Awards Night.

Nina also examined the records of the first cohort of 19 tenth-grade students in this program six years earlier. She noted that during tenth grade, the students' marks improved from first semester to second semester, showing an increase of 2% in the group's average.

Nina also identified the current status of the members of this first cohort.

- Three students had moved out of the school district.
- One student had transferred to another school.
- Fifteen were still in grade 12.
- Seven of these students were planning to come back to do upgrading (taking general program high school diploma courses rather than integrated occupational program courses).
- Twelve were on track to graduate with an Alberta high school diploma.
- Some had plans for postsecondary education (golf management, college daycare program).
- Some were going directly to employment.
- Nina also noted that once the tenth-grade mentorship program was completed, the students and their mentors tended to maintain informal friendly contact for the rest of each student's time at the school, and even afterward.

Looking Ahead

These encouraging signs have led Bev Facey to broaden the program. During 1998–99, there have been 40 student-mentor pairs, and the program is no longer restricted to tenth-grade students. Further, the frequency of "whole-group" social/recreational activities has increased from three times per year to once per month. The many communication pieces needed (memos, letters, contracts, handouts, evaluation forms) have also been standardized and made available in print and disk format (Ellis & Small-McGinley, 1999), and experience will undoubtedly bring further refinements. A selection of these communication pieces have been included in Appendix C.

Many young people coming to high school carry the weight of chaotic, confusing lives and a history of failed relationships with schools. Such students can be at risk of further alienation in large, complex, fast-paced, and seemingly bureaucratic secondary schools. A mentorship program such as the one we studied can offer at-risk students the opportunity for human connection, caring, and material support in such schools.

ℬ Chapter Four ℭ

EVALUATION OF TWO ELEMENTARY SCHOOL LITERACY MENTORSHIP PROGRAMS

*A*ll children need supportive interaction with caring adults to learn and grow. Increasing numbers of children are at risk of not having as much as they need for the mental and moral development that will enable success at school (Brandt, 1992–93). Brendtro and Long (1995) and others have observed that children who are securely attached to adults learn trust, competence, self-management, and prosocial behavior. In the past, educators have generally waited for some children to fail at school and then offered remediation. Slavin, Karweit, and Wasik (1992–93) have likened this approach to a community with contaminated drinking water choosing to spend funds only on treatment of sick people rather than on a water treatment plant.

With the view that prevention is preferable to intervention, we have collaborated with two schools to develop and research literacy mentorship programs for children in kindergarten, grade 1, and grade 2. The programs entailed having adult mentors spend an hour a week with a child to visit, read together, and carry out literature response activities or other language development and literacy support activities. After mentorship sessions had proceeded for six to eight weeks, the researchers interviewed children, mentors, and teachers to learn about the quality of the relationships and the value of the academic support. Given that mentors were not trained teachers and did not have a specific curriculum to follow, there were real questions about how beneficial the literacy development activities would be. Given that nonrelated adults were spending only an hour a week with young children, it was also questionable whether the relationships would have enough intensity to qualify as mentoring ones rather than as more limited tutoring ones. This chapter presents an overview of issues and questions related to early literacy development and to mentorship programs, describes our development work, and discusses findings from this first phase of our research.

Issues Related to Early Literacy Development Initiatives

The Problem

In a review of the topic of preventing school failure, Slavin (1994) has noted the importance of children learning to read in the early grades. Longitudinal studies have shown that disadvantaged third-graders who have failed one or more grade levels and are reading below grade level are extremely unlikely to complete high school (Lloyd, 1978; Kelly, Veldman, & McGuire, 1964, as cited in Slavin, 1994). At the same time, remedial programs beyond the third grade have few, if any, effects (Kennedy, Birman, & Demaline, 1986, as cited in Slavin, 1994).

In his review of preventing school failure, Slavin has underscored the critical role of children's grade 1 experience.

> Almost all children, regardless of social class or other factors, enter first grade full of enthusiasm, motivation and self-confidence, fully expecting to succeed in school....By the end of first grade, many of these students have already discovered that their initial high expectations are not coming true, and they have begun to see school as punishing and demeaning. Trying to remediate reading failure later on is very difficult because students who have failed are likely to be unmotivated, with poor self-concepts as learners. They are anxious about reading and they hate it. (p. 11)

While these are strong words about how children can experience grade 1, our previous video program research with junior high students' memories of elementary grades (Mighty Motion Pictures, 1997) confirms that children in grades 1 and 2 are highly sensitive to both explicit and implicit information about their performance in school.

Forms of Early Intervention

Concerns about supporting children's early growth and experience are not new, and there have been many different kinds of initiatives employed: birth to age 3 interventions, preschool, kindergarten models and day length, retention, developmental kindergarten, transitional first grade, smaller class size, instructional aides, nongraded primary class, one-to-one tutoring, Success for All, and improving curriculum and instruction. In reviewing evaluations of these strategies, Slavin, Karweit, and Wasik (1992–93) noted that approaches that incorporate one-to-one tutoring of at-risk first-graders are most effective for preventing early reading failure. Further, these reading outcomes are largest and longest lasting when the tutoring is done by teachers using well-developed curriculum and instruction such as Reading Recovery. The lasting effects of Success for All were the largest, but this is a multistrategy program that continues through the elementary grades.

Barr and Parrett (1995) have also concluded that the best way to meet the needs of at-risk youth at the elementary level is through school-wide programs that integrate the various approaches into a comprehensive effort. They also acknowledge, however, that given the demands placed on schools by increasing numbers of at-risk children, schools must begin implementing practices that are known to work. A common feature of prevention and intervention programs or strategies is the need for special funding. While some schools serving large numbers of disadvantaged children may be targeted for special funding, other schools may have no special funds for services for at-risk students in their classrooms. While one-to-one tutoring of low-achieving grade 1 children by a specially trained teacher may be the single most effective strategy, this can require hiring an additional teacher for each grade 1 class.

The Mentoring Movement

Flaxman and Ascher (1992) have described mentoring as representing a shift in vision for antipoverty efforts. They noted that by the 1980s, most compensatory education and youth employment programs were viewed as only marginally successful in forestalling academic failure or dropping out of school, or in making youth employable for anything but low-skill jobs. They critique previous intervention programs for having focused solely on imparting skills or manipulating the youth's motivations, attitudes, or behaviors, rather than working with the young people as "complex, physical, psychological and social beings in environments and institutions over which they had little control" (p. 2). Any caring and help that was provided to recipients in these programs was fortuitous and unplanned and not considered part of the programs' effects. Mentoring, by contrast, is conceptualized as a more whole way to respond to the whole child or youth.

> In attempting to duplicate how people behave under natural conditions, its [mentoring's] goal has been to give them something closer to what they need. As an ideal, mentoring bypasses the scientism and technicism of many educational and social programs, which appear remote from lived experiences. In this, it has appeared to be a sensible and socially moral response to the difficulty of growing up in the United States today. (Flaxman & Ascher, 1992, p. 2)

Smink (1990) has insisted that the mentor's most critical function is to provide moral support and a sense of caring. As social learning theory suggests, when younger people feel liked and cared about by their mentors, they will be more likely to identify with their mentors and to want to imitate their behaviors and attitudes. Similarly, Flaxman and Ascher have emphasized the importance of mentors and mentees having joint activity, personal attraction, frequency of interaction, and familiarity in order for trust to develop and for the younger person to be inclined to look to the mentor as a helper or caretaker. The notion of "moral support," as used by Smink above, however, is probably not reducible to things that can be counted and measured like "frequency of interactions." MacIntyre (1981) has explained moral action as action that preserves the continuity of the story one is living—the story of being someone's daughter, someone's friend, someone's teacher. Thus, moral support from a mentor would manifest itself in interactions that preserve the continuity of the story of the mentor being one who cares for and supports the growth of the child.

Brodkin and Coleman (1996) have defined *mentor* as "one who provides one-to-one support and attention, is a friend and a role model, boosts a child's self-esteem, enhances a student's educational experience" (p. 21) and *mentoring* as "meeting regularly over an extended period of time with the goal of enabling a special bond of mutual commitment based on the development of respect, communication and personal growth" (p. 21). Flaxman and Ascher (1992) state that the heart of natural or spontaneous mentoring has always been to provide assistance during a period of transition such as that from childhood to adolescence or from novice to expert and that the goal of mentoring is to help the child or youth gain social learning and command over tasks of everyday life in school, work, or society. This occurs through jointly carried-out activities in which the mentor alternately models, teaches, manages, questions, and structures a task for the child/youth.

Mentorship Programs

During the last several years a number of mentorship programs have been initiated in the United States, and more recently in Canada, particularly in Ontario. The programs vary greatly in size, longevity, target population, and purposes. Described here are programs for elementary students that are based in schools.

Our Lady of the Lake University in Texas has been involved in a mentoring initiative with an inner-city elementary school. Staudt (1995) explains that "this very successful mentoring program involves the matching of college students and at-risk elementary students in order to improve the elementary students' attitudes, behavior and self-esteem" (p. 5). Mentors and mentees engage in a variety of activities "such as reading to their students, taking them to the university, playing games. Field trips are allowed after a trusting relationship is established between the mentor and the student" (p. 7). The mentors can help the students with academic schoolwork; however, "the mentoring program is not to be used as a tutorial program" (p. 7). Ongoing communication between teacher and mentor provides both with strategies to meet the needs of the students. Mentoring occurs primarily at the school but not inside the classroom. The university is located one block from the school. Mentors sign in upon arrival and wear badges for identification purposes. Written permission must be provided by parent or guardian before the mentoring process begins. According to Staudt, this program is making a significant difference in the lives of elementary students.

The CUNY/BOE Student Mentor Program in New York City is a college-based program that also serves elementary children. This program offers course work and academic credit for mentoring. Mentoring is a component of college courses in educational psychology, sociology of urban education, fieldwork in child/adolescent development, and mentoring internships. Training occurs in classes on campus following a model that provides multiple levels of continuous support from peer groups, coordinators, and scheduled weekly mentor/mentee get-togethers. Academic credit serves as an incentive for mentoring (Flaxman & Ascher, 1992).

Excellent Beginnings is an early childhood mentoring initiative that resulted from an understanding that children, particularly African American, lack male role models (Walter, 1995). Teachers and members of the community wished to encourage at-risk students to stay in school as well as increase the numbers of African-American male elementary teachers. High school students were sought as mentors for elementary students. Three of the 14 schools that applied for funding for this program were chosen to participate. Consideration was given primarily to early childhood proposal initiatives that could successfully integrate the school and community. The criteria for all proposals included curriculum and classroom management, parent involvement, high school mentors, higher education collaboration, training, guidance, and staffing. One hundred African-American, preschool, and kindergarten children, as well as students in alternative classes for older elementary students attending the Lincoln Center school in Ruston, Louisiana, participated in this program. Third-graders and younger students were targeted because "research indicates that is a pivotal point when African-American males become turned off school" (Walter, 1995, p. 2). Students came from single-parent families, suffering low self-esteem due to economic hardships.

Although the largest and most widely recognized programs for at-risk students are in the United States, Brown (1995) recently identified a number of Canadian mentorship programs in Ontario. Each program is unique in terms of purpose, context, and age of mentors. Prime Mentors, for example, is an in-school enrichment program for elementary high-risk, creative youth. Big Brothers is an out-of-school initiative that matches boys from single-parent families to men. Big Brothers, Big Sisters (1995) has recently developed an In-School Mentoring Program, which is a partnership program between the BBBS and the Board of Education in Hamilton, Ontario. This is a highly structured program developed after the BBBS model. Community Mentoring is an initiative that involves community volunteers acting as mentors in North York school. Three intergenerational programs include the Seniors Independence Program, which involves matching adults with at-risk youth in Scarborough, Toronto, and North York; the Volunteer Grandparents Program, which links grandparents to children from two to six years old; and the Toronto Intergenerational Project, a pilot project linking seniors with elementary students identified as at-risk.

Programs vary greatly in terms of the relative emphasis given to providing a relationship or providing academic support. In the program at Our Lady of the Lake University described above, for example, there were clear warnings against the program becoming a tutorial one. Some mentoring programs, however, focus specifically on strengthening academic skills. HOSTS—Help One Student to Succeed—for example, is a national program in the United States that helps students of all ages who are experiencing reading difficulty. Each student is matched with a trained mentor who provides "individual attention, motivation and support" (Smink, 1990, p. 12). Similarly, One PLUS One is an initiative with a goal of increasing literacy of at-risk children and youth (Flaxman & Ascher, 1992).

Some programs focus on a wide array of skills or are based on whatever the student needs. The goals in such programs are intended to respond to the needs of the people they serve. As an example, KIT—Keeping in Touch with Students—is a well-established program that has been operating for at-risk junior high students since 1987. In this program, teachers mentor students in their own schools, using weekly meetings to provide personal tutoring and counseling (Flaxman & Ascher, 1992).

Evaluation Issues

Considering how best to research or evaluate literacy mentorship programs in elementary schools has not been a straightforward matter. Typical measures of the effectiveness of one-to-one tutoring programs have been immediate reading outcomes and longitudinal measures regarding retention, placement in special education, or other measures of actual school success or failure (Slavin, Karweit, & Wasik, 1992–93). In a review of five one-to-one tutoring programs, Wasik and Slavin (1993) identified difficulties with both the availability of standardized tests that were suited to the curriculum of the tutoring as well as the practice of dropping children from a program if they were not responding successfully. They pointed out that it can be increasingly difficult for students to demonstrate sustained gains with each passing year because the range of all students' scores on tests also increases. They drew attention to the need for both authentic performance assessments and for more ethnographic studies or micro-analysis studies to reveal the cognitive and motivational processes activated in tutoring; that is, how it is that at-risk children learn to read in tutoring.

In evaluations of mentorship programs, outcomes of interest have been increased academic success and persistence. In a discussion of the evaluation of mentorship programs, Flaxman and Ascher (1992) have suggested that the amount of time the mentor gives to mentoring largely determines how good the mentorship can be. Given the importance of the quality of the relationship in mentoring, they also emphasize that more qualitative studies are needed to clarify or verify the nature or intensity of mentorship relationships. As well, if academic support is intended to be an important component of the mentorship, the planning skills of the mentor warrant attention. Brown (1996) has observed that mentorship program developers have generally lacked funds for substantial evaluation studies. Accordingly, evaluations of in-school mentoring programs have typically used pre- and postattitude and achievement measures. The majority of such programs have been with youth rather than young children.

Description of Program Development

In January of the school year we worked collaboratively with two elementary schools to initiate literacy mentorship programs for young children. Mentors were adults who came to the school for at least an hour a week to be with one child. The hour was spent visiting while sharing a snack, doing a language development activity, reading books together, and doing literature response activities. The children selected books to bring to the sessions and sometimes the mentors also brought books of their own. Mentors included university and college teacher education students, parents, retired teachers and principals, friends and relatives of school staff, and employees of a nearby bank. Mentors were provided with brief orientation sessions and handouts containing ideas for how to establish a relationship with a young child, how to share books with a child, and how to do paired reading with a child.

Both schools were in the same large school district in a major city in Alberta. School A was identified as 40th on the list of high needs schools in the district and School B was fourth on the same list. School A assigned its mentors to all grade 1 children, most of the second-grade children, and a few of the third- and fourth-grade children. School B assigned all of its mentors to kindergarten children. The teachers considered the needs of children and the preferences and characteristics of the mentors as much as possible when matching. For example, children who already had a large amount of relationship support outside of school, but who struggled academically, were matched with university students who were eager to try new instructional ideas that they learned at university. Children who appreciated a lot of personal attention and time to talk with adults were matched with people who offered maturity and a comforting presence. Mentors were also invited to indicate any preferences they had for the characteristics of a child they would like to work with. When possible, the hobbies and interests of the mentor were also considered in matching.

Data Collection

This study reports on the interviews that were conducted with children, mentors, and teachers, six to eight weeks after the weekly mentorship sessions had commenced. In this research we hoped to learn about how the children and mentors were experiencing the mentorship sessions, both in terms of the quality of the relationship and in terms of the academic support being provided to the children.

The interview schedule used with children included the following questions.

- You've been participating in a mentorship program. Someone comes to the school every week if they can to spend time doing things together with you. What do you do together when they come?
- Do you like doing those things with your mentor? Do you enjoy it?
- What would make it better or more enjoyable?
- Is it helpful for you?...How does it help you?
- What would make it more helpful?

Children were interviewed in groups of three, asking each child the same question in round-robin style. Probing questions were used to clarify children's responses where necessary. Both researchers attended all interviews, with one researcher asking the questions and the other recording responses and adding follow-up questions. All interviews were audiotaped and transcribed. Interviews were conducted with all 27 participating children at School A: 15 in grade 1; nine in grade 2; and three in grades 3 and 4.

The interview schedule used with mentors included the following questions.

- To start, could you please introduce yourself? Are you a university student, do you work somewhere else, are you retired?…How did you learn about the mentorship program?
- How long have you been a volunteer mentor at this school?
- How many children do you work with? At what times do you meet with them?
- Can you describe some of the things that you do together with the child?
- How has the nature of the activities and the feeling of the session changed over time?…Was there a particular turning point?
- Can you talk about the relationship with the child a little more? How did it feel at the start? What influenced it? If it changed, how could you tell it was becoming different?
- Have you seen growth in the child? How would you describe it?
- What are the challenges in the role that you have?
- What are the pleasures or satisfactions?
- What would make the sessions work even better?
- What additional preparation would you have found helpful?
- Would you recommend volunteer mentorship work to other people? What would you say to them about it?

Most mentors were interviewed in groups of two or three, asking each mentor the same question in round-robin style. Some of the mentors were interviewed individually. Interviews were conducted with 26 of the 38 mentors: 16 from School A and 10 from School B. (Two mentors worked with two children each.) Two researchers were present for the interviews, which were audiotaped and transcribed.

Findings

Given that the mentorship sessions had been in progress for only six to eight weeks, our first question was whether the children and mentors experienced their relationships in a positive and significant way. We wondered whether there was enough intensity in these relationships for them to count as mentorship ones. At the same time, given the lack of research on mentorship programs with young children, we were not even sure what intensity should be like in such a program. Our second question was whether the literacy development component of the sessions showed benefits or promise. Although we had made some handout materials available to mentors, we had presented these in a low-key manner so as not to intimidate anyone. Our mentors had very diverse backgrounds, and our orientation objective was to communicate that this was something they were all capable of doing. Thus we were interested in everyone's perceptions of the value of the academic support provided by mentors.

The Mentorship Relationships

At this point in the mentorship program it was evident that mentors were finding the relationships to be satisfying in that the children's responses to them were so gratifying. The following excerpts from mentors' interviews give examples of the ways mentors expressed the significance of the mentoring sessions to them.

> And just to be able to see that when I walk into the room he knows that it's our time, and he has a big smile on his face and he's very excited. That just give me a good feeling all over.
> She sees me and she's all happy and smiles.
> When he's with me he talks now the whole time....I get great satisfaction out of knowing that that's going to benefit him too just by having a wonderful, really good interaction with somebody.
> If it brings a little bit of happiness into this boy's life to think that somebody would actually take the time and spend it with him and make a difference, that's where you see the reward.
> If people could realize how little it takes to turn a child around,...their self-esteem,...a half hour a week.

In the mentors' giving to the children, it was clear that the children were giving back so much in return. The children's obvious appreciation of the mentors made the time spent in mentoring significant and worthwhile for mentors.

The children's interview transcripts were replete with expressions of appreciation for their mentors. It was clear that for them, they had new and significant relationships with someone they "loved" or someone who brought them a tattoo (adhesive) or a newspaper article or book on their favorite interest, such as figure skating or cats. Listed below are examples of ways that children expressed appreciation of their mentors.

> It makes me feel proud of myself,...and she's proud too.
> I love my mentor!
> I am happy when she comes.
> I like it because my mentor is nice,...and she's nice to be with,...and I like to read to her.
> I like her coming and because I love singing songs to her, and she loves me.
> It makes me feel good.

He reads books, and he likes me lots.
It's fun to talk to her.
It makes me feel happy and proud when she comes.
I like him very much, and I like it all the time when he comes, and I'm happy.
She helps me read books that I can't read,...and she loves me.

As illustrated in these excerpts, the children were highly appreciative of having someone special who was there just for them. They perceived the mentors as liking or loving them. Conversations with teachers confirmed children's interviews, as teachers described how the children would always be ready early with books under their arms, ready to meet with their mentors. The mentor had quickly become a "someone" in their lives, someone who was nice, someone who liked them and was proud of them, someone who read to them, someone the children could sing songs to and talk to. It was fun to talk to one's mentor. The mentor made the child feel good. Mentors made children feel proud of themselves. Enhancing self-esteem is a primary goal of mentorship programs with a relationship focus.

Academic Support in the Mentorship Sessions
Given that the mentors had not had an intensive training program on how to share books with children or support children's reading, we were interested to learn how children and mentors experienced the academic component of the mentorship program. In our interviews, mentors demonstrated an obvious engagement with the academic component of their sessions. They showed that they were thinking about the child as a reader, the child's skills and progress, and how to support the child's engagement and growth.

The following two excerpts show examples of mentors' thinking about the importance of the child's interests.

Using different reading material has helped. Instead of always just reading him novels, we read comic books or Nintendo stuff and things like that that he's maybe more familiar and comfortable with, so that's helped.
The students' reading levels are not very advanced at this point in time, so I think it's very important that the children have a little bit of say in what they're reading. It has to keep their interest and you certainly want to keep them liking the program.

Mentors' comments revealed that they noticed and looked for growth in the child's reading. The following are examples of such reports.

I also tape record her too when I go see her and have her read. So the last few times that I've been doing this I'll tell her, "You select your book that you want to read."...Then I'll tape record it on the second read, and then I'll go through the words that she doesn't know and write those down. And I played it back for myself last week after I got home, to the very first time she read and to this time, and it's a lot more fluent.

He's much better than he was earlier. It's great. We're working on the alphabet right now, and he doesn't really recognize his letters, but I'll ask him what a letter is, and so then he'll go through A-B-C-D. He'll do a little song.

We've been working a lot with stories right now, and he recognizes now that books have titles, they open, and you read left to right. And I've tried to get him to follow along with the print and stuff with me while I read and recognize certain letters....We're working on the letter S, and he really likes the sound of S, and he always says "snake." And he'll pick out the letter S in the text now.

She usually brings an easy book to read to me. Then I read her one that's a little bit harder. She remembers what I've read and she reads it back to me.

Many of the mentors' stories illustrated their attention to and concern about comprehension and meaning in reading. The following are examples of the different ways they talked about focusing on and supporting comprehension.

He would be a character and I would be a character....He'll pick up cues from me when I'm reading about something, and I'm sure he's thinking about how I'm interpreting.

And I think helping reading stories and stuff like that encourages literacy as well, and talking about your stories and just having an imagination,...just being able to imagine what the story is going to be like or make your own kind of story up, and being able to think about it and then communicate that into language.

What I really find fascinating about her is that she would love to read you a story instead of me reading her a story....And so she would just love to sit there and read the story to me about three different times, and every time using a different version....She doesn't read the words, but she looks at the pictures, and then she just tells the story from the pictures. And then from what she's heard before, if the story's been read to her before, she just kind of makes up her own story.

He usually brings an easy book to read to me—one that he's read before. The book is simple so he doesn't have to concentrate much to comprehend it. I try to read him a more challenging book and make him think and talk about all the details and background and what's going on in the environment of the story. Then I know he has to stay tuned in to comprehend it.

Finally, mentors talked about how they helped children with difficult words in reading. Here is one example.

What we do is, he will try to pronounce the word, and I don't immediately correct him. I'd rather have him try to sound it out, and then if he's just at a roadblock, then, before he has frustration, I'll just go, "Okay, let's look at that word together." And so we'll sort of sound it out by the syllables, and that's how I handle situations like that.

It appears that for each mentor there is a meaningful story about how literacy has been supported in the mentorship sessions. The full stories are likely as different as all of the children and mentors are. It is clear, however, that there is time spent on reading, the mentors work to make sense of the children as readers, mentors have objectives or purposes in mind, there is a responsiveness between children and mentors, and the mentors discern progress.

In School A, where grades 1 and 2 children had mentors, the teachers reported that children showed more confidence in both their behavior and in the work they produced in class. In School B, which was fourth on the list of high needs schools in the school district, only the kindergarten children had mentors. The teacher also taught kindergarten in another school in the mornings. She noticed that the children in her School B kindergarten class were very quiet and not inclined to vocalize in class. She observed, however, that after their first 20 minutes with their mentors, they enjoyed talking to them nonstop in their one-on-one sessions. As the mentorship program progressed, more of the children also started opening up in class, joining in songs, and putting up their hands to answer questions. In the following interview excerpt a mentor from this school describes how a child came to respond very quickly to the one-on-one interaction: "When I first met him, he didn't want to really talk; he was very shy. And the teacher had mentioned to me that he really needed to work on his vocabulary and his language and talking about things, and when I came again, he just wouldn't stop talking."

For young children, confidence and a willingness to try activities presented by the teacher can serve to further support their immediate academic gains and their long-term constructive habits and attitudes as students.

The children told us in many different ways that their mentors were helping them to learn to read. Here are some examples from children's interviews.

She's always there for me, and if I miss a word she's always guiding me, she's guiding me along, she's reading with me, the same word.
She helps me with words I don't know so it's fun!
She helps me with the words when I get stuck because I get stuck a lot.
It helps me read better.
She helps me sound it out when I don't know.
He breaks up longer words into smaller words.

I like it because I can read long words
It's helpful because I can read the big, fat words.
She explains it so it can be something fun!
She shows me the word, then I remember it next time.
And it's fun reading books!! And it's really, really, really fun writing words down on the paper.
I know new words because my mentor read them to me.
She reads it to me, then I can read it back to her.
You learn new words and stuff,…and all the rhyming words and all—you read better.

The child's statement "She helps me with words I don't know so it's fun!" pulls together so much of what all the children were saying. Granted, throughout the interviews the children said that the whole activity of reading with their mentors was fun. We expect that this is likely a general tribute to the one-on-one attention, praise, and mentors' efforts to support interests, challenge, and comprehension. Children also stated that mentors made it possible for them to read harder books than they otherwise could. Overall, however, the children spoke insistently about the value of mentors helping them with difficult words. As we puzzled over this focus in the children's comments, we searched our own experiences for an analogy to help us understand the children's perspective. Finally, we thought about our own experiences of learning to use new computer systems and software. Certainly, having a one-on-one mentor who is nice, who likes us and brings us treats, and who explains every word or step we don't know would make learning new computer skills much more "fun" for us. The children's statements and our own memories of acquiring some computer literacy help us to appreciate how frustrating it must be for some children to try to learn to read without the one-on-one help provided by caring, supportive mentors. One can hear in the excerpts above that reading, the mentor, fun, and increasing competence have become linked in the experience of these children. For these children, mentorship and literacy development have become a powerful combination.

Discussion

These findings suggest much promise for mentor-supported literacy development for young children. The children's appreciation and receptivity serve to keep mentors engaged. It is perhaps because the children are so young that they trust and respond to the mentors so quickly. The children enjoy the mentors' attention and one-on-one time for talking and sharing interests or songs. Time with mentors makes them feel happy, good, and proud. Self-esteem is supported. The mentors make sense of the children as readers and work with their interpretations to try different approaches and to look for growth. The children enjoy reading and learning to read with the support of their mentors. Reading with their mentors is fun. The children's pride in their work with their mentors spills over into increased confidence and participation in classroom activities. As preventative programs, such initiatives appear to warrant further development and research.

In the second and third phases of the mentorship research, we planned to learn how mentors were so successful in such short periods of time. These research components included case studies of a number of mentor pairs to study the mentors' pedagogy (Chapters 6, 7, 8, and 9) and to study the development of relationships between mentors and children (Chapters 10, 11, 12, 13, and 14). Findings from these studies can serve to inform orientation and training of mentors and program coordinators for new programs of this kind.

In closing, we have been strongly impressed with the immediate value and long-term promise of literacy mentorship programs to extend support for the social, emotional, and academic growth of children in schools. It appears that such programs may be able to make a difference to the life chances of individual students. If such programs become more commonplace, our communities may also find such collective caring experiences to be restorative. We will give the last word to one of the mentors, who said: "It's a good program and I'm glad I did it!"

⋙ Chapter Five ⋘

GUIDELINES FOR ELEMENTARY SCHOOL LITERACY MENTORSHIP PROGRAMS

𝕴n this chapter we offer ideas that may be helpful for elementary schools wishing to initiate or expand literacy mentorship programs. These ideas have been drawn from the programs described in Chapter 2 and from our own experience in collaboratively developing and researching programs with schools. The sample letters, posters, and support materials for mentors referred to in this chapter are included in the appendices. This chapter focuses on mentorship programs with a literacy support emphasis. For an example of a program with a social support and recreational emphasis, please see "The Good Guys Program" in Chapter 2.

Starting a Program

Starting with Students' Needs

Schools or teachers tend to start mentorship programs when they have pressing concerns about the unmet needs of certain students. This pattern has been illustrated in the programs described in Chapters 2 and 3. Those chapters described, for example:

- a program in a grade 3 class that was started because a large number of students in the class needed extra help with reading
- a program in a grade 5 class that was initiated because many of the students needed help with writing skills
- a program for grade 4 and 5 boys who didn't have enough attention from or interaction with positive male role models
- a program for a kindergarten class in an inner-city school with a large number of high needs students
- a program for grade 1 and 2 students in a school with an emphasis on early literacy

- a program in a secondary school for incoming grade 10 students who were considered to be at risk of dropping out of school before graduation

The Power of Preventative Programs

There can be many short- and long-term benefits from using whole class mentorship programs in kindergarten and grades 1 and 2. For example:

- Longitudinal research has shown that mentorship relationships have contributed to the resiliency of at-risk youth.
- At-risk youth who had experienced having mentors earlier in their lives were more able to connect with and benefit from mentors assigned to them as part of intervention programs when they were older.
- Mentors for students in early grades can support both self-esteem and academic growth.
- When children in early grades have mentors, the confidence gained from their mentorship sessions spills over into more confident behavior and performance in the classroom.
- It can be faster and easier for mentors to gain the trust and appreciation of young children; consequently, mentors can more quickly become committed to the program and children can more readily accept new mentors when some mentors have to leave the program.
- Literacy research has clarified that intervention programs have maximum impact when used in grade 1 and when they entail one-on-one support for students.
- Remedial programs, typically implemented as technical interventions after students' difficulties are more clearly identifiable in grade 4, have tended to be intensive, expensive, and largely ineffective.

Intact Class vs. Whole School Programs

A teacher may wish to have a mentorship program such as a "reading buddy" program or a "writing partners" program just for his or her own classroom. To keep a program self-contained in this way, it can work well to have all of the mentors come at the same time block each week. This approach requires that a suitable physical space be available for program use. Additional reading materials and other literacy development materials might also be required, since all would be in use at the same time each week. Most importantly, using one single time block each week would require that a large number of mentors also be available at that time. This can be possible if seniors or students from a particular class at a college or university are available. An intact class mentorship program with a single time block each week makes it possible for the teacher to be the program coordinator. Besides planning coffee for mentors, materials, general communication posters and memos, physical space, thank-you cards, crafts and celebrations, and sometimes fund-raising, the most important work of the program coordinator is to maintain a conversational relationship with each of the mentors and to monitor the matches. If all students have their mentors there at the same time, the teacher is free to circulate to accomplish these two most important coordinator tasks.

Operating a mentorship program as a whole school program can mean that more of the work to support the program can be shared. This works particularly well if all staff take ownership of the program and help with recruiting mentors. In a whole school program, specific grades can have priority for receiving the majority of mentors, while some mentors can still be assigned to a few of the higher needs students in other grade levels. A whole school program approach requires that someone be available to serve as a program coordinator. Besides organizing orientations, schedules, matches, refreshments, communication, record-keeping, materials, thank-you activities and celebrations, a person serving as program coordinator must greet and debrief with mentors and monitor matches. To take advantage of a wide range of mentors and their available times, each participating class in a whole school program can choose a unique set of half days as possible times for mentors to meet with children. Then, as new mentors are found, they can be assigned to classrooms according to matching time schedules. In this way, each participating class might have only three half days that are disrupted by some students leaving to meet with their mentors.

Starting Small, Thinking Big
Any school can start a program—name it, make a poster, plan a schedule. A program can be started with only two or three volunteer mentors and a vision communicated on a one-page poster or brochure. While it might seem odd to call something a program before there are a large number of participants, a program plan has to be conceptualized and communicated before people can know about it and choose to participate. Even a sign posted in front of the school can be helpful. Many schools already have two or three volunteers who informally do whatever school staff indicate would be helpful, and they can become the first mentors in the program. Local media, church bulletins, and newsletters to parents can extend program awareness. The first mentors to start can take one-page posters to clubs, work sites, or classes they attend.

While a program may start with only a few mentors, it can be valuable to plan a structure that will work well for the school if the number of mentors increases dramatically. Structural or organizational considerations can usefully include:

- Who will be the school contact person for interested volunteers?
- Who will draft a letter to parents describing the program and requesting parents' permission for students' participation?
- Who will conduct orientation sessions for new mentors as they join the program throughout the year?
- Who will maintain a master list of mentors' names, addresses, telephone numbers, and available times?
- Who will keep master copies of support materials for mentors and copy sets for new mentors?
- What physical spaces in the school are available at what times for mentorship sessions?
- What systematic communication procedure can be established at the outset? For example, if each mentor has a file folder and checks it upon arrival at the school each week, this system can be used for announcements about upcoming special events that may conflict with scheduled mentorship sessions. Also, if the mentor's student is absent, a note can be left requesting the mentor to work with another specified child instead. Some teachers may wish to maintain communication booklets with their students' mentors, and these can be kept in the mentors' folders.
- What refreshments will be made available for mentors and/or students and how?
- Will reading materials and language/math development games and art materials be made available to support mentorship sessions? Where will they be kept?
- Will students and mentors be given folders, scrapbooks, and/or journals for saving work pieces or works in progress from mentorship sessions?
- Who will take photographs of mentor/student partners?
- Who will have debriefing conversations with mentors and when?
- Who will send thank-you cards to mentors (by mail, not passed through students), prepare certificates of appreciation, write letters of reference if requested, help children prepare thank-you crafts, and organize celebrations?
- Who will explore funding opportunities to support program costs?

Planning a Time Frame for the Program

If mentors can be expected to remain in the program for the whole year, then a time frame can be planned with that in mind. If it appears that new mentors will need to be found both in the fall and in January, then that fact will influence anticipated start and stop times for the program each term. Programs of at least eight weeks' duration appear to be worth doing. Programs of 10 to 12 weeks are even better.

Recruiting Mentors

Every school will have different opportunities or constraints for accessing volunteer mentors. Depending on the context of the school and its community, any of the following approaches may be useful:

- School staff members invite friends and relatives to be mentors.
- The school invites parents and/or grandparents of students to be mentors.
- Employees of local businesses or local branches of community services are invited to be mentors (if numbers are large, an adopt-a-class approach can be used).
- Students in classes at local colleges or universities are invited to be mentors (a visit to the class by the principal works well).
- Members of local clubs, church groups, and so forth are invited to be mentors.
- The social coordinator at a seniors' lodge can help with recruiting, especially if transportation can be arranged or sponsored.
- Retired teachers can be invited to be mentors.
- Local media can help to increase awareness about the program and invite participation.

People who are interested but unable to participate can be invited to make a donation to support the costs of operating the program.

Planning Orientation Sessions

If a number of new mentors can be expected to be able to attend an orientation meeting at a single scheduled time, such as after school or at the supper hour, it can be worthwhile to plan to have the meeting attended by the school principal, program coordinator, and teachers of participating classrooms. The meeting agenda can include:

- a tour of the school, with particular attention to spaces that can be used for mentorship sessions;
- a brief presentation about the program's purpose and methods;
- opportunity for mentors and staff to introduce themselves to the whole group;
- refreshments and opportunity to complete a brief survey (address, telephone, times available, interests, hobbies and work experience, and preferred characteristics of a student to work with);
- a brief review of ethical and legal guidelines for conduct with students in the school;
- presentation of mentors' individual packages (may include school handbook, pictures and names of school staff members, information about the program, support materials pertaining to the program);
- viewing of a video program if an appropriate one is available (we helped to produce a 10-minute video program about mentorship programs and it is available from Alberta Teachers' Association) (Alberta Teachers' Association, 1999);
- fielding questions from mentors;
- inviting mentors to brainstorm ideas for activities with students;
- advising how to prepare for first session with student;
- reviewing procedures for program communication and refreshments each week;
- indicating time and method of next contact regarding schedule for program activity.

A modified version of this agenda can be used for individual or smaller group orientation sessions.

Matching Mentors and Students

Since teachers know their students best, it is preferable for them to match mentors with students. It is useful to have mentors complete a single-page survey to identify address and telephone; times available; hobbies, interests and work experience; preferences for the characteristics of a student they would like to work with (gender, age, general ability level, ESL or not, personality). The classroom teacher can meet briefly with a new mentor to review the information on the sheet and then use all information to plan a match. Typically, teachers consider students' needs and choose mentors who seem most likely to be able to support those needs. It is also important to learn what will make the mentorship work comfortable and satisfying for the mentor.

Preparation for the First Mentorship Session

Mentors can be encouraged to bring artifacts or photographs to use when telling the students about themselves at the first session. If mentors are working with young students, they can plan to help the children make "All About Me" posters or booklets. If students are older, they can be asked to write an autobiographical piece and be prepared to read it with the mentor. If mentors are working with older students, it can also be advisable to encourage them to use time during the first two or three sessions for recreational activity to build friendship and rapport before beginning more academic support work.

Maintaining a Program

Informal Trouble Shooting

It is valuable if a person serving as program coordinator can informally touch base with participants throughout the program's operation. Casual observation and conversation can help the coordinator to discover where help or changes are needed. This form of monitoring is not so much about looking for fires to put out, but about looking for wrinkles that rub and then smoothing things out— even small blisters can make people very angry or frustrated with a program. For example, mentor/student pairs working too close to each other simply may not realize that other spaces in the school are available for their use. A teacher who volunteered to put the cookies out for each day's lunchtime mentorship sessions may begin to find the task irritating when days can be so busy—and a student could take this responsibility. A mother who speaks no English and sits in on her daughter's mentorship sessions may be making the mentor feel self-conscious—a little exploration may clarify that the mother has to wait to walk her other child home from school and she doesn't know where else to be in the school; yet she might respond happily to the invitation to help organize the gym equipment. If a couple of mentors are struggling while other mentors working in the same time period are doing well, all of these mentors can be asked to shorten their sessions by 10 minutes to allow time for group sharing and debriefing at the end of each session for a few weeks. Watchfulness and thoughtfulness can help to support a good feeling about a program and the success of the program.

Formal Sessions for Problem Posing and Solving

Key staff participants in the program should plan to meet formally to review program progress, identify problems, and explore possible solutions. If problems are structural, solution ideas may need to be saved for the next time period in which the program is implemented.

Providing Mentors with Attention, Feedback, or Validation

Almost any kind of attention can be affirming for mentors. Even the simple act of someone coming around to take photographs of mentor pairs every once in a while reminds them that what they are doing is special and appreciated. Mentors also appreciate feedback and validation. This can take the form of casual conversation with the mentor while he or she is working with the student, or sharing a few words at the beginning or end of a session. It's easy to reassure mentors that what they are doing with the student is valuable and beneficial in the eyes of other adults or educators. Feedback from teachers about how the student is doing in class or how much the student enjoyed presenting the work completed in the mentorship session can also be welcome to mentors. At the beginning of a mentorship, mentors may not get a lot of feedback from the students, so reassurance from other adults is appreciated. Once mentors do see progress in the child's work, they are very interested to learn whether the student is also manifesting this progress in the classroom.

Matches That Don't Work

With young students, most mentor pairs will take three weeks to become more comfortable with each other, and eight weeks to achieve an at-home-with-each-other interaction that is characterized by focused attention and spontaneity on the part of both the child and the mentor. Leading up to that stage, mentors can often experience some uncertainty about the appropriateness of the activities they use to engage the student and to support his or her growth. Some matches simply will not work at a particular time. When a match isn't working, the mentor and student are not finding a place to be together to attend to the same things at the same time. For example, the child will not pay attention to a book being read to him by the mentor and the mentor will not try to join the child in his attempts to construct a game. To have such a match continue in this manner week after week is frustrating for the mentor and not helpful for the child. The child can be assigned to the next mentor who joins the program, and the mentor can be reassigned to another child who is waiting for a mentor.

Celebrating a Program

Celebrations are important, both to honor the contribution of the mentors and to help students learn the way to use rituals to mark events and relationships in their lives. Students can be supported in making crafts to present as thank-you presents at key times during or at the end of a program. Students can also do a group project such as a wall mural that expresses their feelings about the mentorship program. Appreciation teas make a strong impression on mentors about the school's valuing of their work. For end-of-program celebrations such as a year-end picnic, students can be supported in preparing two-minute public speeches to express their thanks to mentors. Cards from the school principal or program coordinator mailed to the homes of mentors are experienced as a personal expression of appreciation.

Evaluating a Program

Listed below are key questions that can serve to guide an evaluation of a program:

Is students' self-esteem supported?

Is students' academic growth supported?

Judgments about answers to these questions can be usefully informed by the views of students, mentors, classroom teachers, and parents; notes from observations from mentorship sessions; and work samples or records from mentorship sessions. With older students, attendance, behavior records, classroom academic work records, students' relationships with peers and teachers, students' attitudes to school, and students' further educational plans may also be of interest.

To evaluate a literacy mentorship program for grade 1 and 2 students, the following interview questions were used with children and mentors. Interviews were conducted with two, three, or four interviewees at a time using a round-robin approach, although some mentors were interviewed individually. The interviews were audiotaped and transcribed. Two interviewers were present so that one could write down responses as a backup to the audiotape. Students' and mentors' answers to questions were examined to learn about the nature of the relationships and the academic value of the activities. When students said, for example, that their mentors made them feel special or proud of themselves, this was taken to indicate that self-esteem was being supported by the relationship. When students said that their mentors helped them read harder books, sound out words, and learn new words, and that reading with their mentors was fun, this was taken to indicate that academic growth was being supported. When mentors spontaneously described strategies they used to support reading comprehension and provide challenge to the students' growth, this further reassured us that mentors were using students' time in worthwhile ways. For a fuller description of this study, see Chapter 4.

Interview Questions Used with Children and Mentors

The interview questions have been listed in Chapter 4. The questions for both students and mentors are relatively open-ended, with the intent of inviting the participants to talk in their own words about what was most salient or meaningful for them in the mentorship sessions. Classroom teachers can also be asked to offer their observations of any benefits noted in the classroom. Representative examples of answers to questions can be used in reports to give parents, staff, and participants a sense of how the program is being experienced by those involved.

Support Materials for Programs

Please see the appendices for sample recruitment letters, posters, and support materials for mentors.

‹Ð Section B ℘

THE MENTORS' PEDAGOGY

❧ Chapter Six ☙

THE PEDAGOGY OF A FRIEND:
A CASE STUDY OF ONE MENTOR PAIR

In the spring of 1997, we conducted research on literacy-support mentorship programs that we helped to initiate at two Edmonton elementary schools. These two programs are the first ones described in Chapter 2. Six to eight weeks after the programs had begun, mentors, children, and teachers were interviewed. Their comments about how the programs had supported the children's self-esteem and literacy development were so persuasive that we wanted to know more about how this support had come about in such a short time. In the fall of 1997, another literacy mentorship program was initiated at one of the original schools. As described in more detail in Chapter 7, the weekly sessions of several mentor pairs were studied throughout the fall term to learn about the mentors' pedagogy. This is the story of one mentor pair.

Joann and Cindy met Wednesdays at lunch to visit, share treats, read, write, and do art projects from early October to early December 1997. Joann was a fourth-year education student who was eager to gain experience that would be relevant to teaching. When a presentation about this literacy-support mentorship program was made in one of her university classes, she responded with interest. She hoped to try out ideas she had been learning in her courses, with the ultimate goal of supporting a child's literacy. She felt quite prepared for the work on reading: "I'm in reading and writing courses, so I do have the strategy background, and I'm trying to use many of those, just to give her wider experience" (Joann, October 29, 1997).

Joann had carefully researched other available volunteer programs and chose this one, as she welcomed the opportunity to work one-on-one with a child. From colleagues, she had heard stories of programs in which volunteers like herself were simply asked to do photocopying in schools. She had also heard of other programs in which the academics were stressed to such a point that there was no flexibility in the nature of the sessions. There were still other programs in which she could work with a child, but it would not be the same child from week to week. Joann was eager to see what would unfold between her and her mentee over time. By the end of the fourth session, she was already excited about how things were developing.

> It's wonderful. It's great to see that she's—she's very shy, and so it's really good to see that she can open up, feel warmer, just be more responsive and more involved with what we're doing. And she tells me things about her family, so it's wonderful, because she's Chinese, so I get that added bonus of hearing about, yes, her family lives together still and everything like that. (Joann, October 29, 1997)

Joann's mentee, Cindy, was in grade 3 at the time. She was born in Vietnam and her family moved to Canada when she was still a young child. English was her second language and generally wasn't spoken at home, but she was quite competent and was reading age-level books with no difficulty. She seemed rather shy at first and was soft-spoken. When interviewed she was extremely shy, but she was still able to convey her excitement about what had been developing over the course of the program. When asked how she had felt at the beginning of the program and how she felt at this later date, Cindy had this to say:

> Cindy: The first time, like, we just read a little bit, and these days we read lots and lots of books.
> Jan: Okay. Do you feel that you know her [Joann] better now?
> Cindy: Yeah.
> Jan: You feel that you know her better?
> Cindy: Yeah.
> Jan: So you said the very first day you read one book, and now you read lots of books?
> Cindy: Yeah.
> Jan: That's how it's different?
> Cindy: Yeah.
> Lucy: Were you nervous the first time?
> Cindy: A little bit.
> Lucy: A little bit?
> Jan: How do you feel now?
> Cindy: Excited.
> Jan: Excited. You're not nervous now?
> Cindy: No.
> Jan: Do you like it when your mentor comes?
> Cindy: Yeah. (December 1, 1997)

The story of Joann and Cindy's mentorship was based primarily on observations and interviews. At first, we set out to videotape them every week. We soon discovered, however, that it was difficult to hear what they were saying while trying to maintain a distance that was respectful of their space. And since the mentorship program was about working one-on-one, the intrusion with the video camera seemed a little unnatural. They eagerly agreed to have all their sessions audiotaped, and the tape recorder itself became an integral part of their special corner of the library.

Observing each week's session made it possible to understand many aspects of a mentor pair's relationship, the work that they did from week to week, and the issues they faced. In this case study, we follow Joann and Cindy from the more reserved first session through to later sessions full of student participation and enthusiasm, through to final sessions that revealed a mutuality of involvement, attachment, and learning. This is how their story unfolded:

October 15, 1997

Joann and Cindy have met two times before today, the first time we are observing their session. Joann fills us in on the nature of the first meeting they had.

> The first session we had together I made sure that that was a real open, "Let's talk; let's find out about each other." We did a mobile, and on the mobile it was "Favorite Things," and she had a color and I had a color, and so on each hanging mobile, little leaf or whatever they are, she was on one side, I was on the other with our favorite things, and it's hanging in the mentor-program room. Yes, and that way, at least, we talked about favorite foods, and then that way I know what not to bring her for the treat and things like that. (Joann, October 29, 1997)

Today, as we approach them with the video camera, they are just finishing *I'll Love You Forever*, a huge class-size version of the book by Robert Munsch. Cindy is propped up on one knee, leaning into the story as Joann reads. She is wide-eyed from beginning to end, speaking only when Joann asks her a question. They discuss the story a little afterwards. In particular, they focus on the passing down of a traditional song from one generation to the next. Cindy is very quiet and doesn't say much. Suddenly, the tone changes and Joann prepares to shift to the next activity. "That's the end of that story," she announces. They turn to the craft that Joann has planned for the day—sock puppets. Joann pulls out bags and bags of buttons, beads, and fluffy stuff to decorate their puppets and gives Cindy complete freedom to choose her materials. They sit side by side, concentrating on their work. They mainly work in silence, which is broken every now and again by small conversations about family, Joann's dogs, dollar stores, and jokes. Joann asks about the morning in class with a substitute teacher. She wants to know if they had given her a hard time by switching name tags, desks, or some such trick. Cindy giggles and denies any such goings on. They return to silence for a bit.

Usually, Joann initiates these conversations with a question or a bit of information about herself. It's still difficult to hear what they are saying and their voices sound almost tentative. Perhaps it's the influence of the video camera. Or perhaps it's just the feeling of two people still getting to know each other, searching for common topics of conversation. Once they have finished, they each choose a name for their puppet. They try them on and introduce them to each other. The conversation between puppets is a bit awkward and doesn't really go anywhere. After this brief encounter, the puppets are taken off and laid side by side so the glue can dry.

"You can eat the rest of your lunch because I don't want you to be hungry this afternoon." Joann's suggestion introduces the next activity. She will read another book to Cindy—*Big Pumpkin*. The cover is stunning and she draws Cindy's attention to it. "What do you think it's about?" Cindy guesses and Joann asks her more questions to elaborate her response. Their hands dance over the cover illustration as they make a few comments each. Then Joann begins to read. Cindy sits back and reaches for a container that has been sitting there since the beginning of the session. She opens it and starts eating as she watches the turning of pages and listens to the words that accompany them. Joann finishes the story and comments on the accuracy of Cindy's predictions. She is full of praise and amazement. Then, abruptly, she pulls out a small notebook and says, "But now, you've got to do the boring stuff. You've got to write in your journal, put what day it was, and you have to write what we did….You don't have to make it long. Write whatever you feel." As Cindy writes, Joann searches in the library for one more book to share. When she returns, she asks Cindy, "Did you like my homemade apple pie?" thus explaining the contents of the container.

In a similar fashion, they discuss the cover of this new book, *A Porcupine Named Fluffy*, and then Joann begins reading. There's something about the way she reads that draws Cindy completely into the story. I am drawn in as well and find myself resorting to video playback for other details of these moments, their body language, their conversations, and so on. They are still quiet as they discuss the book and its meaning. But they seem more relaxed. Afterwards, Joann reads what Cindy has written in her journal. Cindy doesn't want to write more, but Joann prods her. "You have to write what your favorite thing is every week. 'Cause then that way I know what you're liking and what you're not. What if you didn't like what we did today?"

Joann explains the importance of the journal in an interview two weeks later.

> At the end of our sessions we write in her little journal—she writes in her jour-
> nal—and it lets me reflect on what she's liking and what she's not. I tell her to
> write what we did, and then her favorite thing. And so I can see our activities, our
> drawing or reading of a book or something, and then I can tell what kind of books
> she likes more than the other ones, and it just gives me more of an insight.
> Lucy: Is that something that you wanted to use for your course as well?
> Joann: No. I just thought it would be a good way to track and see, for my own use.
> Hopefully, I'll be able to put it in my portfolio and keep that with me, because it's
> kind of important, I find. (Joann, October 29, 1997)

The session ends with the two drawing their favorite animals on bright pieces of paper. Joann talks a bit about herself, about her many pets, her temporary cat, and the like. And in a gesture of reciprocation, Cindy reaches into her backpack and shares its contents with Joann. This moment is interrupted by the school bell, signaling that lunch is over. They hurry to gather up their things. Joann calls after Cindy, "Is there something you want to do next week?"

October 22, 1997

It's the next session and Joann and Cindy are already sharing treats and bits of news. Joann has brought two treats this time for Cindy and asks her teasingly to guess what they might be. Cindy is correct in assuming that one has been made with chocolate—the obvious result of some previous discussion. Then the conversation shifts to the many things they have planned for today. Joann has brought four books to share and this time Cindy has brought one as well. Joann has also brought colorful paper, felt, pencil crayons, and so forth for their art project and they discuss how to divide up the time.

> Joann: So we've got five books. We can read some of them. Or we can read all of
> them, depending on how much time we have. Then we can draw a picture of
> whichever book we like best. Sound like a good idea?
> [And for the first time, I hear Cindy assert her vision of the session.]
> Cindy: We can just read one or two and then we can start drawing the pictures and
> afterward we can read another one.
> Joann: That sounds like a good plan to me.

Joann displays the selection of books and Cindy chooses the first one they will read, *The Ghastly Guest*. In what has become a habit, Joann asks Cindy to predict the nature of the story from the book's title and cover. Cindy replies with more confidence and in more detail. Joann still prods her for more. At the end of the story, Cindy draws Joann's attention to an expression she finds odd. Joann explains that it's a play on words and they look back in the book for more examples. As they do so, Cindy spontaneously points out characters and retells small parts of the story.

Cindy chooses *Ira Sleeps Over* as the second book and Joann explains how a professor had just read the book to her class. She liked it so much that she hunted it down to share with Cindy. The book begins in the usual way, with the prediction, and Joann asks if Cindy knows what a sleepover is. Her response takes off in a different direction and Cindy talks about how she sometimes sleeps over at her aunt's house, how her aunt just got married, how this aunt used to live with her, and how she moved out when her other aunt and grandma moved in. Cindy is opening up with details of family history, her life at home, and so on. After they read the story, Joann picks up on Cindy's eager-ness to share more personal stories, and she asks more questions that relate the book to Cindy's life. Each of the two main characters in the book were rather attached to their teddy bears. And so, Joann and Cindy discuss their respective teddy bears. Cindy describes the ones she takes to bed every night. Joann de-scribes the names and origins of hers.

As Cindy is still eating her lunch, the reading continues. Cindy is eager to pick the next book, but first, she talks about a book she's reading at home. She is encouraged to bring it next week, as Joann wants to know more about Cindy's favorite books. They move on to the next book—*The Mare on the Hill*. Cindy's predictions are even more detailed and Joann's questions and Cindy's elaborations flow much more naturally. The conversation becomes related to something Cindy has lost. They talk about how she felt when that happened. Joann shares a similar story and then they turn their attention to the book. This time they don't proceed quickly through the book as they often do. Instead, the story is interrupted by many little conversations about the pictures, about what might happen next, about their feelings as the different events unfold.

The word "favorite" is becoming a staple in these sessions. Today, for their art project, they will draw their favorite scenes from one of the stories. They plan to display their creations in the mentor room. As they turn to the task, Joann apologizes for the squished paper and for the old pencil crayons. They begin drawing and sharing conversations about the morning's activities.

Joann: Do you like drawing pictures?
Cindy: Yep.
Joann: I thought you liked drawing pictures. It seemed like you did. Because you said you wanted to draw last time I was here. So . . .

[Silence.]
Joann: So are you dressing up for Halloween?

And the conversation continues on to cover everything from Halloween to cooking and more. At one point, Cindy comments on how the tape (my tape recorder positioned nearby) is still running. She feels they should talk more to get it on tape. It's interesting to see how she seems less and less conscious of the camera and of the tape recorder and how she seems to take pride in the importance of their shared contribution to the study. They use the tape as an excuse to make more small talk. When the drawings are finished, they plan to hang them in the classroom. The pair doesn't use the mentor room since, as Joann explains, there are always meetings there on Wednesdays. "So that's why we're always stuck in the library. But that's okay. That way we have our own little private area."

They wind up the session with a discussion about what to do for next week. Cindy plays a more active role and they decide to relate next week's activities to Halloween. They make plans to decorate a Halloween tree. Cindy describes decorations they can make and colors they can use. As time runs out, Joann is quick to remind Cindy of the one task that must be done: "But I do need you to write in your journal. What we did and your favorite part. And you can write the date. And bring your other favorite book next week. The one you were talking about and then I'll be able to read your favorite books." And so the session ends.

October 29, 1997

The next week I find Joann apologizing to Cindy, as she wasn't able to bring the tree they had planned to decorate. She explains the different attempts she made to find the tree and how none of them worked out. Cindy has remembered to bring the book that Joann requested and she proudly shows it to her. Together they plan the session's alternate activity—recreating one of the stories they will read by printing and illustrating a summary. Joann introduces the idea:

Remember we read about Franklin and his blanket and you really liked that book. So I brought my Franklin Halloween one. And since it's Halloween this week, I thought that would be a good idea. Do you think? [Pointing to the treat she has brought for Cindy] Is that a good chocolate doughnut?

Joann may not have brought the materials for the activity they had planned, but she did make sure to put some thought into what she did bring, drawing on the enthusiasm that Cindy had shown for a book they had shared earlier. When interviewed, Joann talks about the planning being the most difficult aspect of the sessions. And while Joann makes the planning process as collaborative as possible, it still involves organization outside of the sessions to prepare materials and alternative activities.

> Lucy: Do you find anything difficult in the sessions?
> Joann: Coming up with different things every week. We were going to do a little tree, like a Halloween tree, and I never got around to getting the tree. So this morning I was thinking, Oh, my goodness! What can I do with her? So we're going to write a book today— (Joann, October 29, 1997)

Today, the transitions seem to be rougher and there's a little less chit-chat. Perhaps they are thrown off by the change in plans. Or perhaps they are distracted by the other events taking place in the library. A mentor pair is carving a pumpkin, another is acting out a Halloween story, their loud monster voices carrying over to Joann and Cindy's private corner. Cindy picks colors of construction paper to make their book. Joann reads the Franklin story to Cindy and asks her to retell it in about five sentences. The first sentence reminds Cindy, for some reason, of her sister and a story about trick-or-treating. They follow that thread a few minutes and go back to their work. Cindy retells the story and Joann writes sentences on scrap paper for her. Cindy elaborates so much on the details that they have to pick out four more pieces of paper to accommodate the writing.

Joann asks Cindy to copy the sentences on the construction paper and Cindy suggests making a cover for the book when they are done. As Joann realizes that it is taking too long, she takes over the copying of the sentences and asks Cindy to illustrate. Joann hands each page over to Cindy and asks her to read, making sure she will understand what she is to illustrate. They exchange small talk and pass different colors of markers back and forth. As the book progresses, the conversations are interspersed with the praise Joann gives Cindy about her illustrations. Twice Joann encourages Cindy to draw her own pictures and not copy what is in the book. She comments on how Cindy can draw much better. Then, out of nowhere, Cindy blurts out, "I like Wednesdays the best." Joann says, "Pardon." Cindy repeats, "I like Wednesdays the best because I have mentor day, library, drawing, and sharing also." "Holy cow! You're really lucky," Joann responds.

As Cindy finishes up the cover page, Joann gets the journal ready for Cindy to write in later. But before they go to this activity, Joann suggests they read their book in its entirety for the tape recorder. Cindy excitedly asks if she can be the one to read it and she does so proudly.

With the journal almost staring her in the face, Cindy asks if it would be okay to read a library book. With Joann's approval she scoots off quickly to find one. They begin the story, but the school bell goes off and their session ends abruptly. They make plans to finish the story later and Joann reminds Cindy that she will have to catch up with her journal the next time.

November 5, 1997

Joann and Cindy are talking about Halloween. Cindy tells her proudly how she managed to get five bags of candy. Joann asks a few questions about Cindy's trick-or-treating before she brings the conversation back to unfinished business. "Okay. We have some stuff to do from last week. Remember? What do we have to do? Can you tell me?" Joann helps Cindy recall what they did last week, and more importantly, what they didn't do as she brings out the journal.

"I brought you some cookies. I made them last night." The laborious nature of the task is mediated by Joann's offering. When Cindy has finished the entry for last week, Joann quickly looks at it and says, "Okay. We'll put it away until later today. Remind me a little before the end so we can do this today like we're supposed to do."

Joann tells Cindy that she found today's activities in the support book given to all mentors as part of their orientation and she proceeds to explain the activities to Cindy. She also brings out three books and asks, "So, what should we do today?" Cindy chooses the fingerprint activity that Joann described. Joann suggests that they do it as the second activity so Cindy can eat her lunch before her fingers get ink all over them. Cindy chooses a book for Joann to read, *The Gypsy Peasant* by Phoebe Gilman. Joann reminds Cindy that they read another book by the same author the very first time they met. She describes the story, the pictures, and what they talked about at that time. Joann tries to describe the term gypsy to Cindy. Cindy doesn't seem to understand. Joann draws parallels between gypsy potions and witchcraft. She talks about horse-drawn caravans. And finally, Joann thinks of something relevant to Cindy's world and speaks of the character Jasmine in the film *Aladdin*, which she knows Cindy has seen. At last Cindy gets the connection. As Joann reads today's book, she stops now and then to look at the illustrations and to ask for Cindy's help pronouncing difficult words and names. Cindy gets most of the words on her own. The one or two more difficult names are worked on as the two voices pronounce the syllables together.

When the book is done, they go back through and Joann explains words that she imagines Cindy would find difficult to understand. Then she asks Cindy for the "meaning" of the story. When Cindy has trouble, Joann illustrates, with examples from the book, the importance of accepting who you are. They decide to read one more story before the fingerprints so Cindy can finish her lunch. When Joann mentions that it's an older book, Cindy interrupts and talks about the year she was born and "old, old" books she has read. Joann responds, "Well, this book was written a year after I was born, so it's a really old book!" When that one is finished, Joann offers to read one more while Cindy eats. But Cindy, concerned that they might be running out of time, asks to do the fingerprint activity. They sit in their corner of the library, coloring their fingertips with markers and making impressions on pieces of construction paper. When they've made several prints, they settle down to the task of making drawings out of these impressions. Cindy giggles at Joann's stained fingers. They comment on how silly they look and yet they keep on doing the activity. They compare their fingerprints on the page and then turn their hands over to compare palm size and so forth. Then, they turn their attention back to the prints. Joann explains that they are supposed to look at them for an idea of what to draw—sort of like the Rorschach inkblots. They check each other's images now and then and Cindy explains that one of her characters is skipping or something like that. They use the word "silly" so much today and Cindy giggles almost nonstop. As they chat, Joann asks Cindy for the location of her parents' store. "I'd like to stop in and say I'm Cindy's mentor so they know who I am."

Joann talks about the activities they could do in future sessions and asks for Cindy's input. She really wants to know what Cindy would like to do. They make plans to possibly build a gingerbread house. Then Joann shows Cindy her drawings.

> Joann: You have to guess what this is.
> Cindy: A duck.
> Joann: No!
> Cindy: A bird.
> Joann: No!

Cindy's laughter gets louder each time Joann exaggerates her frustration. Joann tries to point out the tail, the feet, and so forth. Cindy laughs some more and seems to tease Joann with her inability to guess. And finally, I hear Joann exclaim, "Yes, it's a pig!"

There is a momentary break in the fun as Joann says, "So, you were going to tell me what we are going to do."

Not really in response, Cindy shows Joann all her fingerprint drawings and asks her to guess what they are. Cindy then asks if they can make more and shows Joann how they can do patterns with different colors. She carefully teaches Joann by example and seems very proud when Joann thanks her for teaching her something new. They make plans to do a really big drawing next week before Joann changes activities. "Now the boring part. You can continue your patterns after that. But please do that" [she points to the journal]. Joann tells Cindy that she has to keep a journal for each of her classes and describes it as a lot of work.

As Cindy writes, Joann asks, "Cindy. When's your birthday?" When Joann discovers that it was just before they began meeting she suggests, "My birthday has just passed too. So maybe I'll bring a little birthday cake for us next week so we can have a little party. You know what? I'm going to write it down so I don't forget what we're doing. Do you want chocolate birthday cake?" Cindy nods. "Yeah, I figured that. So we'll sing happy birthday to both of us since we missed both our birthdays."

Cindy asks to finish today with one more book. She brings a book called *Cindy's Neighbors*. Joann tells her to sit back and eat her cookies while she reads. The bell rings and Joann restates the plan for next week. "Shhh. Don't tell anyone about the birthday cake."

November 12, 1997

This week Joann is away. Cindy reads books with another mentor whose student is also away.

November 19, 1997

The day starts with an exchange of presents. Cindy has made something for Joann and has brought small gifts—a Barney button and some cards. There's a buzz of attention around the pair as the session is clearly a celebration. Joann has brought the promised birthday cake. Joann is hesitant to take all of Cindy's gifts. They decide to put them in their mentor folder so they can both share them. It's become clear that Joann and Cindy's sessions are full of moments of sharing and reciprocation.

> Lucy: Can you tell us, was it the last time now or two times ago, you had a kind of special day, Cindy. What was that that happened? I saw cake, and I saw that you brought Joann a treat. Why did you do that?
> Cindy: Because she's a nice friend.
> Lucy: Uh-huh.
> Cindy: And she always brings *me* a treat.
> Lucy: So you wanted to bring her something too?
> Cindy: Yeah. (Cindy, December 1, 1997)

A lot of time is spent talking about the gifts and taking pictures. Cindy asks Joann to help her with writing today. As she goes off to sharpen her pencil, Joann explains her absence last week to one of the mentorship researchers. Her computer crashed and she lost an entire 15-page paper. She spent from 5:00 A.M. to 6:00 P.M. redoing the project that was due that day. This week, Joann is coughing, but she is here nonetheless. She feels badly enough about having missed the previous week's session and refused to skip today, especially since she had promised a birthday celebration.

It's unclear why Cindy wants help with her writing today. She tells Joann some story about how her brother told her she is spelling her name incorrectly. She then brings her writing workbook to share with Joann. But first, while Cindy eats lunch, Joann will read her the books she has brought. She introduces the first one by recalling an earlier book they had read (*A Porcupine Named Fluffy*). Today's book, *Tacky the Penguin*, is by the same author. The name of the author makes Cindy's eyes light up and she proceeds to tell Joann about the friend she has by the same name. She describes her friend, how she knows her and that she is a twin.

Cindy, still eating her lunch, chooses the second book—*Mrs. Claus's Crazy Christmas*. They finish the story and lunch and Joann asks Cindy what she'd like to do first. She replies, "Eat cake!" They turn and offer some to us.

As they eat their cake, the discussion returns to the writing assignments. Cindy explains that she is practicing writing letters. Cindy doesn't want Joann to write, but wants rather to write and show Joann. It's as though she is proud of this new skill she is learning and wants to show it off. Joann compliments her on her letters and then offers to read another book while they finish their cake. Before they get started, Cindy talks about the books she has been reading at home. Joann explains that she read some of them when she was a child, and they discuss the stories together.

By now, Joann doesn't have to ask Cindy to make predictions. Instead, Cindy speaks spontaneously and often about ideas that come up before, during, and after the reading of the books. Cindy makes an observation about how all of today's books involve animals. They talk about the animals and classify differences and similarities. A little later, Joann goes off to find their folder. When she returns, Cindy has laid out the contents of her bag so she can show them to Joann. She shows her different kinds of paper, toys, etc. Then Cindy brings out something from her choir. She tells Joann that the choir will give a Christmas concert and Joann asks for details of when and where so she can go. Joann then asks Cindy questions about how her family celebrates Christmas. She is eager to find out about their traditions.

Cindy, for a change, proposes a discussion of next week's activities. She asks to make a mobile, something like the one they made the first time they met. Cindy then proposes an animal theme. She asks Joann to bring animal books so that they can look at them before they draw. As the bell rings Joann gives Cindy a letter to read later.

November 26, 1997

Joann and Cindy are reading a book full of dreams of monsters and worms and bugs. Their reading is interrupted by Cindy's teacher. She wants to know if Joann will be back at the school next term to continue her mentorship sessions with Cindy. Unfortunately, Joann will be doing her long-term practicum and it will be impossible for her to get to the school. The same is true for all of the student teachers who have volunteered this term, and new mentors will be matched with the students. Although it's sad news, Cindy is able to see both the advantages and disadvantages of the change.

> Jan: What do you think, Cindy, about having another mentor?
> Cindy: Good.
> Jan: Yeah? It would be good for you?
> Cindy: 'Cause it's good too. I like to know other people.
> Jan: Mm-hmm?
> Lucy: That's very good.
> Jan: Yeah.
> Cindy: And it's sort of depressing that you don't—but it's sort of depressing that you're losing your favorite mentor. (Cindy, December 1, 1997)

When Cindy's teacher leaves, Cindy tells Joann the date of her Christmas concert to make sure that Joann can come. Cindy describes last year's concert and she is clearly excited that Joann will be able to see her perform this year.

> Lucy: And she's excited because you're going to the Christmas concert, right?
> Joann: Yes.
> Lucy: When is that?
> Joann: The eighteenth.
> Lucy: And you're going?
> Joann: Yes, I'm going to go. She just has to find out the time for me. But that was the first thing she told me. I told her to find out the day; that's the first thing she came with: "It's on the eighteenth! It's on the eighteenth!" I didn't know what she was talking about at first. I was like, "What?" (Group, November 26, 1997)

This excitement, juxtaposed with the earlier conversation of departures, returns a certain lightness to their session and they turn back to their book. When the book is finished, Cindy suggests making musical instruments next week. There's no mention of the mobile discussed last week, although they seem to be reading books about animals.

Joann introduces the next book, *The Rat and the Tiger*. "You just sit back and eat your lunch." After a few minutes of reading, Cindy tells Joann stories about Vietnam, rats, and war. She describes the place she was born with stories told to her by her parents, grandparents, aunts, uncles, and so on. She then goes on to tell Joann how her father just bought a book for her and she begins a play-by-play of its plot. She is talking more and more about what she is reading at home these days and she tells Joann how she reads these books by herself.

This turned out to be the last time we observed Joann and Cindy's sessions. We were away the next week, which unexpectedly turned out to be their last session together. Two weeks later, Joann waits quite a while for Cindy to turn up. She doesn't and Joann discovers that Cindy was absent from school in the morning. She also discovers that there will be no session the following week as there is a special event taking place in the school. She leaves disappointed that they did not get a sense of closure to their weekly meetings. Earlier in the year, Joann had envisioned revisiting the journal on their final day together:

> Lucy: Do you think she likes the writing activity, then?
> Joann: It's probably her least favorite, but I make her do it anyway, because I think she needs to write it down and think about it herself, and then if we may want to go back, we can look and see what she's really liked. Maybe the last session we'll look through all the journals and see, "What was your very favorite session?" (Joann, October 29, 1997)

A few minutes later, Cindy runs into the school looking for Joann. Whatever the reason for her absence in the morning, she has rushed to school to make her session. Her face sinks when she finds out that she has missed Joann and she joins another mentor pair to read. But perhaps there is no need for closure to this story. Already, Joann has promised to attend Cindy's Christmas concert and she hopes to visit and keep their friendship alive. Cindy is doing quite well with her reading and Joann is not worried about that. And while Joann worked hard to make the "academic" aspects of their sessions interesting and challenging, she was always aware that this was only part of what they were accomplishing. For her, reaching Cindy through her interest in art activities, through conversations, and so forth, was as important as any measurable reading outcome. Joann wanted reading to be fun and to not take away from Cindy's time to eat and relax during her break.

> Joann: Yes. I'm just there if she wants to talk, if she wants to read, if she wants to write, that's okay. Whatever she—if she just wants to just sit and draw together, then that's okay. I don't want her to feel like she has to work and be pressured into

reading and pressured into doing her math homework there or whatever. (Group, November 19, 1997)

Lucy: If there's one thing...you hope [Cindy] got from this, what would it be?

Joann: Friendship. I hope Cindy thinks of me as a friend. And I want to take some pictures so that she can remember that, and she always is talking about how Wednesdays are so great because she has library and then mentor and then computers, and it's just the best day of the week. So it's nice to hear that actually they want us to be here, not just, "Oh, mentor day again. Great. I have to go read a stupid book." (Group, November 19, 1997)

In the end, Joann's plans to attend the Christmas concert and her plans to keep in touch reveal that the friendship will carry on beyond the schedule for the structured program. Her sentiments regarding their friendship reveal that all their learning has taken place within the structure of this relationship—within the pedagogy of a friend.

Chapter Seven   ⋆

PUTTING ON MENTORS' SHOES

he case study of Joann and Cindy presented in Chapter 6 is one example of a mentor pair's development in weekly one-hour sessions over nine weeks. It described the weekly unfolding of events, emotions, decisions, and circumstances that determined the directions in which the pair traveled. Although only one example, Joann and Cindy's story had much in common with the stories of other mentor pairs. In this chapter and the next, we will examine in more detail the thinking and feeling at the source of mentors' actions. In particular, we will follow what mentors did in sessions, why they did what they did, what they found challenging, what decisions they made, what considerations they took into account, what feelings they encountered, what rewards and results they perceived.

In this chapter we examine the meaning of mentorship to the mentors, how and why they came to participate in the program, and how they experienced the role once they were in it. For most mentors, taking this role was like putting on a comfortable pair of slippers; for a couple of mentors, it meant recognizing that mentors' shoes are more like slippers than oxfords and need to be walked in accordingly. We continue the analysis in Chapter 8, where we examine the nature of the mentors' pedagogical work.

In this component of the research (Chapters 6, 7, 8, and 9), our focus was on the pedagogy of the mentor. What influenced the mentor's pedagogy, and to what extent was it shaped by or responsive to the child? As reported in Chapter 4, our research on eight-week programs in two schools had indicated that mentors quickly became effective in supporting the children's literacy development. Six to eight weeks after mentors had begun meeting weekly, one-on-one with the children to read books and do other literacy support activities, mentors and children were interviewed to learn about the quality of the relationships and the value of the academic support. The results of these interviews showed that, in a relatively short period of time, mentor pairs experienced mutually satisfying relationships, with both mentors and children articulating the significance of these relationships. Furthermore, even though there were no prescribed activities or specific academic objectives to be met during the course of the program, mentors and children identified areas of progress in reading and other related skills. Positive results with respect to the children's enhanced self-esteem and increased participation in regular class activities were noted by mentors, students, and the teachers as well.

Description of the Research

These successes, particularly in such a short period of time, motivated the researchers to take a closer look at the weekly conduct of mentorship sessions. Therefore, in September of 1997, another mentorship program was initiated at an Edmonton elementary school. Mentors were placed with all children in a combined grade 2/3 class and each mentor met with the same child once a week to visit and snack, read books together, and do other literacy support activities. Researchers visited the school three to five times a week from September through December to observe mentor pairs and conduct interviews. This analysis is based primarily on the observations of mentor pairs in action. Occasionally the mentorship sessions were also videotaped and/or audiotaped. A large part of the data also consisted of audiotaped and transcribed interviews with mentors and with children.

There were regular weekly interviews with a group of four to five mentors who were students in education at the University of Alberta. These were mentors who agreed from the outset to remain at the school after their sessions each week to accommodate the interviews. Over time, the interviews evolved from semistructured question-and-answer sessions with the interviewers to venues for debriefing and sharing among the participating mentors themselves. All participants in this group were white female students in the fourth and final year of the elementary education program. They were beginning to search for employment for the following school year. Although all of the children they worked with came from the same grade 2/3 class, they varied considerably in reading abilities, maturity, social skills, and backgrounds. The following is a brief description of the mentor pairs.

Joann and Cindy

Joann, the mentor in the previous chapter, exuded confidence and friendliness. She had previously earned a diploma as an esthetician and had worked for a short time before returning to school. She worked with Cindy, in grade 3, whose family moved to Canada from Vietnam when she was a baby. Chinese was the language mainly spoken at home, but Cindy could speak, read, and write in English quite well.

Jean and Stan

Jean was a very outgoing woman. She readily agreed to participate in regular interviews, but was not interested in having her sessions videotaped or audio-taped. She worked with Stan, an extremely shy and quiet child of a visible minority background in grade 2. He had more difficulties with reading than many of his classmates.

Marie and Cole

Marie was a friendly woman from northern Alberta. She was about to return there to do her practicum in January and spoke fondly of her hometown. She was participating in another volunteer program at the time and went there immediately after her mentorship sessions at our school. She was matched with a grade 2 boy named Cole, who was often restless during their sessions.

Diana and Ben

Diana was a soft-spoken woman who was very eager to participate in the weekly discussions. She worked with Ben, a quiet Vietnamese boy in grade 2. Although English was Ben's second language, he was not experiencing difficulties in reading.

Cathy and Gina

Cathy was a warm woman who called her family's farm, outside of Edmonton, home. She worked with an outgoing grade 2 girl named Gina, and the two seemed to bond instantly.

We also conducted interviews with other mentors on a less regular basis. These other mentors were also white and female but came from more varied backgrounds. The following is a description of other mentor pairs discussed in this chapter:

Jane and Joy

Jane was a youthful grandmother figure who left her position as a junior high school teacher several years earlier. She had begun working with Joy—now in grade 2—the previous school year and wished to continue working with her. Joy was a boisterous child who had a few difficulties with reading. She much preferred doing other activities to reading and writing.

Irene and Chris

Irene was an older, strict grandmother-type. She had been retired for some time and had also participated in the mentorship program with another child the previous year. This year she worked with a grade 3 boy named Chris. His reading was probably well beyond grade level. He was an extremely intelligent and active young boy.

Sophie and Debbie
Sophie was a fourth-year education student. She worked with Debbie, an outgoing young girl in grade 2.

How Recruitment Took Place

Although poster advertisements for the mentorship program were placed around the university campus and in the community surrounding the school, in-class presentations, made to both beginning and more senior teacher education students, seemed to have the best results for recruiting. These in-class presentations about the program were made by the researchers and/or the school principal. Many students mentioned the importance of having the principal come out to speak to them rather than hearing about the school and the program second-hand. Recruiting was also done by the staff members of the school, who approached friends, relatives, and retired colleagues. Such enthusiasm on the part of the principal and other staff members gave the program a very upbeat profile.

As a result of these efforts, mentors were mostly university students, parents of children or of teachers in the school, retired teachers and principals, and so on. Although all of the volunteers in the fall of 1997—our primary data collection period for this phase of the research—were female, there were several male mentors during the term beginning in January 1998.

Why Mentors Came to the Program

The mentors expressed many reasons for participating in this program. Most of the university student volunteers learned about the program from presentations made in education classes on campus. In some courses, specific assignments were given with the expectation that mentorship program participation would provide the hands-on experiences needed to complete these assignments. In other courses, there were no specific assignments, but students were urged to participate in the mentorship program to enhance their *curriculum vitae* and support their own personal growth.

> I'll be doing my practicum in January, so I thought that this would be a really good opportunity, even just to deal one-on-one with kids, because I know that as a teacher you don't get to do that that often. I heard about it from language learning class, a class that we're in together, so the principal came to the classroom, and she

had a little speech, and it seemed really positive in something that I was interested in. (Jean, October 15, 1997)

My name is Sophie, and I got involved in the mentor program through a class of mine at the university where we have to meet with a child and read different pieces of literature, poems, whatnot with them and have them respond to the literature in different ways. (Sophie, November 10, 1997)

And just as Joann expressed in the previous chapter, and Jean above, many of the mentors were particularly interested in the experience of working one-on-one with a child and how it could benefit them professionally. These mentors felt that this experience would foreshadow aspects of classroom teaching from flexibility, to behavior management, to familiarity with what's important in a child's world.

Lucy: Can you talk a little bit about how you feel the program benefits you as teachers, even though this is a different situation from being in front of the class?

Diana: I think the one-on-one relationship. The big thing was the flexibility and having to change on the spur of the moment to suit their interests. You could be in the middle of a lesson, and all of a sudden, okay, a kid asks a question: "Oh, okay, we'll go along with that," and I think that's really good experience.

Lucy: Yes, I think you're right.

Marie: Yes, it's very good experience. And plus, behavior management and stuff, that's the kind of thing that I have to work on a little bit. But like proximity and eye contact and stuff. I'm trying to be aware of these things and trying to reinforce them to see if they're working with him and stuff. But it's just, the experience is just awesome.

Jean: Yes.

Marie: That's the best—and like what we were talking about before about spur of the moment trying to change a task, like, "Oh, this bombed. I've got to think of something else to do" or whatever, and that happens so often in teaching; that happens all the time. So it's good practice to get your frame of mind to that kind of thing, because that happens all the time.

Jean: Also keeping them on task. Once we've decided to do something, halfway through he'll be—like the spider: Halfway through he decided he wanted to do a spider. "Well, no, now we're going to do this first." And even just to know what level, I guess, kind of to—not to expect, but when you're in a school you're out of touch pretty much, *I* think, with what's going on out here. What are the kids interested in today? What is it like in the classroom for the kids nowadays? You have no clue when you're sitting in the classroom and you're reading out of a textbook.

Marie: That's right, and it's so different than from when we went to school.

Jean: Oh, yes!

Marie: Things have changed so much.

Jean: Completely, yes.

Marie: Different kinds of problems.

Jean: And you forget about what a big deal it was to take the book home to read to your parents and to sign it out and everything, or just all the little things you just forget, and it's good to see before you actually go out and do it. (Group, November 5, 1997)

Mentors outside of the university community participated in the program for various other reasons. For one mentor, it was a love of literature and the role it played in her life that inspired her to share reading time with a child.

My whole family are readers, and we're almost all writers as well, even though it's not necessarily commercial, but we all have, in one way or another, expressed ourselves in writing. When the children were little I made up stories for them and I wrote them down and they read them. And we're very opinionated, so we have letters to the newspaper fairly frequently. Although I write under my maiden name, because my husband's very well known, and people don't think I have an opinion of my own, so I write under my maiden name when I write to the newspapers. And actually, I have had a few poems published in just mostly *Alberta English*, but there too I started writing as a single person, so I kept my maiden name when I write. So I haven't published anything for a long, long time. The *Journal* only seems to print things that I write if I'm sarcastic, and I have a rather snide streak that comes out very well in written form, and when I write anything else they seem to think it's very sentimental, so my letters to the editor are quite sarcastic as a rule. (Jane, December 8, 1997)

Jane also expressed, as did some of the other senior mentors, that the program provided a way to keep working with children in a more relaxed one-on-one situation.

Lucy: You told me when we talked before, I think; has it been about 10 years since you've been in this school?
Jane: Actually, it's 13.
Lucy: Thirteen. How does it feel? What does it feel like? What does it mean to you coming back in this way?
Jane: For a long time I couldn't come back, because I burned out very badly. But I used to teach junior high, and I don't know if I could do the same thing at the junior high level, but reading with Joy is a little like baking cookies with my children when they were little. (Jane, December 8, 1997)

Some of the retired teachers and principals admitted to being cajoled into participation by staff members with whom they had worked in the past. This same admission was made by mentors who were relatives of school staff members, and it confirms the importance of the active involvement and support of school staff in initiating and supporting a mentorship program: "My name is

Ron Miles and my daughter is the intern teacher here and she kind of twisted my arm. I'm very glad she did because I'm enjoying myself immensely" (Ron, May 1998).

Thus, university students who planned to be teachers came to the program hoping to learn about children and their own capabilities in working with children. Other adults came to appease enthusiastic school staff members or because they knew they would in fact enjoy working with a child in this way for the purpose of supporting literacy.

Mentor as Friend or Buddy

Once mentors began their participation in the program, they often spoke of a certain negotiation between more specific goals related to reading improvement and more general goals related to fostering a love of reading, developing rapport with the child, and so on. After a period of time in the program, mentors spoke very clearly about how they experienced their role to be very different from that of a tutor. They felt that being mentors allowed them to focus on the positive aspects of sharing books, rather than on, for example, taking formal responsibility for addressing any specific weakness a child had in reading. Some mentors were very clear about this distinction in roles and purposes from the outset.

> Jean: Tutoring, to me, would be like one subject, going through material they're already going through. Not as fun, I think. I don't know if that's bad; I'm sure you could make tutoring fun, but it's at a different level, I think. Again, tutoring, that whole different aspect of respect probably, more the teacher figure rather than buddy figure. *Mentor* is a really good word, or *buddy* is a really good word for what we're doing. (Group, November 12, 1997)
> It's not structured like this, when it's more of a buddy thing, not so much student-teaching thing. (Jean, October 15, 1997)
> Jean: I don't know how to—just somebody, I guess, to be a role model, but not in a very imposing way; very loosely structured; a role model where he can see, "She likes reading, and she likes—look at all the stuff" and being imaginative and taking risks, like you said. But it's not in an imposing way; it's not in a structured way. Yes, a role model, I guess, if anything. (Group, November 12, 1997)
> Diana: Definitely with mentoring the structure isn't there; there's not a set objective to follow like "We have to get this done today" or "There's a specific thing to work on." And you're free to change sort of in the middle, as we often do; just that flexibility in it. And mentorship is just, you're more there as a friend, as someone to open up, just to talk to, share events of everyday life. It's not like a school situation. (Group, November 12, 1997)
> Jan: Would you say the goals are different for mentoring and tutoring?
> Diana: A little bit, I think. You're still there to encourage them, but as you say, you don't have a set—

Jan: Agenda.

Diana: Yes, an agenda, yes. It's just more flexible.

Jan: Do you think that mentoring is less stressful than *tutoring*?

Diana: I think so, because tutoring, you picture the student-teacher roles. Sometimes it could be intimidating when "I've got a *teacher* or something there." It's just one-on-one, and you're sort of nervous about working or opening up. It doesn't put as much stress, I don't think.

Jean: It means a specific subject to me, do you know what I mean? It's tutoring, tutoring in math, in English; it's very specific things.

Marie: Particular problems.

Marie: Yes, a weakness or something.

Jean: That's a really good point, tutoring is just focusing on their weaknesses and trying to—

Marie: Strengthen them. Yes. Through strategies and stuff. (Group, November 12, 1997)

Although mentors demonstrated that they took responsibility for the more academic aspects of the program by coming prepared for sessions with carefully chosen books and literacy support activities, it was clear, by the way they spoke about the program, that they saw this work as secondary to the relationships they were developing between themselves and the children. The way they articulated this hierarchy echoed the research, cited in Chapters 1 and 4, on the importance of providing moral support, of caring and of establishing friendship and trust in mentorship relationships (Smink, 1990; Flaxman & Ascher, 1992; MacIntyre, 1981). In fact, these university students felt the greatest demand for structure in their sessions came not from the program, but from certain requirements outlined as part of their university course assignments. This issue will be discussed in Chapter 9.

There were some mentors, however, who came in with somewhat different expectations or emphases regarding the mentorship program and its goals. These mentors were more focused on strategies for reading improvement and on monitoring the immediate results of their interventions. More relaxed activities related to building a relationship and just having fun were of secondary importance to them.

Gail: I wouldn't mind working with a child that actually needed the paired reading, because then they're sort of at a different level and need more of the practice, because I think Anthony could read on his own perfectly fine and still comprehend it and all that.

Lucy: And you don't think he needs—the other aspect of the mentorship is the friendship and the relationships and *confidence* end of it, and he's doing quite fine with that as well.

Gail: Yes. His family is a very stable family, and he's not one of those kids that is lacking in confidence or anything. (Gail, December 8, 1997)

For the most part, such attitudes shifted considerably over the course of the program, and mentors who were rigid about the focus on reading improvement became more open to the other benefits of mentoring a child. Jane, a retired teacher, who worked with Joy in the first and second mentorship program at the school, described the concerns she had felt during earlier sessions with Joy and how these changed in response to Joy's needs and interests.

> I felt a little uncomfortable in the beginning because I didn't think I was pushing her enough, because some of the little people that are reading are reading so much better—or were last year—reading so much better than she was, and I thought, "Oh, am I not pushing her enough?" But actually I think the pace that we've taken is good for her, because she looks forward to this time of reading. And if she's a little bit reluctant to read, I've been able to find ways to divert her attention back to it after a bit of coloring or something else.
> Lucy: That's great. I think that you bring up a valid point, because so much of this mentorship program is the one-on-one and giving her the chance to work at that pace and feel comfortable and so on, which is great. (Jane, December 8, 1997)

Over time, Jane stopped worrying so much about her student's immediate progress and concentrated more on working at the pace Joy set. She worked on motivating Joy to enjoy reading and giving her the strategies that would support reading by making these activities fun and interesting. She devised games, found newspaper articles related to Joy's interests, planned artwork related to the reading, and so on.

> I always think that you learn a lot by doing things together, and motivation is important for us, and I think if you can motivate a child to love reading, to find the imagination in books, that's probably a big key to their lifelong reading habits. It certainly is not the only key, because there are things like dyslexia and other learning disabilities or difficulties that can interfere. However, curiosity is just a natural thing, I think, for children, so arousing their curiosity is really a special treat for me to see in Joy. (Jane, December 8, 1997)

And when asked about how she felt about the term mentor, it was clear that she no longer felt pressure to push Joy beyond her capabilities. Jane, like the mentors discussed earlier, had come to understand the nature of her sessions with Joy as primarily rooted in friendship.

> I don't mind the word, but it does evoke ideas of vast wisdom, like a guru, and I don't see myself in those terms. I like it better than *tutor*, though, because tutor

implies too much of a rigid idea that there are standards to be met, and I'm not always sure I will meet them; whereas mentor is more of a friendly, has a more intimate connotation—less formal. So actually I like the word *mentor* better. (Jane, December 8, 1997)

Jane's reflections, and her earlier mentioned analogy of reading one-on-one being like baking cookies with one's own children, resonated with the experience of another mentor, who also redefined her initial conception of the program from one focused solely on improving reading skills to one that rooted reading in the types of activities that friends and family share. In an interview early in the fall, Irene described her student Chris as someone who "has trouble sitting still. He also wants to play outside and that's not what this is about" (Irene, November 12, 1997). She expressed frustration with his distractibility and with the fact that they often did not accomplish everything she wanted do in a session. Although Irene and Chris's sessions remained focused on reading, as the weeks passed, the pair could be seen reading the instructions for the kite they were building—the kite they would fly outside. Or the pair could be seen reading the recipe for the cookies they were baking, the origami they were making, etc. And Chris was almost always completely absorbed in the reading, the activities, and the many conversations they had together over lunch.

When I first saw her I thought she was like a little bit grumpy; like, she might be grumpy or something. And once I got to know her again, she *wasn't* grumpy at *all*. She always wanted to try new things. Like, she wanted to start reading a chapter book, and that was a good idea. And we started to read books, and then we would make the characters that we—the main character or characters that were in the book. Like, we would make a Zoomoo, which was a rabbit. (Chris, November 14, 1997)

Similarly, other mentor pairs maintained a focus on reading but did so in ways that were enjoyable and engaging for the children. Mentors chose books that were of particular interest to their students, while also ensuring that the reading level was always appropriate. They also encouraged students to choose books as well, exploring their worlds and their interests. And they prepared activities that would draw on the children's creativity and would encourage other ways to appreciate the written word. One pair read the rules to board games and explained them for comprehension. Another pair retold a story by illustrating it in clay. Many pairs retold stories through pictures, role-play, etc. And often the stories became starting points for more personal conversations about each other's lives, developing the bond between them and grounding the learning in ways that were relevant. In a sense, the sessions reflected a pedagogy of friendship based on mutuality, enjoyment, interests, respect, trust, and relevance to their lives. Many mentors articulated the importance of this friendship as the basis for learning. In one of the weekly interviews with the group of fourth-year education students mentioned above, mentors elaborated on how the notion of friendship came to be the key consideration for the way they conceptualized the sessions.

Jan: Would you all agree, do you all think it's best to follow the student's interest?
Marie: Mm-hmm.
Diana: I think so.
Jean: That's the only way anything's going to come of it.
Lucy: Or they're going to learn anything that you—
Jean: Or the trust to be—that's just something you have to deal with.
Marie: Yes, that's where the trust comes from, I think, as you show interest in what they're doing in things they do outside of school.
Jean: Yes, yes.
Marie: Then they'll say, "Hey, this person really is a person, not just someone just instructing me or trying to do activities and stuff."
Jean: Exactly, because it's not our time; it's their time.
Marie: That's right. Yes, it's lunch time, so—
Jean: Exactly.
Marie: —you want to try to do a little bit of different things, fun activities and stuff, compromise.
Jean: Yes, I agree.
Marie: Lots of compromise.
Cathy: I said friendship, to me, just embodies the whole thing, and everything good comes out from that. It's more than just a relationship; you can have any kind of relationship. To me it's a really, really special friendship, and we talked about today—it really took off at the end, where she had ideas like, "From this book I want to make *our* memory book about this," because she had this special idea with her orange peel and this memory coming out of it. She's *really* creative! So I said, "I'll bring the stuff in next time," and it was really important for her to tell me that she wants two copies, one for her and one for me, so that we'll have this memory book—
Lucy: To share.
Cathy: —to have, and I didn't even say anything about it. But it was going on in my mind too, but for her to think ahead like that and to want to have something, I thought that was really good and quite surprising for a seven-year-old. But it was fun; it really warmed my heart to hear her say that. And I look forward to it because it'll be fun.
Jan: You look forward to coming too, always?
Cathy: Oh, yes, definitely. Yes, I do. And I look forward, like I said, to making this book with her and having it. And she even said, "And then when you're a teacher

you can read it to the kids in your classroom!" She's so, she has just always got ideas. She's a bright little girl. (Group, November 5, 1997)

Jan: Okay. You would define mentor as like a friend?

Joann: Yes. I'm just there if she wants to talk, if she wants to read, if she wants to write, that's okay. Whatever she—if she just wants to just sit and draw together, then that's okay. I don't want her to feel like she has to work and be pressured into reading and pressured into doing her math homework there or whatever. And I think if I was tutoring, I would have to take that approach, that the kid would have to be *learning* something, whereas Cindy can just sit and talk with me and not learn anything, learn about what I did yesterday and that sort of thing. (Group, November 19, 1997)

In essence, the value that mentors placed on the relationship and the care with which they planned sessions that would engage their students in reading, fun, and new experiences reflected the nurturing attitudes the mentors had toward the children. And although a humble Jane expressed concerns that the term mentor evoked the idea of "vast wisdom," these mentors lived up to the important distinction they articulated between mentor and tutor, proving themselves to be worthy of the title. The mentors who shared their perspectives in this research have helped to clarify the thoughts and feelings that guide mentors working with young children in a literacy support program. They wanted the children to enjoy the sessions, experience the mentor as a friend or buddy, and engage in growth-oriented literacy activities in a motivating and enjoyable way. Mentors appreciated the opportunity to be semistructured and flexible in their sessions so as to have the freedom to relate to the child as a person or friend rather than as an authority figure with a set agenda and prespecified responsibilities. The majority of the mentors in our research came into the program hoping to be able to experience the role in this way. A few of the mentors took more time to recognize the need for this way of relating to the children they were paired with. Once they did, they became increasingly responsive to the children and more creative in devising enjoyable and motivating ways to engage the children in literacy activities.

ᛞ Chapter Eight ᛒ

THE PEDAGOGY OF MENTORS

In this chapter we offer our analysis of the pedagogical work of mentors. The research study that provided the basis for this analysis was described at the beginning of Chapter 7.

Interestingly, when mentors were asked to discuss what they were doing in mentorship sessions, what they were trying to accomplish, and how they were trying to accomplish it, their responses emphasized establishing or maintaining the child's friendship through working with the child's interests and always being flexible with plans for the session. They specifically commented on resisting structure, preset expectations, prescribed activities, evaluation, or "bringing stress into the sessions in any way." As we observed their sessions and listened to their other comments in interviews, however, we noted their care in actively supporting the children's academic growth. We also discerned the facilitative role of routines in their mentorship sessions. Each of the mentors spontaneously generated routines for sessions and these enabled them to learn students' needs and recognize progress.

Listening for and Incorporating Children's Interests

As shown in Chapter 7, establishing and maintaining a friendship with the child was or became a priority for mentors. A friendship relationship was seen as the way to ensure successful experiences in the sessions. Given that the mentors eschewed anything they perceived as impersonal, structured, strategy-based approaches to supporting literacy, a different but very specific and common type of planning took place. It revolved around the child—the child's interests, the child's suggestions, moods, and so on. Thus, in the beginning, sessions were planned with the goal of getting to know the child and establishing a rapport. This did not, however, take the form of one-way interviewing of the child; for many mentors, establishing rapport entailed reciprocating with stories and details about their lives as well.

On display in the mentor room were several posters made by various pairs. These posters often marked a pair's first session together, with a picture and descriptions of each of their hobbies, all their "favorites," and so forth. Joann and Cindy shared personal stories and learned about each other by making a mobile of favorite things. Another pair completed the opening pages of a scrapbook they would use for their sessions. Their names headed the first two pages of the book, where they charted everything from favorite foods to favorite music, TV shows, and more. They discussed and compared all of their entries during the session. All of their sessions included making a contribution to this scrapbook, and it became a keepsake to treasure when their time together was done: "He decided that maybe he would like to have a collection of what we did during the year. It'll probably end up quite okay. Hopefully somebody gives us a picture that somebody took" (Irene, November 12, 1997). Mentors continued to get to know the children more indirectly through conversations over lunch. They listened carefully for any interests the children mentioned in these conversations.

> Lucy: You spoke last week and you're speaking again about finding his area of interest, so do you mostly come upon those through conversation?
> Jean: Mm-hmm, I'd say, yes, through his stories, or he'll just say, "I have that at home" or whatever. (Jean, October 22, 1997)
> What I'd like to do is go more into his interests. He really shows interest in hockey, so we shared a couple books now, and maybe next time I'll bring something to do with hockey. I don't know. Something to do also with the weather changing. It's the first snowfall and stuff like that that interests me. (Jean, October 15, 1997)
> I can tell that his grandfather is a big influence on him. He talks about him a *lot*. He doesn't talk so much about his parents, but his grandpa, so that's something interesting, maybe to get a story on grandpas, because that's something special to him. (Jean, October 22, 1997)

This focus on the child's interests and on the mutual nature of the sessions included the direct involvement of the child in the planning. Joann often asked Cindy what she wanted to do from week to week, and she repeatedly asked for Cindy's input as each session went along. Other mentors also involved their students in many of the decisions. As pairs became more comfortable with each other, the children began to contribute more and more to the planning and initiation of activities. And although children like Cindy may have been reluctant at first to give their input, after the first two or three sessions they could be seen bringing books, suggesting activities, directing conversations, and so on.

You can just tell where he doesn't want to go, do you know what I mean? "Uh, no. How about we do this?" And sometimes, especially with the writing today, he's like, "How about you write today? I wrote—" (Jean, October 22, 1997)

But if he chooses to read his library book, then he reads his library book to me. (Irene, November 12, 1997)

Lucy: Who generally chooses the books? Do you, or does he?

Gail: Oh, I let him. He brings one from the classroom, but we read that, and then he scans through the library, and we read a few more. And he laughs about them, and, yes, it's kind of fun. (Gail, December 8, 1997)

Diana: We started doing a picture on dinosaurs. We were going to read a story; it was a dinosaur each day of the week. And so he's going to do a picture, a collage, and then he decided, "Oh, I want to write my own story." So he started, went off on a tangent, so it was about a sick tyrannosaurus rex, and he wrote about five or six sentences by himself without any help, so we're going to finish that next week, I think. (Group 11/5, p. 4)

Jean: And he's suggesting things that he wants to do now, which is something. It's not, I know that he just doesn't see me as somebody there to "We're going to do this, we're going to do this." He's like, "Okay, how about we do this?" He's giving ideas and suggestions now, and I'll follow through with them. (Group, November 5, 1997)

The children themselves expressed their awareness of their involvement in the direction of the sessions. They perceived the choices that were made, in particular about the books that were read, as very much shared between both members of the pair.

I have fun with her and—I learn these things every day. She does the fun things with me. She reads nice books to me. I read nice books to her. (Gina November 12, 1997)

Lucy: Who usually picks the books when you read?

Chris: Me or her.

Lucy: Both? Mm-hmm. (Chris, November 14, 1997)

Lucy: Who usually picked the books?

Debbie: Sometimes I did, and sometimes she did. Some books, like, ones that looked like they were made out of plasticine, she would kind of go and look for those ones, and some are already hers, so we couldn't really find some, but some almost looked like plasticine. (Debbie, December 1, 1997)

Lucy: So you would read or you would have your mentor read? You love that. That's great. When she comes, who usually picks the books? Do you pick them, or does she?

Sara: Both of us.

Lucy: Both of you? Uh-huh.

Sara: We take turns picking.

Lucy: You take turns picking.

Sara: Mm-hmm. (December 15, 1997)
Lucy: Do you sometimes choose books to bring? [Child nods.] Yeah? Every week do you bring books too?
Gina: Yeah.
Lucy: How do you choose your books? From the library or—?
Gina: Some are from the library; some are from my class. (Gina, November 12, 1997)

Many of the mentors felt that this openness to the students' input and focus on the students' interests not only ensured that the students enjoyed their sessions together, but also helped to promote on-task behavior and decrease discipline problems. Jane related the following positive results of accommodating the child's needs and interests.

Oh, yes. In the beginning she was a reluctant reader; she really didn't like to read. She wanted to play games, and she told me that her favorite parts of school were recess and gym, so she's obviously an active little girl and likes to move around quite a lot. So I devised a game where she would be able to play hopscotch, and we would put flash cards down on the hopscotch squares, and as soon as she could read the word, then she could step or jump on that square. She usually steps; I think she doesn't want to disturb the card. But she likes that once in a while because it helps her get rid of some of her energy. (Jane, December 8, 1997)

In the following interview excerpt, Irene commented on the need to discover and incorporate her child's interests.

But I feel I have to be one step ahead of him, above him. And I see that I have to be ready with many activities for him, because his interest span, I find, is very short. He gets bored very easily. I have not at this point really discovered what his interests really are. (Irene, November 12, 1997)

As shown in Jane's and Irene's comments, mentors sought to minimize distracted behavior by keeping students interested and actively engaged in the literacy support activities. Maintaining interest was understood to be of prime importance, since most sessions took place at lunch and the children had already spent a full morning in the classroom and would spend a full afternoon there again. Keeping children actively engaged not only helped in the pairs' accomplishments during the sessions, but it kept distracted children from disrupting the sessions of other pairs. Early in the program, when Chris was distracted, he would visit his classmate Cole, who sat nearby with his mentor. This was not productive for either pair. In later sessions, when Chris was busy making his kite, making origami characters or having his first experience of baking cookies, he had little time and desire to wander.

Learning Flexibility

A committed focus on the children's often fluctuating interests, their changing moods, and other possible distractions often made planning difficult. Mentors often came prepared with many activities but expressed the need to master a certain flexibility in the execution of their plans. On many occasions, mentors had come with books and activities, only to set them aside to follow the children's leads. Jean, for example, having discovered through many conversations that Stan's grandfather was an important person in his life, prepared a session on grandpas that was complete with reading materials, art projects, and so forth. As she brought out the books and attempted to move toward the topic, Stan moved toward the monster house they had begun the previous week. When she tried to divert his attention back to the book on grandfathers, he chose instead a book on fish.

> Jean: The thing that I was always going to do with the grandfather and stuff like that totally just bombed. I don't know whether it was the book, but I brought this book, and it was *When I Grow Old with You* and all this sort of stuff, and then we were talking about his grandpa, and he *loves* to tell stories. He just tells stories, and it's so funny. And then finally I'm like, "Okay, well, how about now we—?" and we discussed what he likes to do, what his favorite thing is to do with his grandfather. "Okay, so let's maybe draw. Would you like—?" "No." Mm-hmm, he just said, "No, I don't think so." Okay. "No, no." He's like, "Let's work on our monster house again." I'm like, "Okay." We worked on that quite a bit, but then he brought a book about fish, so I'm like, "Okay, scrap that whole—" Whsht! "Next, fish book." We focused on a couple pages in there, and then went off and did an activity with that, just to learn more about them or whatever, but had to scrap that first plan.
> Jan: When you brought that book I thought that was so wonderful, because I know, that's exactly what you said last time: He loves his grandfather, and that's all he talks about, and all his stories about his grandfather.
> Jean: Yes, yes, yes.
> Jan: So you brought that book. I mean, that was a brilliant idea! Really, it was.
> Jean: And he was just like, "No, I don't think so," and I'm like, "Okay!"
> Lucy: He doesn't want to make Grandfather the center of it.
> Jean: No. I'm like, "All right, fine, whatever." So we did a fishy thing.
> Jan: But you handled that really well when he didn't want to do it. I noticed that you didn't look upset or anything, and I—
> Jean: I was pretty choked! It was like, Okay, fine! There goes everything. Whatever. That's what I'm so prepared for. (Group, November 5, 1997)

Similarly, other mentors spoke of the need to often let go of planned activities.

> Jan: You keep a notebook with a plan? That's neat.
> Irene: What I expect to do that day; whether I'm going to do it or not is another
> thing. (Irene, November 12, 1997)

Planning and flexibility were perhaps two of the most demanding aspects of being a mentor. Joann, for one, spoke about the difficulty of finding interesting and motivating things to do every week. The time that mentors devoted to preparation showed that the program was more than a one-hour-per-week commitment. Abandoning plans in which mentors had invested so much was, as Jean stated above, difficult to do.

Mentor Goals

As discussed above, mentors emphasized the importance of having fun, being flexible, and following the student's lead. With these goals in mind, they expressed a desire to resist evaluation or other structures that could bring stress into the sessions. At the same time, what mentors actually did in sessions revealed structures they constructed as they informally assessed children's capabilities and deliberately encouraged and supported new learning. Whether or not these learning goals were articulated, observations of sessions revealed mentors' intentions that gave direction and purpose to the sessions.

A Focus on Literacy

The books that the mentors chose took not only the students' interests into account, but also their particular reading levels. If students chose books that were too easy, they were sent back to pick more appropriate books. And students who had more difficulty reading were often encouraged to try more of the reading themselves, in ways that would build their self-esteem. Mentors made use of many strategies to enhance reading comprehension. Students were asked to predict, retell, finish sentences, explain words, and so forth, often with illustrations as cues. And there was a constant cross-referencing of stories and their relevance to the lives of the children. This helped to ground more abstract concepts and make connections across books and experiences. Although much of the time the pairs spent together revolved around the sharing of books, mentors planned other activities—crafts, conversations, writing—as vehicles to extend the reading and help the child experience the role of reading and writing in other areas of daily life.

Diana: Today with the writing, though, I was discussing the story last week, and I was coming up, "Okay, what happens next?" about his dinosaur, and so we said something, so I wrote it down. He was like, "Oh!" and he looks at it, and then he writes it down himself, and it was easy. And then he started writing on his own just after that, so he's really good with the writing; it's just preferably try to come up with something. (Group, November 12, 1997)

We wrote a letter to her cousin in Kelowna that I think is nine or ten; I don't know if she's got a reply. It wasn't a very big letter, but I just thought the idea of writing a letter would give another example of how reading and writing are important and necessary for our day-to-day lives. (Jane, December 8, 1997)

We are currently writing a story; I can't quite remember what it's about. Oh, we had some words last week; we wrote some words down, and it occurred to me that if we put some of these words together we could come out with a story. So the story so far has evolved around Christmas and children, and a dragon who comes down from Mars, and I think he takes the toys from the tree. I'm not sure exactly; we haven't finished it. But Joy has pretty much dictated it, using the key words that I have given her, which I think is an addition to developing her imagination. (Jane, December 8, 1997)

Sessions were indeed, as mentors had hoped, focused on having fun, but they were also dedicated to the child's learning.

Role of Routines

Mentors also used routines well to make the most of the short amount of time they had with the children during the lunch period. As the weeks passed, fewer explanations were needed for regular activities and the transitions between them. The children could even be seen reminding mentors now and then of what was to come next. Routines were established to deal with all kinds of things: when they were to eat, who would read when, when to resume unfinished work, and so on. These routines also seemed to support a sense of security and trust despite the fact that sessions took place only once a week. Students had a sense of what to expect and how to proceed in each situation, which supported a learning environment geared to success.

Gina: I felt kind of nervous the first time. [sighs]
Lucy: Yeah, you were nervous?
Gina: But now I feel okay. I don't have to take deep breaths when I do it, when I go with Cathy. I have fun. (Gina, November 8, 1997)
Lucy: It's fine. Is meeting at lunch time a nice time to meet too?
Chris: Yep.
Lucy: Yeah, you like that.

Chris: 'Cause you get to eat together, and if I'm finished first I read her a story while she eats her lunch, and if she's finished first she reads me a story while I finish my lunch.
Jan: Wow! You have a good rhythm worked out, don't you?
Chris: It's usually her finished first, 'cause she just brings two cookies. (Chris, November 14, 1997)

Some routines were established almost spontaneously over the course of the sessions. For some pairs, each session's opening had a particular ritual, bridging the transition from classroom to mentorship session. Joann and Cindy began with an exchange of treats—a homemade dessert brought by Joann and candy from Cindy, or a drawing or a trinket from home brought by Cindy: "Joann: Yes, she always brings, though, something, candy or something, so I bring her a treat, she brings me, and it's kind of a nice share" (Group, November 19, 1997). For Stan and Jean, it was the yellow activity box (a toolbox that Jean had decorated) that set the mood for the session. The box carried the materials for their art projects and was usually placed on the table beside the books. Stan could look inside at the beads, glue, Popsicle sticks, or whatever and anticipate the activities to come.

Usually while he's eating, that's when we read the book. He interjects every once in a while, helps me. It's not like I'm always just reading or anything. And then we'll usually go into a craft or talk about stuff. That's basically routine. I know that the big yellow activity box has to be there. I had it underneath the table, and he goes, "Did you bring that yellow thing?" I'm like, "Yes, yes, yes. Don't worry about it; it's here." (Jean, October 29, 1997)

Others, like Joann and Jean, created a certain flow to their sessions.

Sophie: I like picking a book or two and then reading it together and then doing an activity about the book, so I'd like to keep that up. (Sophie, November 10, 1997)
We usually start with a joke or a riddle and get things going while he's having his lunch. Then I read to him while he's eating, and he has a book that was a gift, I guess, from somebody called *Teacher's Pest*, and he calls it his *chapter book* because it has little chapters. So we're reading that now, and if he feels like it after he's finished luncheon, he'll read maybe a chapter to me. But if he chooses to read his library book, then he reads his library book to me. But we both read. So we have a riddle or a joke or this kind of thing. And then we have a scrapbook that we do, keep things together, kind of thing, so I thought that would be fun. (Irene, November 12, 1997)

Maintaining Continuity Through Absences

When routines were broken due to absences or the end of their time together, mentors found other ways to establish some continuity. When Jane was away on vacation, she would always make sure there was a letter left for Joy to open on the day they usually met: "When I do have to be away because of—or *choose* to be away I suppose is a better word—I try to leave a letter for each Monday that I'll be away so that she'll have something to read anyway at the lunch hour that is a part of the two of us" (Jane, December 8, 1997). And similarly, when another mentor, Cathy, had to go home one week to her family's farm, she left Gina something to anticipate their next session together—a promise of something to see and of something to keep. The following session, they shared pictures and stories of her farm, her family, her horse, and so on. And then she presented Gina with a friendship bracelet to keep. When their sessions ended in December, they decided to be penpals, continuing the writing and reading they have shared in a different form.

> Lucy: Are you going to be sad when they have to stop coming? Because soon they have to go out and do their practice teaching, right?
> Gina: Yeah.
> Lucy: Yes? But Cathy and you are going to keep in touch. How are you going to keep in touch?
> Gina: Writing letters to her. (Gina and Cindy, December 1, 1997)

For Joann and Cindy there was the Christmas concert to anticipate after their sessions had ended.

Clearly, although many mentors expressed resistance to structure or expectations when discussing their focus on responding to the children's needs and interests, structures based on routines, planning, and multiple goals were indeed in place. Ultimately, the structures created by mentors contributed to the positive experiences they wanted for the children, both by providing continuity and security and by serving as vehicles for challenging students with more demanding tasks or activities.

Mentors Highlight Student Progress

The structured nature of mentorship sessions also gave mentors the opportunity to assess and monitor the children's progress with many kinds of activities. Watching the children work through routine activities and master certain skills made it possible for mentors to highlight examples of learning and celebrate these accomplishments, thereby supporting the child's self-esteem and confidence. In a relatively short amount of time together, mentors were able to establish a sense of their students' abilities. Although they acknowledged these abilities with praise, they also gently encouraged students to work in areas that required further progress. For example, Jean often worked with Stan on completing current activities before beginning new ones.

> He really wanted to go outside today. That was his—so I'm like, "Okay, just, let's write in our book." (Jean, October 29, 1997)
> Jean: It was going back and forth and stuff today, and he really wanted to do instruments, but I really wanted to follow through and finish up from the spider stuff that we did last time, so I said, "Next time we will do instruments." But I wanted us—"We said we were going to do the spider web, we're going to do the spider web, and we're not going to start halfway through, and I'd rather do one thing with instruments next time."
> Lucy: That's good. So at least you're getting him to learn about finishing up.
> Jean: Yes, yes. (Group, November 19, 1997)

Joann worked with Cindy on writing her journal entries and on opening up both in her writing and during the sessions: "I want to see her even warm up more to me, and hopefully her journals get longer and more in depth, because even from the first one that we've written and to the fourth session, she's written a little bit more, a little bit more each time—" (Joann, October 29, 1997).

Chris was already an excellent reader, but Irene recognized a need to work on having him stay on task.

> Oh, I'm easy to get along, but as I said, being a grandma, my expectations are a little—you know how grandmas are: They expect the children to behave, and I find that I do this to him, that I expect a lot, where maybe a young mother would say, "Oh, well." I think that the young people anyway, young parents, *I* feel that way, that the children have their way a little too much. But I'm a grandma, of course; I see them that way. But a little of that is good for children, I think.
> I honestly feel that the children really enjoy to know their limits, because they know where they stand, don't they? You give them too much freedom, they're kind of lost souls. So I'll play grandma to him. (Irene, November 12, 1997)

Jane focused on motivating Joy to read in general.

> Even if she's sitting still, her preference was for games that often have no reading attached to them, but they do deal with colors and shapes and stacking things, so they're eye-hand coordination still. So we would do some of that, and then I would either tell her she could do this after we had read a book, or I would let her do that and then we would read, because that way it wasn't so continuous at the same activity. And when you think that these children who last year were in grade 1 sat most of the morning with a little bit of movement, but not too much,

and after all, noon hour was a time to be free and exercise their muscles, it struck me as a little bit tedious for her to be sitting reading constantly. But this year she seems to have settled into reading a lot more. She tells me she borrows books from the library. (Jane, December 8, 1997)

In many cases, mentors noted improvement in areas where they had had concerns. For example, Jane noted significant changes in Joy's reading.

Now, I don't know whether it's just the school library or whether she goes to the public library. She's reading more in a smoother fashion than she did last year. Last year was word by word; this year it's usually smooth and in sentences, and, of course, that indicates her confidence as well as her ability. So some of the books that I select are perhaps a little more challenging for her, and she occasionally misses a word or stumbles over a word, and if I correct her, she says, "I know." (Jane, December 8, 1997)

In Joann and Cindy's reading, prediction had become such a regular strategy that Cindy quickly began predicting and elaborating without prompting. Diana, like Joann, had to work harder in the beginning on getting her child to engage more freely in the discussions. Just as Joann did, Diana noticed a satisfying transformation over their time together.

I guess with me with Ben, I noticed a big difference between the first two sessions, and then the last few he's talking a lot more. But I find that he is in general a quieter kid. I usually have to prod him with questions, and I feel like he's going to be tired of all these questions, but he doesn't say much. I know he doesn't talk much about his family, but Vietnam he likes to talk about every once in a while, so I ask him, "What's it like there?" and then he'll go off into a story. But sometimes I have a hard time understanding what he says, a lot of the time. But he has opened up a little more to talk. I'm just trying to think of ways to help him a bit more. (Group, November 5, 1997)
And he was telling me stories today and just on and on; he just talked nonstop. (Group, November 26, 1997)

The mentors found these changes to be very rewarding and celebrated the children's progress with praise and encouragement. Outside of the sessions they talked about these experiences as extremely rewarding. And just as the mentors perceived all learning to be rooted in friendship, their friendships, too, were rooted in learning.

We're having tons of fun and learning how to write Chinese. We're doing all kinds of fun things for special days. All kinds of Irish things for St. Patrick's Day. I'm learning all kinds of things about the Chinese culture I didn't know. We're becoming fast friends. (Ron, May 1998)

Children's Perceptions of the Experience

The children themselves expressed their enjoyment of the time they spent with mentors and identified the benefits of participating in such a program. Given the choice, many of the children would have liked to meet more often with their mentors.

> Lucy: What would be ideal? What would be the best for you, once a week or more times a week?
> Sara: More times a week; every day a week.
> Lucy: Really? You'd like to miss—
> Sara: Yeah, I love it.
> Lucy: You love it?
> Sara: Mm-hmm, yeah.
> Lucy: You'd even miss your going outside every day to read?
> Sara: Yeah.
> Lucy: Yeah, you really like reading. Great.
> Sara: Mm-hmm. (Sara, December 15, 1997)
> Lucy: Was that perfect, or would you like a mentor to come more times—every day, or what would be perfect and still give you time to eat lunch and play outside and all of that?
> Debbie: We usually just say we don't go outside until the bell rings, and I would like to see if she can come three times or two times a week.
> Lucy: So a mentor two or three times would be even better? (Debbie, December 8, 1997)
> Lucy: Would you want to meet at a different time of the day? Or would you want to meet more times in a week if you could?
> Gina: Yes, and spend more time with Cathy.
> Lucy: Yeah, you'd like to. How many times a week? Every day?
> Gina: Mm—
> Lucy: A few times?
> Gina: One week after another, so it goes Monday, Tuesday I skip, Wednesday, Thursday I skip, Friday.
> Jan: Every second day. (Gina and Cindy, December 1, 1997)
> Lucy: I know we already asked Gina this question: Cindy, would you like your mentor to come just once a week, or come more times a week or every day?
> Cindy: More times.
> Lucy: Yeah, how many times a week? What would be good for you?
> Cindy: All the days.
> Lucy: Every day? You like it that much, huh? Why is it important to do that every day? How does it help you?
> Cindy: Read.

Jan: Helps you read, mm-hmm. How else does it help you?
Cindy: To learn more things. (Gina and Cindy, December 1, 1997)

Although many of the children's comments were simply stated, it was very evident that they appreciated the time with their mentors and would like to have even more. The following interview excerpts provide examples of the ways that the children articulated the benefits of the program.

Cindy: The first time, like, we just read a little bit, and these days we read lots and lots of books. (Gina and Cindy, December 1, 1997)
Gina: I have fun with her and—And I learn these things every day. She does the fun things with me. She reads nice books to me. I read nice books to her. (Gina, November 12, 1997)
Jan: How about you, Gina? How does it help you when your mentor comes?
Gina: It helps me print more 'cause we do a lot of writing. We read a lot. Sometimes I even bring two books. And that's all. (Gina and Cindy, December 1, 1997)
Jan: Okay. Do you like it, Chris, when your mentor comes?
Chris: I do!
Jan: You do. Why do you like it?
Chris: I like it because when my mentor comes we have a chance to pair read or read different kinds of books, and we sometimes make different kind of crafts that go along with books, and sometimes we make little rhyming poems with five sentences. And what I have is, I have a scrapbook, and it's full of crafts and writings and pictures. And for Halloween we did a spider, two black cats, and an alien dog with three eyes.
Jan: Wow! Is there anything else that you like that you do with your mentor?
Chris: I like it because we just make different kind of crafts, and we read a lot. (Chris, November 14, 1997)
Chris: 'Cause we have a turn to have somebody like a mentor.
Lucy: And that's important, isn't it? Yeah. Why do you think that's important?
Chris: 'Cause lots of kids need to improve on writing and do better reading skills, so—and I did it. I already had pretty good reading skills, but still, it gives me a chance to improve if there is anything wrong. (Chris, November 14, 1997)
Lucy: Tell me why you like having a mentor.
Gina: Because it could help us to get higher grades and achieve more things.
Chris: And you get to play fun games and if you're a person who's not very good at reading and you're shy and you're not really friendly with people it could help you with that. (Chris and Gina, May 1998)

From the children's comments, it is evident that they experienced the sessions as both fun and helpful. They mentioned fun activities and doing "nice things." They also mentioned their own progress with reading, writing, and becoming less shy.

The only negative sentiments communicated by the children had to do with the difficulty of having sessions end and of saying good-bye to their mentors. They spoke of sadness, but despite this, the children looked forward to keeping in touch with their mentors and to meeting the new mentors they would have the next time around.

> Jan: What do you think, Cindy, about having another mentor?
> Cindy: Good.
> Jan: Yeah? It would be good for you?
> Cindy: 'Cause it's good too. I like to know other people.

Cindy and her next mentor, Ron—whose mentorship work is discussed in Chapter 9—hit it off famously. Losing mentors may have been very difficult for some children, but it is important to consider how their sadness at the ending of a positive relationship differs from the experience of rejection or abuse. Tully and Brendtro (1998), who have worked with children with severe attachment problems, have argued that children benefit from many close relationships in their lives and that their grief at leaving those relationships is a measure of how much they have been loved. They also explain that once children with attachment problems establish a bond with a professional caregiver, it is important for them to extend this fledgling trust to other significant adults and peers. Thus it could be argued that if children can successfully establish a bond with a mentor in a two- or three-month program, it may in fact be to the child's benefit to have a new adult as a mentor in the next term of the program. Each mentor who bonds with a child communicates to that child that he or she is lovable. Conversely, if a child and mentor have not formed a strong bond in two or three months, it perhaps is not an ideal match and it may be just as well to offer the child a different mentor in the next term of the program. The children in our mentorship program communicated their understanding of why mentors had to go, whether it was at Christmastime or at the end of the university school year. They seemed to incorporate these changes into the overall picture of schooling, which is marked by changing teachers and changing classes. In early January, realizing that most of them would be assigned new mentors, the children were often heard to ask "When are the mentors coming again?"

Reflection

While the mentors' planning for academic support in the mentorship sessions was an important component of this program, this research revealed that there was much more going on in the weekly interaction of a successful mentor pair than the execution of a well-designed plan. The adult became a glimmer in the eyes of the child and the child became "a glimmer in the eyes of the adult" (Tully & Brendtro, 1998, p. 153). The mentors came to see the children as bright, creative, and engaging, and the children made it clear that their time with their mentors was special and they wanted even more. The significance of the mentorship experiences for both the mentors and children went beyond an academic involvement to incorporate a genuine bond, a friendship that was rooted in learning.

The very fact that so many mentors were attracted by the specific design of the program—meeting one-on-one with the same child weekly—suggested from the start that they were there to work with the whole child and not just with her/his reading skills. For most mentors, much of the fun and success of the program was in getting to know the children and in learning to create literacy experiences specifically for them. Given the varied backgrounds and needs of the children, these were not literacy experiences that could be anticipated, but rather were ones that could only be imagined once the children opened up in ways not possible in the classroom.

> Unlike traditional teaching where everyone is supposed to learn the same curriculum, often at the same pace—despite personal interests, abilities, or conflicts—mentoring asks that these very interests and conflicts be the heart of the relationship between the adult and the youth. Thus personalized care and attention to individual needs lie at the core of mentoring. (Flaxman & Ascher, 1992, p. 11)

Mentorship sessions were mutual learning experiences in which mentors were challenged to abandon the more traditional roles of teacher and student, replacing them with more equal roles of collaborators and friends. These roles enabled mentors to discover children's needs and interests and to respond with collaboratively constructed activities to which both parties became increasingly committed. It follows, then, that there is no prescription for guaranteed success in mentoring sessions. One can learn much from the examples in this chapter to anticipate the possible nature of the mentorship experience in a literacy-support program for young children, but ultimately, the success lies in the magic that can unfold between mentor and child.

❧ Chapter Nine ☙

PROGRAM DESIGN AND SUPPORT ISSUES

In studying the literacy mentorship program described in Chapter 7, we identified a number of issues that are worthwhile to consider when planning such programs. These issues pertain to recruitment; university students completing course assignments in the context of mentorship work; prescribing activities for mentorship sessions; scheduling sessions; physical space for sessions; role of a program coordinator; matching; and race, language, and cultural issues.

Recruitment

Recruiting mentors, particularly for whole class or whole grade programs, is perhaps the most difficult task that program planners face in the early stages of initiating a mentorship program. In the case of the program we studied, we were able to recruit enough mentors to work one-on-one with each child in a combined grades 2/3 class for the fall of 1997. As the year progressed, mentors were also found for all of the grade 1 students. In January of the previous school year, we found mentors for all the grade 1 students and almost all of the grades 2 and 3 students in the same school. A few of the original mentors continued their participation in the program for three terms. As discussed in Chapter 4, the research on early literacy highly recommends one-on-one support to children in grade 1 and in grades 1 through 3 if possible. Achieving this goal through a volunteer mentorship program entails dedicated, creative use of existing opportunities.

It is unlikely that a school would find the number of mentors needed solely through impersonal modes of advertising—putting up posters, newspaper ads, and so forth. Instead, as proved more successful in this school's example, the personal involvement of the school staff and researchers in recruitment was needed. In this regard, the researchers filled the role that would otherwise be carried out by a program coordinator if funding were available for one. Several education classes at a local university and college were visited by the researchers and/or the school principal for the purpose of making presentations about the program and the school. Many of the mentors came from these classes, and they commented on the positive impact of the principal's enthusiastic presentation. The principal's presentation persuaded them that the school environment for the program would be upbeat and friendly, with staff and mentors working collaboratively for the children.

For recruitment plans, each school would have to consider its community resources and program funding. In some instances, funding for transportation could create opportunities for otherwise inaccessible mentors, such as seniors living at a distance. Cooperative programs can be established with college or university classes. An adopt-a-classroom approach can be taken with a department or unit in a local business or other organization. Community clubs and societies can also be approached. It is our firm conviction that there are many adults in our communities who could spend an hour a week to contribute to the life of someone else's child. Elite athletes, for example, can find this a satisfying way to give back to the communities that have supported them.

One of our most effective mentors, Ron, was a real estate agent who became a real grandpa figure to the child he worked with. Although the recruitment of university and college students greatly contributed to the program we studied, it is important to recognize that children can benefit from mentorship relationships with other members of the community as well. It is worthwhile for program planners to consider ways to encourage participation from other institutions and individuals. Ron was encouraged to participate in the program by his daughter, an intern teacher at the school. He worked full-time in real estate but once a week was able to organize his day around his mentorship session with Cindy. In a videotaped interview, Ron discussed the importance of community involvement.

> I think everybody who has a love for children should be involved in a mentor program. You don't have to be a teacher to be involved with children. You don't have to have a degree in education. You don't even have to have a university education. All you have to do is be yourself and have a love for children. It's very simple. Things just develop on their own. Get involved. (Ron, May 1998)

Many recruitment possibilities can be explored by a program coordinator once funding for such a position is obtained. In the meantime, even a small program can be initiated by drawing upon any parents who regularly volunteer to help at the school. Often such parent volunteers would welcome the meaningful work of being friends with a child and doing reading and writing together. The idea of "build it and they will come" can be very true for these programs.

In the program we studied, there was no formal screening of mentors. All of the mentors were known to the school staff or to the researchers and their university colleagues. In programs where mentors are not so well known, it is advisable to use official police checks and child welfare checks.

Mentors Completing Course Assignments

In the program we studied, the mentors who were education students raised important concerns with respect to their course commitments and the mentorship program. As mentioned in the previous chapter, some university instructors encouraged participation in the program by treating the experience as fieldwork that would contribute to specific assignments in their courses. These assignments often required a specific structure for the mentorship sessions. For example, some university students were asked to read to the children and complete particular "reading response" activities. They were also required to keep a journal describing the sessions and to submit these reports along with a written analysis at the end of the course. Encouraging mentor participation by connecting the program to education course requirements was crucial to the success of recruitment efforts.

Unfortunately, university education students experienced conflicting obligations when mentorship sessions had to be described for course work. Mentors from these classes spoke of the difficulties of trying to complete the course assignments and still preserve the flexibility and fun in the sessions. They worried that the demands or structure of the course assignments would interfere with building relationships in the student-centered approach they preferred to follow. In the end, many of the mentors chose to not compromise the flexible the nature of their time with the children, but instead admitted to embellishing journal entries to suit the written assignments they had to complete. It would be valuable if course instructors could consider how assignments could make the best use of the education students' opportunities for learning when they work as mentors in such programs. Now that case studies such as those in this text are available, it may be more feasible to design course assignments that are better suited for education students who work as mentors in literacy-support programs.

Prescribing Activities for Mentorship Sessions

The case studies in both Sections B and C of Part One of this text revealed the importance of allowing and requiring mentors to do their own planning for sessions. Mentors wanted children to enjoy the sessions. They worked hard to accommodate children's interests and were flexible in changing their plans according to students' needs or desires. As highlighted in Chapter 14, mentors used various activities as needed to help them to get to know the child, encourage the child's comfort and spontaneity, and keep the child engaged. Just as the previous section clarified the difficulty in accommodating structured university course requirements in the mentorship program, any apparently "convenient" booklet of weekly activities would undermine the potential of the mentorship sessions.

Before Mentors and Children Meet

In the program we studied, mentors and children knew nothing about each other until they met at their first session. In group interviews, mentors discussed this approach and considered alternatives. On one hand, mentors thought it would be useful to know more about the children in advance, especially since they had a relatively short time to work together. On the other hand, mentors worried about the kinds of assumptions they might have based on any information they might be given. That is, they wanted to resist preconceptions around certain labels and, in a sense, spend the first few sessions getting to know the child through their own modes of interaction. Ultimately, they agreed that it would be good to jump-start the program and alleviate some of the tension of the first meeting by exchanging letters of introduction before the first session. Given the amount of time that can elapse between pairing and the scheduling of the first session, a letter exchange could function as a nice ice breaker for the sessions to come.

> Lucy: I'm just curious if you had suggestions in how mentor-student pairs are introduced.
> Diana: Helpful just to get maybe a list of interests or something about the child beforehand, just to have a general idea for the very first session.
> Jean: You mean like, once they've paired you up, that you have something? Is that what you mean?
> Diana: Yes. Or just to know some background about the child, where he's at with his reading, is he a good reader, is he a poor reader, that kind of thing.
> Cathy: I kind of agree with you in some ways, but in other ways I kind of like the way it happened, like this, because I didn't have any predetermined, "Oh, she has this problem with reading. I'm going to expect that, and then I'm going to work on that." This way it was good for me because I'm going to have to be assessing kids when I get to be a teacher. And also, like I said, it didn't put her at any sort of a disadvantage—or advantage. I didn't know if it was a girl or a boy, what age; I had no idea. And I think it was important—and I assumed—there was no way she could have known anything about me either, because nobody did, really. On the

other hand, it might be something to base it on, to get a head start in the relation-ship, but I don't know.

Cathy: Yes. I think you'd have to be careful. I don't know what kind of system would be best for [preparing the mentors and children to work with each other]. I personally didn't have a problem with the way we did it.

Jean: No, I think because it's just like the way it would be in a classroom.

Cathy: Yes.

Jean: You have to really adapt quickly to see what's going on in their heads.

Diana: Or you could ask the child, say, just get the child to write a few things that you would like your mentor to know, or for *you* to write it.

Cathy: That's a good idea, a letter exchange. [Several speak at the same time.]

Jean: A letter exchange? That's a great idea.

Cathy: That's better, yes, definitely, the same from the teacher.

Jean: Saying, "My name is …. I'm looking forward to meeting you," kind of thing. And then you can write back, "I'll see you soon, and this is what I'm kind of thinking," yes.

Lucy: And what questions they have about you.

Cathy: Yes. And the teacher wouldn't do it, but they could help structure it, and they could say, "Tell them what you like and what you're good at" and stuff like that. I think, yes, that's a great idea.

Diana: Yes, that would be good.

Cathy: And where you're from and what your name is, and your age. Yes, that would be an excellent way to do it, and that would get around a couple of the problems that I had thought might happen.

Lucy: Hmm! That's a good idea.

Jean: Alleviate a little of the anxiety. (Group, November 5, 1997)

Scheduling Mentorship Sessions

In the program we studied, mentors were asked to come during any lunch pe-riod from Monday to Friday, but to use the same day each week. There were two or three mentor pairs whose sessions were conducted outside of lunch hours, and these were carefully scheduled by the teacher to both accommodate the mentors' time constraints and minimize disruption to the child's school week. Teachers have told us that they can work better with the disruption of students leaving the class for mentorship if, for example, six students would be leaving at the same time. Thus, if a school would prefer to not use the lunch pe-riods for mentorship sessions, it might work to identify one-hour blocks at three specific times during the week for any one classroom, and ask mentors to choose from those times. If one had a group of mentors who could all come at the same time, such as a college class or a group of retirees, it expedites scheduling, although it places heavier demands on the use of space and materials for mentorship sessions.

When the mentors in our program discussed the use of the lunch period for mentorship, they noted both advantages and disadvantages. Mentors typically expressed concern about the time that eating took away from the sessions and their feeling that children needed the time to go outside and burn off energy before returning to the classroom for the afternoon.

> Jean: An hour is a fair time and everything, I think. Unfortunately, it's at lunch, and that's where it kind of gets thrown off because we're not doing something right away; it's kind of held off for lunch, and he doesn't always finish his lunch. It's not as if he minds or anything; it's just, you know. And today he *really* wanted to go outside, so you kind of shorten everything up, because he does need a break, being in the school all day and he's looking outside and the sun's shining. So I think it's the lunchtime thing. If it were during school, like after lunch or something, I think it would be different in that way.
> Lucy: That's something to keep in mind, this sort of thing, when negotiating with teachers and so on, I think.
> Jean: I realize it cuts into their time. It's only fair to do it at lunch, but it does, it does put a time pressure, for me anyway. I don't know what you guys find.
> Cathy: Yes, I tend to agree with that lunch thing, because I'll read while she eats, and then she'll want to talk, and again, it's not fair when they go through all those classes and then not have a noon break, because kids need that. (Jean, October 29, 1997)
> Lucy: And anything difficult or frustrating?
> Sophie: Just a lack of time sometimes. Remember, you know, we're eating lunch, that takes a while; and by the time we're done eating lunch and we start to get into stuff, before you know it, the time's up and you're still in the middle of making your picture. Yes. I think I would have preferred to do it not at lunch, actually. (Sophie, November 10, 1997)

Many mentors dealt with time constraints by having the children eat while the mentors read stories. Others simply took advantage of that time to chat with the children and learn more about their lives and their interests.

The main advantage of having sessions at lunch period seemed to be that the meal led to precisely the kind of casual atmosphere where mentor pairs could chat and learn more about each other, share treats, occasionally go outside, and pursue activities and a relationship that would not be possible within the structure of the regular classroom.

> Cathy: I was just going to discuss one thing about the lunch thing, that one of the pros is it makes for a more casual atmosphere.
> Jean: That's true. Then it's not like teaching time. (Jean, October 29, 1997)

Using the lunch period for sessions may, in fact, have made a significant contribution to mentors' willingness to exercise flexibility and responsiveness to the children's needs and interests. Given the enthusiasm with which the children met their mentors, and the comments they made when interviewed, it was apparent that the children did not miss going outside.

Short-Term Programs

In the program we studied, a large number of mentors were education students, who could participate in the fall term or the winter term but not both because of practice teaching in one of the terms. Mentors and children who did work together for a full year or even longer expressed satisfaction in their relationships, but so did mentor pairs who worked together for only the one term. As discussed in Chapter 8, the children understood why they would be changing mentors after the Christmas holidays, and they looked forward to meeting new mentors after the positive experiences they had had with the previous ones.

Physical Space for Sessions

Since the particular value of one-on-one mentoring depends on focused interactions between pairs, the spaces in which sessions were held were important. Having several mentor pairs meet at the same lunch period made it impossible to restrict those pairs to any one room. In one case, where several pairs tried sharing a small room, the atmosphere was full of distractions and lacked intimacy. One pair, Joann and Cindy, found a corner of the library that partially closed them off from the others in the room. This was their "private space." Other mentors spoke of distractions and the need to create a space where they could celebrate their learning.

> Today was productive. We went to the library instead of sitting in the normal room. Sometimes I find being in that room is a little too noisy, and we've got lots of distractions. (Sophie, November 10, 1997)
> Diana: Today I mentioned with Jean, he would always look over to see what she was doing, and she found the same with her child. They were always, "Okay, what's going on over there?" And then I'd feel like his attention span was gone. It was like, "Okay, what am I doing wrong that I haven't—?" (Group, November 5, 1997)
> Joann: I've found, though, that if you guys are doing something more interesting than what we're doing, her attention's focused there. So if you didn't have anything really structured today, maybe that's why he was looking at there, because they were doing the craft or something, and over at Cindy and I, because we're

playing with stuff…. I know, yes, because she was always looking at you when you were doing the pumpkin, or one of you did the pumpkin, because it was more exciting than what we were doing. And so you just have to just let them look. (Group, November 19, 1997)

Marie: I just find that it's really distracting with anybody else in the room. It's like a negative cohesiveness, the two of these kids. And I find it tough, because he comes up and asks me how to spell this. They'll be doing an activity and he'll come up—her boy will come up to me and ask me things, and it kind of breaks our flow of thought or whatever. (Marie, October 22, 1997)

What did work well was having access to several locations throughout the school. Although there was a dedicated mentor room, complete with a comfortable couch and the artwork of mentor pairs on display, it was too small to accommodate more than one or two pairs at a time. So some pairs worked in the classroom while others worked in the mentor room, the music room, the library, outside in good weather, etc. In general, pairs seemed to return to the same place each week unless there was a special activity that took them elsewhere.

Program Coordinator Role

As we outlined in Chapter 5, there are many tasks for anyone who assumes the role of coordinator for a literacy-based mentorship program for the early grades in an elementary school. In the program we studied, many people, including school staff and the researchers, performed the tasks for which a coordinator would have responsibility. Very importantly, the program was supported by the enthusiasm of the school staff as a whole. As researchers, we helped with recruitment of mentors, providing support materials for mentors, and conducting orientation sessions for mentors. We were also at the school on a regular basis speaking with school staff, mentors, and the children. This ongoing involvement with the program helped us to appreciate the important work that only a program coordinator could undertake. Although it might be possible in some schools to enlist parent volunteers to help with program coordination work such as scheduling, record-keeping, relaying information, and arranging special events such as thank-you socials and the like, there were certain aspects of program support that could not be completed by school staff or other volunteers. In addition to the efforts required for recruiting mentors, a program coordinator would provide important program support by conducting orientation sessions, monitoring matches, and debriefing with mentors. The potential scope of recruitment efforts has been discussed in the first section of this chapter. Coordinators may sometimes also be responsible for fund-raising to cover the costs of materials, refreshments, celebrations, and "thank-you crafts" for children to make. Below we discuss the important work of conducting orientation sessions and debriefing with mentors.

Orientation Sessions for Mentors

At the beginning of this program, an orientation session was conducted by the school principal, teachers of participating classrooms, and the researchers. This session included an introduction to the school and a discussion about the program's goals, methods, and procedures. Handout materials included a school handbook and a literacy mentorship handbook, which suggested good practices for sharing books with children and activities for getting to know children. Some of these materials are included in the Appendices.

School staff noticed that mentors who were not university students felt intimidated by receiving a large amount of print material, as they felt this implied that literacy mentorship might require expertise they didn't already have. It might be useful to make a brief video about sharing books with children to show a model of good practice in a way that reminds people of what they already knew, but might sometimes forget. Once they enter a school building, some mentors may think that they are supposed to leave their "family literacy skills" at home, not realizing that we are hoping that they and the children will experience reading as a social event with lots of interaction and discussion.

The orientation session closed with having mentors brainstorm ideas for activities with children and with suggestions for how to prepare for the first session. Mentors completed a brief form giving their contact and scheduling information, their interest and experience areas, and their preferences for the characteristics of a child they would prefer to work with.

As one would expect, some mentors were unable to attend the large group orientation sessions. The school principal generously conducted individual orientation sessions for these mentors. A coordinator with a good background in the research on mentorship and other literacy-support programs could conduct orientation sessions and become an ongoing source of encouragement and support for mentors.

Debriefing with Mentors

Mentors found it welcoming to be recognized and greeted when they were in the school. At the end of their sessions they seemed to enjoy chatting with the principal or any of the researchers about what they had been doing in their session with their child that day. They seemed to appreciate receiving affirmation and reassurance that what they were doing would be beneficial to the child.

Early in the program, children don't give mentors a great deal of clear feedback, and mentors work with a lot of uncertainty as they search for the most appropriate or helpful activities to do with the children. Later in the program, children can be seen approaching everyone in the hallways to show off work they completed in the sessions with their mentors. Until those spontaneous celebrations are occurring, mentors appreciate validation from other adults. Once mentors do see progress in the children's reading, writing, or task completion, they are eager to learn if the child's increased capabilities are noticeable in the classroom. At that stage, they are happy to learn any news the classroom teacher can share. Sometimes, for example, the child will have taken great pleasure in reading to the class a story that he or she wrote in a mentorship session.

As part of our research with this program, we had weekly group interviews with several education student mentors who came at the same lunch period each week. These group interviews showed the benefits of mentors having the opportunity to visit and debrief with their mentor peers. In part, they used the group interview for visiting and sharing course planning or job search ideas. But they also used the interviews as a place to discuss mentorship issues and seek each other's advice. These group meetings seemed to fulfill a certain need mentors had to share information and reflect on the experiences they were having with their children. The "group interview" began as a regular scheduled interview with just one mentor. Soon members of her car pool joined in. Then other education students mentors did as well. The mentors discussed, for example, problems they were having in planning and with children's responses or distracted behavior.

> Diana: I was just going to ask, how do you encourage your child to—[speak more spontaneously]. I was working with Ben today with one book, and I'd always ask him questions: "What do you think's going to happen?" or "What are they going to say?" kind of thing. He's, "I don't know, I don't know," he shrugs. I tried to cover the words today, which is good; he looks in the text to see. But just to come up with his own ideas, I have a really hard time encouraging him to come up with things.
>
> Marie: Yes. I would maybe model it, say, "Oh, look at the picture here. You see what the bear is doing here, and it looks like they're going to play a game of soccer" or something—he's holding a soccer ball—and just kind of show him what you see and just talk aloud so he knows, "Oh, okay," and then he'll look at the pictures, and maybe he'll make some kind of prediction from that. That's what I do; the modeling just seems like the easiest thing so they know what they're looking for. Maybe they don't know, depending where they're at. (Group, November 12, 1997)

It was interesting to note that the same mentor who could be seen giving advice in the above excerpt was asking for it during the next session. There were many useful suggestions from her peers.

Marie: I don't know. I'm just having a hard time getting him focused and stuff. I've been trying different things, and today we did a bookmark and stuff, and then he wanted to draw a picture, so I said, "That's okay." He drew a picture, and we did a snowflake, and he thought he knew how to do a snowflake, so he just folded it up and it turned out to be like nothing; it was just kind of, he was looking at it and "It doesn't look like a snowflake." He just folded a piece of paper and I said, "Hey, that looks like a tree," because the trunk, and then it had the top. He was like, "Yes, okay." So he started to color it in, and he thought that was all right. And then I read him a book and we talked about it a little bit, and that was about it. And then he just wanted to play with cars, so I didn't really know—I just thought, It's fifteen minutes left or whatever, so I thought, Okay. I don't know. I'm not sure what—I don't know what—he's so hard to have focus. He's always like, you're sitting there reading and he'll get up and throw something in the garbage, and then he has to go to the washroom. I don't know what I'm doing wrong.
Jan: Hey! What about getting down on the floor and playing cars with him? Is that something that you've thought of?
Lucy: Anybody have suggestions? Anybody else? I mean, everybody's got different kids.
Jean: Books about cars, I don't know. Make a car.
Joann: How about playing with him outside? Taking a ball and just throwing it back and forth and—
Marie: Or having him run around.
Joann: —wearing some energy off maybe, because the hour break, he needs to run around maybe instead of sitting in a class.
Lucy: Have you ever been in any space without anybody else there?
Joann: Maybe you could have games set up for him outside, and "Let's make a snowman. Let's build a fort. Let's find things under the snow. Let's do a treasure hunt." Go fifteen minutes before and put things out so that you can do this little treasure hunt around. Then at least he'll be involved, because he's got a goal—
Marie: Yes, he's done something.
Joann:—whereas just reading a book is kind of—[boring for him].
Joann: Did you ever try maybe—is there a rocking chair? I saw a child that really wasn't focused on anything ever, and as soon as they were in a rocking chair they would have that action constantly going, and then the teacher could teach the kids something. So maybe you could read a book while he's doing that, or get a Rubik's cube or something so he's figuring that out, and just have it in the background.
Marie: Have him doing something else, yes.
Joann: But something that is challenging more than just crashing around, sort of do something. (Group, November 19, 1997)

This kind of debriefing proved to be very important to the group of mentors that met weekly. They did more than provide ideas for activities. They also offered emotional support, encouragement, and reassurance to their peers. Both helpful ideas and reassurance and praise can be important for new mentors who are finding their way in working with a new child. A program coordinator could plan to provide or facilitate such support with benefits for the mentors, the children, and the program. By holding tea and coffee sessions at the end of time slots used by several mentors, the program coordinator could open up intergenerational communication among mentors who were retired teachers, education students, and other adults not in the teaching field.

Matching and Monitoring

Most mentors and children were deeply satisfied with their matches for the program. These were more or less done on a random basis, with the teacher perhaps making a few choices based on her knowledge of the children and whatever information she had about the mentors. Some mentors, however, were not as satisfied with their match. For example, Gail—the mother of one of the children involved in the mentorship program—expressed a desire to work with a child who needed more help with reading. While she enjoyed Anthony's company, she wanted to feel she was making a difference to a child who needed a lot of help in reading.

> I wouldn't mind working with a child that actually needed the paired reading, because then they're sort of at a different level and need more of the practice, because I think Anthony could read on his own perfectly fine and still comprehend it and all that. (Gail, December 8, 1997)

Gail's experience reminds us that it is useful to ask mentors to indicate the characteristics of a child they would prefer to work with.

Given the focus on enjoyment in the mentorship program and the program's situation outside of the regular classroom time, mentors faced difficult decisions with respect to responding to "off-task behavior." They had to consider appropriate ways to encourage on-task behavior while always evaluating the appropriateness of the tasks, the amount of attention that should be given to them, and how much time should be spent on "just having fun." Most mentors did not encounter serious difficulties. As discussed in Chapter 8, sessions that were geared to the students' interests and abilities and that were organized in ways that were engaging kept the students involved and happy. There was, however, one pair who never achieved a shared focus during their sessions. Marie and Cole's sessions were always noticeable to passersby because of Cole's distracted behavior. Teachers were impressed with Marie because she always came so well prepared and organized, and they were impatient with Cole because of his inattentiveness. Marie was a fourth-year education student. Cole was in grade 2 at the time. Cole's mother was also a mentor in the program, and that gave both Marie and the researchers a chance to talk with her about her son on different occasions. Marie occasionally expressed feelings of frustration. She always came well prepared with books and reading support activities, but Cole would often sit rather quietly in the sessions or he would sometimes wander off, disrupting their session and the sessions of mentor pairs nearby.

> Marie: And with Cole, I talked to his mom after, and sometimes I'm having a hard time keeping his attention; he's just so rambunctious and hyper and stuff. He's only six, and he's in grade 2, so his attention span, I can't expect much, I don't think, like a lot from him in that sense. But she said that she has problems at home too to get him to stay focused on a task and stuff like that. So I didn't know if it was just me or if it was the material I was bringing wasn't interesting to him or what, but I tried some different things. I brought books on dinosaurs and stuff today, and next week I told him I was going to bring—he likes magic, so I'm going to maybe do some card tricks and bring some books about magic and stuff like that. But his mom said that the biggest thing is, she thinks that—he brought cars and stuff and he wanted to play with his cars, so I said, "Okay, we'll read these books and we'll do the activities, and then we'll play cars," I said. It was kind of a compromise: "After we get this stuff done, then we can do that." (Group, November 5, 1997)

There were a couple of moments in the program where Marie sensed progress, as though she had finally reached Cole a little through his interests and through compromise. These feelings of progress, however, continued to be interspersed with various setbacks and frustrations, and as Marie was just about to complete her commitment of one term to the program, she was still expressing concern that Cole wouldn't focus on what she asked him to do.

After observing the pair, tape recording several of their sessions, interviewing Marie, and speaking, in passing, to Cole's mother, we have tried to understand what may have prevented this pair from being as successful as many of the others.

One aspect that stood out was the way Marie articulated her ideas about planning. While almost all of the mentors, including Marie, discussed a tension between planning more academically structured sessions and being flexible enough to abandon plans and "just have fun," the way Marie spoke about this tension seemed to indicate less flexibility than many of the mentors. And while Marie talked about trying to appeal to Cole's interests in the sessions, she also revealed in an interview that the sessions were not wholly designed for Cole. Each session's plans were similar to those of a reading diagnostic program in which Marie was also volunteering. When asked about planning, Marie had this to say:

> I find it really quite easy because some of the activities that I do with him are the same activities I do at [the other school]. So I kind of incorporate—because they're basically, although they're different grade levels, they're at the same reading level, etc. So, a lot of the stories and even different things to get him to read are the same, so it's all in one—inclusive. (Marie, October 29, 1997)

Marie's description of planning being somewhat easy contrasted sharply with the statements of many of the other mentors who, as reported in Chapter 8, found researching the children's interests and planning with these in mind to be a lot of work. As further contrast, Marie's discussions failed to emphasize collaborative input from the child; and instead revealed her sense of being in control and having an agenda to follow.

> I have him draw every time. (Marie, October 22, 1997)
> I had him draw, we had a practice writing and sentence writing. I had him write two sentences on Halloween. (Marie, October 29, 1997)

Marie, like other mentors, spoke about compromising to incorporate activities that Cole wished to do, but she somehow seemed much more committed to her plans than many of the other mentors.

> Lucy: Are there particular things you want him to get done?
> Marie: Yeah, usually like the things I have planned out, like this writing thing. This [over here] he wanted to do, so we managed to fit that in too…. As long as I get the things that I had kind of set to do, or mostly done I think that's a pretty good compromise. (Marie, October 29, 1997)

Whether this was indeed enough compromise for Cole was difficult to know. Gail, Cole's mother, talked about how much he enjoyed his sessions, except the reading part.

> Lucy: Great. And Cole's all finished with his mentor, I know too.
> Gail: Yes.
> Lucy: How does he feel?
> Gail: He really enjoyed it. I don't know that he enjoyed the reading part, but he enjoyed Marie's company, and he was just extremely proud. She'd given him a little book when they were done, and he was just thrilled to death. He carried that

book all over with him, reading it and reading it and reading it after. (Gail, December 8, 1997)

The next term Cole had a new mentor and he seemed like a new person. He was attentive and involved. We wondered why this new match was such a success. Perhaps Cole had matured over the Christmas break. Marie noted above that he was young for grade 2. Or perhaps the shift had to do with his new mentor being male. The many possible factors were likely interconnected, but Marie and Cole's case does serve a useful purpose in underscoring that planning alone does not guarantee success in a literacy-based mentorship program. The one-on-one focus in a literacy mentorship program requires mentors to find a shared space where the mentor and child can connect, enjoy each other, and collaboratively develop engaging routines and activities that serve to support the child's love of reading and related literacy activities.

Race, Language, and Cultural Issues

As reported in Chapter 8, during the fall term of the mentorship program all mentors were female and white. We are interested in issues related to cross-cultural mentorships, given that so many of the children were of visible minority backgrounds and so many of the children's books were written by authors of diverse backgrounds as well. This discussion does not intend to discourage the pairing of white mentors with nonwhite children. Nor does it intend to encourage the exclusive pairing of mentors of the same backgrounds. Instead it attempts to open up issues around the many ways that the invisibility of whiteness affects the children in our schools. In the mentorship program, language was a key issue, as mentors were helping children to learn to read in English. And while all, or almost all, of the mentors were extremely well-intentioned in celebrating diversity, cultural and linguistic biases slipped out in various ways. These ranged from simple side comments to the effect that an ethnically different author's name sounded "funny," to a more complex nonrecognition of the politics of learning English and learning English as a dominant world language, to, in one case, unacceptable racist statements about a child's background. One example, however, of cultural respect and learning is presented here to help us think about the ways we can deal with racial, cultural, and linguistic differences in such a program.

After the Christmas break, Cindy was paired with a new mentor. Aside from being a bit older and male, he was different from her first mentor, Joann, in many ways. Nonetheless the pair was an immediate success story. Ron brought Cindy lunch each week (after he discovered she preferred the meals from a popular fast food outlet to her usual wholesome fare from home), and their sessions were always full of smiles and laughter. He was great at being a grandpa figure, playing board games with her and teasing her about the rules and her ways of winning. It was clear that the two, like other mentor pairs, had formed an important bond.

> For me it's a real love. I think people are missing something who are not in a mentorship program....We laugh, we joke, we tell stories about each other and we get along fantastically. We're more than a mentorship relationship, we're pals. And that is what it's all about. You have to be a friend before you can be a mentor.

Ron also spoke to us about the kinds of learning they did together, and in particular, he spoke at length of learning about Vietnam and Cindy's cultural background.

> I hear all about her relatives and stories. We've done being Chinese from Vietnam, we've done some geography, we've discovered which animals are only from Vietnam, they don't live anywhere else, we discovered where Vietnam is in the world, she didn't know that, we've done some history lessons on what Vietnam did, the various cultures that have come through and how they've changed the culture with the French being there, the Chinese being there, which has been a real eye-opener for me because I didn't know all that stuff. (Ron, May 1998)

Ron not only showed an interest in Cindy's family and in more general cultural information, but he also went to great lengths to learn more about where Cindy was from and how this fit into her identity. What was interesting about the learning that Ron did with Cindy is that he explored the cultural influences and differences within Vietnam, rather than reifying a unified image of the cultural other. And furthermore, this unified image was also fragmented by Cindy's ties to what one might call a Canadian identity. Ron understood this as he learned alongside Cindy about the many things that she also did not know, thus undoing a common assumption that the minority child somehow inherently represents everything about that culture. Perhaps the most important lesson in Ron and Cindy's example is how this friendship or love motivated the desire to learn such things in these ways.

Because mentors work one-on-one, they have an exceptional opportunity to support a child's self-understanding. Children experience themselves through the screen of interpretation held by significant others. Mentors can become very significant to children. It may be that when a mentor takes a serious interest in the nature and significance of a child's cultural heritage, the child too can take herself and her heritage more seriously. Conversely, silence on these topics can inadvertently communicate strong messages about the nonsignificance of histories not celebrated in the Western Euro-centric tradition.

In Chapter 8, Ben's mentor noted that he only opened up and started talking to her "nonstop" when she asked him to tell her stories about what it was like "back home." Ben's mentor mentioned that she sometimes had trouble understanding him. She could have asked him to draw pictures for these stories, and together they could have drafted the sentences to go along with these picture stories. Finding common language with shared referents can be the strongest way of building solidarity in a relationship. Feeling awkward or incompetent can get in the way of mentors working well with the opportunities that are there. If it were possible to arrange, it would likely be beneficial to have mentors who are paired with visible minority children attend debriefing group discussions together to share experiences, concerns, and ideas.

The issues discussed in this chapter are intended to provide some insight into areas of concern in literacy-support mentorship programs for young children and to stimulate discussion among people involved in initiating or operating such programs. The potential of these programs is enormous. With a little care, and the proper support, such programs can enable young children to begin their school years with strength and confidence.

❧ Section C ☙

MENTORS BUILDING RELATIONSHIPS WITH YOUNG CHILDREN

ʚ Chapter Ten ໐

INSTANT SOUL MATES:
CASE STUDY OF TIARA AND JOEL

This case study, and those presented in Chapters 11, 12, and 13, were conducted with a focus on learning how relationships are developed between mentors and the children they work with. The mentorship between Tiara and Joel began on January 30, 1998. Tiara met with Joel once a week during a school lunch period. There was a six-week break in their mentorship (May 3–June 17) when Tiara studied French in Quebec. Their mentorship resumed on June 17 and was still continuing outside of school through recreational activities two years later. To complete this case study, Jan had a total of 10 interviews with Tiara on the following dates: January 30, February 9, 25, March 11, 18, 25, April 6, 15, 24, 29. Three of the interviews were audiotaped.

Tiara was a third-year university student in a faculty of education She had enrolled in university immediately after completing high school. Joel was an eleven-year-old boy in grade 6 who was enrolled in a special grade 4–6 class with a literacy emphasis. Joel was older than the majority of the children in the mentorship program. Students in his class, being of high need for literacy support, were selected for the program after all the children in kindergarten and grades 1, 2, and 3 had mentors.

In the pages that follow, Jan shares her study of this extraordinary mentorship relationship.

"I met my little guy today. We have so much in common."

It was a snowy Tuesday afternoon in January (Jan. 30). I was sitting in my office on campus getting ready to go to class when I heard a knock on the door. It was Tiara. "Hi! Jan, can I come in for a minute?" Tiara, who had signed up to be a mentor in the mentorship program, was also a student in a course I was teaching that term. "Of course, Tiara, come in." She took off her coat, plopped her knapsack on the floor, sat down and began talking: "I met my little guy today. He's older. He's in grade 6. I told him that my grandma lives a block away from the school and that my mom went to that school. So it was kinda neat going there and telling him that" (Jan. 30). "What's his name?" I asked. She began, "Oh! I didn't even tell you. It's Joel. And we have so much in common." Although she did not come in for a scheduled interview, I grabbed a pad of lined paper and my tape recorder and said, "Do you want to talk about it? Mind if I tape this, take notes?" "Sure Jan. I don't know if I have anything important to say. I just met him. But I did sign that sheet [the consent form]. So it's okay. I don't mind." I said, "So, I want to hear all about it." She began:

> We have so much in common. His parents divorced when he was seven months old, same as mine. Except I was six months old when my parents divorced. But it's the same thing. He remembers sitting by the window at 6:00 and 7:00 o'clock Saturday morning waiting for his dad to get him for the weekend—just like me, and his dad never showing up, just like mine. He knows about broken promises, lies, lies and lies. We really understand each other. We have so much in common. (Jan. 30)

"Interesting," I said. "Start from the beginning. Was this your first visit to the school? What happened when you got there?" She replied:

> Well, yes, except for the first night, that orientation session, you know, you were there. There were no kids there that night. So yes, it was my first actual time to the school, when there were kids there. When I got there I had no one to mentor; I had no idea if I was going to get one [a student] or anything like that. And then there was this little boy running around the room, and I didn't even know; I just thought it was this kid. I wasn't sure why he was running back and forth, but I guess he was waiting for his mentor, and he was this cute little grade sixer, just adorable, and we clicked; we totally clicked. I found out that we were both only children, and our parents were both divorced, and just everything. We like the same sports, and we like the same movies, and it was mostly just, we found out about each other. (Jan. 30)

"Tiara, that's wonderful. I'm so happy that you clicked like that. I want to talk to you more about this [mentoring Joel]. Can we meet—have an interview after your sessions?" I asked. "Sure," she agreed.

"I love him already. Our time together is special."

The next week (Feb. 9) I was at the school during Tiara's mentoring session, and I looked forward to meeting Joel. I went into the library; they weren't there.

I went into the mentor room; they weren't there either. I tried the music room next and there they were. Tiara saw me and called me to come over to the corner where they were sitting. She said "Joel, this is Jan. She is my teacher." I greeted him, "Hi, Joel, nice to meet you." He smiled and said, "Hi." I asked them if I could take a picture of them together. Joel raised his eyebrows, smiled, and put his head down. "He's shy. He doesn't like his picture taken, Jan." "That's okay," I said. "I'll leave you two alone," and then I left the music room. In our interview after the session, Tiara began by saying:

> I love him already, Jan. He's so sweet—such a nice kid. He's shy. And he doesn't like having his picture taken. Last week, someone came in, I think it was a teacher, and wanted to take our picture and he hid, put his head down, so that's why he did that. I applied for the French Bursary program in Montreal and I really want to go. But if I get it I will miss him so much. So I don't know what to do. And, oh—today, we read and we got through so much of the book that the teacher was even surprised, so it was really good. We had fun. Our time together is special. We've only known each other, seen each other twice. But our time together is special. (Feb. 9)

At this early stage in their mentorship, Tiara and Joel were already very comfortable together. In fact, the following week, when neither Tiara or Joel was there, I learned that they were already rescheduling their sessions if the assigned day didn't work for one of them any particular week.

"She always brings me something."

During my visit to the school on February 25th I found them sitting together in the music room again. Joel was not quite as shy this time. He greeted me, "Hi! Do you want one?" offering me a Skittle [candy]. "Oh, no thank you," I said. He beamed and said, "She brings me something, she always brings me something. She gives me everything," poking her in the shoulder. "Ouch, Joel!" she giggled, poking him back. "She always brings me stuff. You're soooo nice," he said, leaning his head on her shoulder. "You're right, she is nice," I said, adding, "Can I take a photo today?" Tiara looked at him. "It's fine with me…Joel?" His head still rested on her shoulder; he didn't look up, but agreed, "Sure, I don't mind." I took the picture, said good-bye, and left them to enjoy their time together.

Tiara enjoyed bringing a treat for Joel each week. Later in the mentorship she reminisced about bringing him a treat the first day they met.

> The first day, I took him candies, cookies, or something, I can't remember, and he said, "Why did you bring me something? You don't have to bring me something."

And I'm like, "Well, I want to," and he goes, "But you don't have to. I feel bad."
I'm like, "Don't feel bad." Maybe he doesn't get extra things sometimes. So, I'll
take him a package of M & Ms or Skittles. I took him Valentine cookies and I
took him cookies when I made them at home. (Mar. 11)

As Tiara learned more about Joel's interests, she gave him personal gifts as well:
"My cousins went to the Drillers game, and they got these posters, and I gave
him one of them. I got them to bring me one for him because he loves soccer,
and he said he put it up in his room" (Apr. 6).

"We really understand each other.
It's just being together that's important."

When I met with Tiara after their session on February 25, she looked at me,
smiled, and said, "I just love him so much. We really understand each other."
She had said this before and I asked her to say more about her statement, "We
don't have to say words, we just understand each other."

> Yes, we don't. I know that he's reached his limit in reading, he doesn't have to say,
> "I don't want to read anymore," and I don't have to say, "Do you want to read
> some more?" I say, "Oh, okay, let's go on to something else." It's not like a formal
> thing with us. We get along good. (Feb. 25)

When I asked Tiara what they had done in their session that day, she tried to
explain that it was just being together that was important.

> It's hard to explain, Jan. It's not what we do—it's just being together that's im-
> portant. Just being there, sitting there, talking about stuff, all kinds of stuff. It's
> really, the just being there together. We just want that time together where we can
> just be. I can't really explain, Jan. You would have to [experience it]—I don't
> know. (Feb. 25)

"What does it feel like?" I asked. She said, "You'd just have to be there, to feel
it, to know, to truly understand. Do you get it? We just clicked." "What do you
mean, you clicked?" She replied:

> It just felt like—I feel something like I'm his sister or something. I felt actually
> more like I related to him the same way I relate to my little cousins, and I'm really
> close with my little cousins, and so I don't have a cousin-cousin relationship with
> my cousins, I have a sister relationship or a brother relationship with them, and
> that is the same way with him. He's got more of like an adult personality, and I
> think maybe too because he's had to be grown up. It's hard when your parents are
> divorced, and he'll understand things; he'll joke about things. (Feb. 25)

Tiara went on to say that Joel can tell if she is upset and that he cares about how things are going in her life: "You could talk to him; he knows if you're not happy or something like that. He knows that" (Mar. 11). I asked her, "How can you tell that?" She said, "Just he's like, 'Are you okay? Sure you're okay?' Yes, I'm fine. 'Okay.'"

Joel showed that he cared about how Tiara was doing and Tiara showed that she valued Joel's knowledge and judgment. Over the course of the mentorship, Tiara shared her completed assignments (for methods courses) such as games, picture files, and so forth with Joel before she handed them in. She said:

> For my assignments even, if I'm there, I'll show him what I have to hand in and he always gives me his opinion on it, so he's just like my little friend. We get along really good; I think we get along really good. I showed him my French assignments. My games, I asked him, "What do you think? Do you like it?" And he goes, "Yes, Yes. They're pretty! They're cool!" (Apr. 6)

Curious about the significance of this sharing, I asked Tiara if she thought that showing him her assignments made a difference. She responded: "Yes, because he knows I'm still a student and I'm still learning, and it brings me down a level too, I think. But it also gives me an insight: Are these games appropriate for a grade sixer?" (Apr. 6). Tiara's comments also suggested that Joel could feel accepted and understood by her.

> He just acts older, like he's kind of like one of the jocks at the school, I think. And with girls. Girls will walk by and he goes, "That girl likes me." So he's funny. And other people [mentors] would be like, "Well, now, Joel, we're not talking about that. Don't say that. And I'll let him tell me stuff like, that because why should I be strict about it? This is his lunch hour and he's doing homework; that's more than most kids are doing on their lunch hour. (Mar. 18)

"I did make some jokes to make him relax."

Tiara and Joel were so natural and comfortable with each other that I asked her to reflect on how they got started in such a good way. Tiara recalled her thoughts upon meeting Joel for the first time:

> I knew he was going to be, "Who's this stranger coming into my room?" I knew he was going to be like that. I knew he was going to be wondering, "What does she want out of this?" Little kids think like that: "What's this person getting out of this? Why are they doing this? Why are they taking their time out to help me?" And I knew he was going to be scared; I knew he was going to wonder. And I

thought, "Okay. Make a couple of jokes, relax him a little bit." And it was fine, we got along great. And he knows that I'm there for him. (Apr. 15)

Tiara had also described the first session itself.

Totally at ease. He laughed at my jokes and he said, "You're funny," and I think that made him—I did make some jokes to make him relax. Then we were reading the book *The Titanic*, and he hadn't seen the movie yet, and I was telling him about the movie, and he seemed to want to know more. And I was telling him about some of the funny parts of the movie, and then we'd go back and we'd read some more. And he's asking questions: "Why is the ship like this?" Or "Why is that?" And I'd tell him, "I don't know, but what I do remember from the movie,"…and it was just really comfortable. Everybody else [the other mentors] seemed to say that they took a couple of weeks just getting comfortable with their little mentor person, and I got comfortable right away. (Mar. 18)

"We don't have a teacher-student relationship. We just have a friendship."

Tiara tried to explain how she experienced and understood her relationship with Joel.

We're just so comfortable with each other. I feel like I'm his teacher, but I know that I feel like a teacher, he knows I'm like a teacher, but we don't have a teacher-student relationship; we just have a friend relationship. (Apr. 6)

For me as a teacher, I'm always warm. I think that's the way I am. I'm always there for my students. No matter who they are—whether they're Joel or the kids during my practicum or the kids at the school that I volunteer at. If they're upset or something, I sit there and I talk to them about it. If they're happy, I let them tell me why they're happy.…With Joel, I'll let him joke around with me, I'll let him say silly things or whatever; whereas if I were a teacher I wouldn't let him do those things, and that's why it's a little different when you're a mentor. You're more like a friend, you're a big friend to the kid. And there's certain lines he could cross. (Apr. 6)

When asked to explain further what she meant by "friend," Tiara replied:

It's not, "Let's go partying together," it's not that. But it's just kind of, "You can come to me if you have any problem." And I know students can, whether it be Joel, whether it be anybody, they come to me if there's anything; that's just the way I am. If somebody needs me to be there for them, I'll put their needs right ahead of my needs, and I'm like that with my friends, with anybody. (Apr. 6)

The relationship was clearly a blend of friendship and teacher-student relationship, as revealed in Tiara's discussion below of how she and Joel demonstrated respect for each other.

> He respects me as a mentor. He knows that I'm going to be a teacher and he's excited. He says, "You're going to be a good teacher." Yes, stuff like that. We have a good relationship, and he listens to me. If I tell him, "Okay, Joel we have to get back on this," or a lot of times he'll tell me, "We have to get back on topic here," but when I tell him, "We have to get back on this," he'll listen right away. He listens and basically he does what I want, or if I say, "Let's go sit in here today," he'll be like, "Okay, yes, that's good." He doesn't say, "No I don't want to go there." He doesn't argue with me about anything. And I respect him. And I think that's probably more important than anything. I respect his differences; I respect his difficulties; I respect his limits, what he can and can't do; and I build on that. We'll do things that if I know it's hard for him, I'll push him, but I won't push him too much. For example, I'll tell him, "Okay, you don't understand? You don't know what that word is?" I won't tell him what it is; I'll try different ways of having him sound it out or looking at it, maybe looking at the picture to try to figure out what the word is. If he still can't get it, I'm not going to make him look like an idiot; I won't do that. I'll just say, "This is the word," then five minutes later I'll go back and I'll say, "Do you remember what word that is?" And it's good because I've respected his boundaries, because I've respected what he can and can't do. But I think that you just need to be there and show that even though you're an authority figure, you're still a friend. (Apr. 6)

"He enjoys reading now."

As the mentorship progressed, Tiara observed that Joel came to enjoy reading. It was often he who kept them on track: "And like I said, he wants to, even if sometimes we're reading and we get off topic, and we talk about things, and he'll be, 'Okay, we've got to get back to reading,' and he enjoys that [reading] now" (Apr. 6). As Tiara learned more about Joel's likes and dislikes, she was able to use this knowledge in keeping him comfortable with reading: "In terms of reading, I know what kinds of things he doesn't like to read, and even in terms of subject areas, talking about things" (Apr. 24).

"He tells me things; I tell him things."

And he feels comfortable to tell me things. And I feel comfortable enough to tell him things. And I know what he likes and he knows what I like, and I know what he doesn't like and [I] stay away from the things he doesn't like. (Apr. 6)

Tiara often said in passing that she and Joel were comfortable telling each other things. When invited to elaborate, she replied:

> Like just personal things that we did over the weekend, and he'll tell me about the time he'd spent with his dad and stuff like that, when he goes over to his dad's house for the weekend. Actually, I started a little journal with him, and sometimes we forget to write in it because we're so busy with other things, but it's usually he'll tell me what he did on the weekend and it just so happens that it's the weekend he's been with his dad, so he'll tell me what him and his dad did. And just things just about what he's done and about where he's gone, or family life, where his grandma is going. And I tell him things too....I told him about my relationship with my dad and how I don't see him; he thinks that's not good, and stuff like that. (Apr. 24)

During one of my visits to Tiara and Joel in the music room, I encountered one of these "telling each other things" episodes. When I entered the room, Joel exclaimed: "Tiara's mom is leaving for Montreal this morning. She [Tiara] is having a big party at their house!" He looked at Tiara, who appeared surprised that he was telling me this. She said "Joel!!!" He said, "Oh, yes. A party which she has told her mom about." "That's nice, who's going?" I asked, looking at both of them. Joel took the lead, "Half the university." I looked at Tiara, and said, "What!!??" Tiara put both hands up, as if to surrender, then began, "Okay, okay. No, I invited half the faculty though. Mom knows I'm having it, nothing crazy or wild happens. I'm really responsible." Joel couldn't contain himself, "Yeah and she loves chips and nacho chips, so she's having them. Or, no, you're not, because it's Lent and you can't have them still, right?" I asked Tiara, "Oh? Is that what you are doing for Lent, Tiara?" "Yeah," she admitted. Joel continued, "Yeah, because she loves chips. Why not have pretzels at your party instead?"

"You need an extra person around—just someone you can talk to."

In our interview after the session, Tiara reflected on the significance of her and Joel's sharing their news with each other.

> I think that it's important, because teachers don't have that—sometimes you need just an extra person around that's not your parent or your aunts or your uncles, just somebody you can talk to,...and with Joel I know he comes from a close family, but I think the extended family is not really that much there. So we just talk, not just about school things, about life. And like I said, I'm more like a big sister, I feel to him. (Mar. 18)

"I've formed a bond with him. We come from the same place."

On April 29 Tiara telephoned to talk about Joel. She was going to the French Immersion Bursary program in Montreal soon and was very happy that she was accepted but was concerned about not being there for Joel.

> I feel really bad about going to Montreal because I won't see him. I missed him on spring break [a week in the springtime when there is no school for students]. He gave me a letter that said, "I hope you can mentor me next year." I just love him. It means so much to him and his mom is really happy about the program. I asked him, "How does your mom feel about you having a mentor?" And he said, "She loves me having a mentor." I've formed a bond with him in a way that others can't. It's hard to explain, Jan! We just understand. We don't talk about our parents being divorced. We talk about sports and doing things. But we just understand each other. And I think it's because we come from the same place. I think that he sees me and he thinks, "Well, her parents are divorced, we came from the same place and she's made it. So maybe I can make it too." (Apr. 29)

"He should have had a mentor a long time ago."

Although Tiara enjoyed the comfortable friendship with Joel, she was equally focused on his academic needs. Tiara explained how a mentor could have made a difference in terms of helping Joel with his schoolwork at an earlier point in his school career.

> I think it's kind of sad that he's in a special literacy class [literacy in the morning, regular program in the afternoon] which see, that bothers me, because I think, How could a student be in grade 6 and have problems reading? Because I've never been exposed to that. I was reading when I was three years old. I was reading books, reading at home, and so I think that he should have had a mentor a long time ago....You have to get students wanting to learn, and if you spend one-on-one with them you get them wanting to learn. They want that; they like that special attention, and they do extra things to get that special attention, I think. He'll pick out the books; he'll pick out two or three books and bring them over. I help him with math too, and sometimes I think he just pretends he doesn't know the math questions just so I'll help him with it. And then he does really well. And it's too bad because he's in grade 6 and he's going into junior high next year. Is he going to always be at the bottom of the class because nobody noticed that this little boy has had problems reading until now? (Apr. 6)

In interview conversations such as this one, Tiara showed her awareness of Joel's academic abilities and needs and her concern about them.

"I don't want to disappoint him or let him down."

During our later interviews, Tiara (Apr. 6, 15) was primarily focused on how her leaving for the six-week French program in Montreal would affect Joel. She also said she was trying to find someone to have mentorship sessions with Joel till she came back.

> I'm going to really miss him when I go away, I know that much; really, really miss him. I hope I can find someone to be his mentor. I'm going to talk to my friend, because he deserves that, deserves somebody to be there with him once a week. (Apr. 6)
>
> And I'll come back and finish up the last two weeks before school is finished because his teacher—even the principal said, yes, she's noticed an improvement in him. I just feel like I'm letting him down by not being there.... I'm still going to go back there for those last two weeks when I come back. I've already arranged it at work, that I won't work until after [school gets out]. And probably our last day we'll go play soccer outside or something. Do something fun. And if he wants to get his other friends to come play too, that would be great. (Apr. 15)

A Continuing Relationship

Four months later... In September Tiara came to my office and told me about her trip to Quebec. She also told me that she did mentor Joel when she returned and that she still has a relationship with him. He called her whenever he wanted to go swimming and they still did things together. They also wrote letters back and forth.

Twelve months later... When I saw Tiara the following April, she said that she and Joel talk on the telephone often and that they still see one another. When together, they go swimming, to the mall, or to a popular fast food outlet. Tiara and Joel became genuine friends—a natural match.

১০ Chapter Eleven ৫৩

LIKE A COURTSHIP:
CASE STUDY OF CAREY AND DUSTIN

The mentorship between Carey and Dustin began early in February 1998 and continued until the end of June 1998. Carey met with Dustin once a week during the school lunch hour. Jan observed them on nine occasions—February 6, 13, 20, March 6, 13, 20, April 3, 10, and 17—and interviewed Carey seven times on February 20, March 6, 13, 20, April 3, 10, and 17.

Carey was a third-year student in a faculty of education in Edmonton. She grew up in a small town in the United States and moved to Alberta with her family after completing high school. Dustin, a six-year-old boy, was in a combined grade 2/3 class. In the following pages, Jan shares her case study of their mentorship relationship. Although Carey experienced many self-doubts at the outset, the relationship quickly became a very satisfying one for both of them.

"I want him to like me and I want him to enjoy it."

I had been observing Carey and Dustin for a couple of weeks when I decided to ask her if I could talk to her about mentoring Dustin. She responded without hesitation, "Sure—right after, at 1:00 o'clock, that'd be great" (Feb. 20). As soon as Dustin had gone to class, she started talking.

In this first interview, Carey emphasized that she wanted Dustin to enjoy their sessions: "In order of importance, it's: I really want him to enjoy it. So that's the most important thing. I want to be able to visit with him and have fun with him. And I don't know if I'm getting done everything I'm supposed to be doing" (Feb. 20).

Carey knew that her emphasis was on visiting and enjoying each other during their sessions, and she worried that she was not giving enough attention to the literacy support dimension of the mentorship: "But see, the biggest thing to me is I want him to like it. *I want him to like me,* and I want him to enjoy it, but I also want him to improve in his reading and writing" (Feb. 20).

In each of the first two interviews, Carey was insistent about her desire to have their sessions focus on Dustin's interests.

> I'm not sure what other people are doing, but *I want to do something he likes.* (Feb. 20)
>
> I want to do something he wants to do. (Mar. 6)

"Do you have anything on automotives?"

Although Carey wanted Dustin to like her and to find their session activities interesting, she was at first very intimidated by the differences in their life experiences. Carey had attended small private Christian schools with little funds for equipment and facilities and Dustin seemed very sophisticated and precocious to her.

> I wasn't sure where I'd start with him, and he's smart, really smart at things that I'm not that great at. I never saw a computer till I was in grade 10 or something, so I don't know much about it. But there's things, I don't feel competent in. But it's gradually gotten better. (Feb. 20)

When I asked her, "How did you start with him? What was it like the first time you saw him?" she said,

> The very first time I asked him what kind of books he liked; I was just curious. He said, "Do you have anything on automotives?" And I thought, Oh, no! I don't know! I'm not that into cars!! Like, I have a little car; who cares? And I thought, Oh no!! and he said, "Oh, like Hummers." He said something else that I didn't even know about; I've never heard of it!! And I asked him again what it was. (Feb. 20)

Carey thought that Dustin seemed more mature than his classmates. Dustin was a big boy, that is, physically big for grade 2; he was the largest student in the class. He was athletic, solid, strong. He dressed in long black oversize T-shirts and baggy jeans. His head was shaved.

> But sometimes I look at what other people are doing and I think it's hard because Dustin is at an age where you don't want to do things that make him feel like a baby, like younger-type things like different crafts. He's really into cars so I think, okay, I want to do something he likes. (Mar. 6)

She continued by offering a contrast with another mentor pair: "Carmen's little girl loves flowers and butterflies and doing different little things" (Mar. 6).

Carey said that she couldn't bring Dustin a Kinder Surprise (candy packet) each week as other mentors do because, as she put it, "He wouldn't like that. He's into Hummers, automotives and stuff like that" (Mar. 6). Carey said twice that Dustin "seemed old," and that "he doesn't want to do these little things really—like he's just mature a bit. So this is good for me—because I need the experience with kids like him" (Mar. 13).

Carey was concerned about Dustin's apparent sophistication and whether her different life experience would limit her ability to be an engaging mentor for him.

> And he seems old. And he's talking about kind of how the girls liked him, and he's just—wow!! Maybe I've just lived a really sheltered life, he seems really smart and just like—he was talking about his new computer games. He has Quake and he has a mouse and I don't know much about them because we don't have a good computer. And I thought, I wonder if I'm going to make it fun for him. He seems like he is used to a lot, and *I wonder what he's going to think of me!!* (Mar. 6)

All the while that Carey was preoccupied with bridging their different life experiences, she continued to be concerned about her effectiveness with literacy support.

> I try different things to give him different strategies that maybe he would use to help him and stuff, but I wonder if I'm doing enough, I don't know exactly. (Feb. 20)
>
> I wonder if I'm meeting his needs. (Mar. 6)

"He has a totally different life than I've had."

Carey tried to explain how the life she had lived made her feel so different from Dustin. She described the town where she grew up living with her mother, father, sister, and brother.

> The town is really religious. How do I explain it? Out of the people—there's a thousand and one hundred people, so that's like a thousand people. There's six churches in that town. It was Dutch, so there was a big windmill in the town and it's just really Dutch. So you figure how many people there were and how many churches. (Feb. 20)

She talked about how safe and secure she felt growing up there during her childhood.

> And we could do anything. Ever since I was little, we could take our bikes wherever we wanted in the whole town. There's no crime, no nothing. So when we

were little, we'd go, "Oh, I'm going to go buy candy." We could go uptown and buy our own candy and do whatever and go to the swimming pool, take our bike. We'd do whatever and we had fun and I loved it. But then I move here and it's really different for me. (Feb. 20)

Carey moved here immediately after completing high school. Her father is a pastor and they moved here because of his work in the church.

Carey also talked about how her school experience was so different from Dustin's.

He has a totally different life than I've had, and so that's the big thing for me. I look at this school even, and it's a wonderful school. I look at the stuff they're doing; just from the hall I can see what they're doing, and I think my life was totally different, I wouldn't give it up, what I experienced too because I love that life. (Feb. 20)

Carey went on to describe the surprises and difficulties she currently encounters in her teacher education program because her experiences of subject areas had been constrained by "old books," few art materials, and the absence of indoor facilities and equipment for physical education. She also had no experience of school celebrations of holidays.

"Oh yes, he liked it, yes!!"

Out of concern for her and Dustin's different life experiences, Carey set forth to identify Dustin's interests and become knowledgeable about these topics as a way to create some common ground for them and to make the sessions enjoyable for him. Then she proceeded to tailor the mentoring sessions to Dustin's interests: "So I asked people What's a Hummer? What's a Prowler? I think they are cars. What is icing? Why do they only sometimes start the game in the center?" (Mar. 20). Carey spent time at the library learning about dirt bikes, Hummers, Prowlers, and hockey. She even watched a few hockey games on television to learn more about the game. In no time at all, she took a genuine liking to hockey and the Oilers. In fact, once she started, she never missed a game. On one occasion, she wore a hockey jersey to the mentorship session.

Another time, Carey brought Dustin a poster of a Prowler, Dustin's favorite car. Her father had brought it home from a boat show. It was even florescent purple, Dustin's favorite color. When her father gave it to Carey she was delighted.

So I thought, "Perfect for Dustin!!" I wanted to bring him stuff before too, but he seems so mature, like he wouldn't want little-kid-type things. He likes cars and stuff, and you look in stores and there are all these new-type hot rods, and he likes Prowlers, so it was just perfect! It worked good, yes!!! (Apr. 3)

I reassured her, "Yes, he liked that." She went on,

Oh yes, he liked it, yes!! I could tell he liked it. Right away he was like, "I bet it's a poster of the Titanic," and I'm like, "No. I hope you like it as good as the Titanic." And then he opens it and he's like, "Oh, cool!!!" and I'm like, "Do you like it better than the Titanic?" He's like, "Oh, yeah!!!" He liked it better than that, so I was glad. (Apr. 3)

It was hard to tell who was happier, Dustin or Carey. She was so happy that he liked it, and he was so pleased that he immediately ran from mentor pair to mentor pair, down the hallway to teacher, to parent, to principal, showing it to everyone he could see. And after their session, Dustin came back three times to say good-bye to Carey even after the bell rang. Three times, he came back and poked his head in the door where we were having our interview, looked at her and said "'Bye, Carey, and thanks for the poster." The following week, Dustin began their session by telling Carey: "My dad really loved the poster. He is buying me these rods with strings to hang it up in my room so that it won't get wrecked or ripped" (Apr. 10).

"He's not so different after all."

As the weeks passed, Carey and Dustin changed noticeably as a mentorship pair. They no longer sat across from one another at the round table. Instead, they sat beside each other and close together. I also heard laughter, teasing, and joking back and forth, much like a new couple's flirtations with one another. Dustin's behavior gave Carey reason to feel that Dustin liked her and enjoyed spending time with her. She seemed pleased and almost relieved by Dustin's response to her. Carey also talked about how she had become more comfortable with Dustin and less intimidated by his apparent precocity: "And it's gradually gotten better. As I got to know him, I see he's not this genius boy; he's average, and he's nice and he's fun" (Mar. 20).

"He likes me."

Carey finally believed that Dustin liked her and enjoyed their sessions. It was the way he greeted her when she arrived—happy and smiling and full of news to share—that convinced her.

I think he enjoys it too [the visiting], because just the fact that right when I come, he comes up and says, "I'm doing this." That makes me feel happy, because it means—instead of just ignoring me—he could just come out of the classroom, get his lunch, and come in here; but he comes up right away before he gets his lunch, and he says stuff. Just the fact that he does that, it makes me—every time I'm waiting outside that room before he comes out I think, okay—you always have this feeling like—I hope he's glad I'm here. At least that's how I always feel. And then you see right away that thought is gone, because I can always tell. He'll be like, "Hi!!" He always has something to say, it seems like. (Apr. 10)

The following week Carey said,

I don't know if you've noticed that every time he walks, he's skipping, and he's happy and I love him; I really enjoy it. So that's the most important thing I've seen. I want to make sure he's happy. The other thing is that when he comes out of class and I am standing at the door waiting for him, he comes out beaming, bursting with news to share with me. (Apr. 17)

Once Dustin was eager to talk to her about things that he was doing away from school, Carey felt that he liked her and wanted to spend time with her. As Carey became more confident in the relationship she also began to spend less of the interview time talking about whether Dustin liked her and instead talked excitedly about activities they did in their sessions.

"And he wanted to write this time…"

Carey's pleasure with the progress of the relationship was matched by her pleasure with the progress of the literacy activities. One day, when discussing that day's session, Carey said that she "didn't have to coax Dustin to write at all!!" (Apr. 10). This both surprised and pleased her because she had said many times that "Dustin does not like writing." Today, however, was different.

And he began right away. And he wanted to write this time right away. And I usually sometimes have to give him ideas or a way to start a sentence, and he just started going, by himself. It even surprised me because I thought it would be a hard time to get him going. It did surprise me. (Apr. 10)

Carey was very pleased because Dustin typically did not enjoy writing. He struggled with writing and admitted that he didn't want to do it. Perhaps he enjoyed the writing more now because Carey was there to help him when he got stuck, or perhaps he felt that his writing was improving because she has been helping him, encouraging him, and praising him for his efforts, or perhaps he wanted to please her by showing interest in the writing. Whatever the reason, he seemed more willing to take risks and had grown to quite enjoy the writing process.

Although Carey had always invited Dustin into writing and had offered support, she hadn't pushed him. If he wanted to look at magazines and simply "talk, joke, and stuff," that was fine with Carey. For example, one day, Carey had planned on writing a story with Dustin. They had just started and he said to her, "Why don't we just read and stuff?" and she said, "Okay." Now it seemed that Dustin was ready to ask for help and to initiate working on his writing.

Carey was very pleased and surprised by Dustin's growing enthusiasm for writing.

> We sort of spontaneously do things. You never know what to expect because he always wants to do different stuff. And it surprises me, he always wants to write this story, because sometimes I say, "Do you want to read?" and he always says, "No, I would rather do this." And generally he doesn't like writing, he likes reading better, that's what he's always told me, but it's kind of crazy, I can't understand it. (Apr. 17)

"And we didn't end up shooting any gophers."

Intimacy, trust, and mutuality became more and more apparent in this relationship. When Dustin was going to a farm for a weekend and was anticipating shooting gophers, Carey told him that she didn't want him to do that. The following week, Dustin told her, "And we didn't end up shooting any gophers." Carey said, "And so I was happy." She added,

> He goes, "We just shot pop cans," and I said, "Okay, that's good." And he talked a bit about that. And then I told him how when I was little I never wanted to shoot animals. So I was telling him I used to just shoot tomatoes and just watch it all spurt out and he thought that was funny. (Apr. 10)

Dustin had been very excited about the trip to the farm. It had its disappointments, however, and he disclosed these to Carey: "I think he remembered he told me he was going to go there [the farm] because he said it wasn't fun. He goes, 'I didn't have fun,' and I'm like 'Why?' and he goes, 'Oh, these two mean boys came, and they kept trying to get us or chase us.' And I said 'What?'" (Apr. 10).

"I'm always thinking about him."

Carey developed a significant friendship with Dustin. Their relationship was very special to her. She said that on Friday mornings, she did "nothing but think about and anticipate my time with Dustin. I can't study or focus on anything. On Thursday night, I think, I get to go see Dustin tomorrow" (Apr. 3). She also said, "I tell my boyfriend everything about Dustin. I'm always thinking about him" (Apr. 17).

Carey understood her specialness to Dustin as being someone who was there just for him: "By being his mentor, I'm the person that's just for him. Nobody else in the class knows me the way he knows me; I am his. And so we can talk about stuff, and he can tell me what he's doing and stuff like that" (Mar. 20). Carey recognized the friendly, accommodating way that Dustin could experience learning in their sessions.

> And yes, I'm the person that—it's different than like a teacher even, because he can talk about what he wants to talk about, even as we are working. He can say something out loud—I don't care if he's writing and all of a sudden he thinks about something. Dustin—well, all children—cannot do that in a regular class during class time. And that is one of the differences about spending time with a mentor. (Mar. 20)

Carey went on to explain how mentorship is about both learning and friendship.

> A mentor relationship is different than teacher and the child and the kids, their relationship to each other; it's just something different, and I like it a lot. I want to help him learn, but I also just want that friendship to be there. . . . [It's] a friendship, but also I do want to teach him some things too, because I can see he has some problems in some of his reading. I think the main thing is probably just the friendship, because that's what I enjoy the most. It's just that you don't feel that pressure that there's tons of curriculum you have to get through or there's all this stuff. It's more relaxed, but also you can teach things. (Mar. 20)

Early in the mentorship, Carey gave priority to the development of friendship. She worried about not focusing on literacy and said, "That's why I wonder if I'm doing this right because I spend a lot of time just blabbing with him or joking" (Mar. 20). She worked hard to learn about dirt bikes, Hummers, Prowlers, computers, and hockey to give them common ground and to have sessions focus on Dustin's interests. Dustin responded with increased enthusiasm for writing and clearly enjoyed seeing her and sharing his news with her.

ঙ Chapter Twelve ও

LIKE MAKING A NEW WOMAN FRIEND: CASE STUDY OF KRISTEN AND CASCANDRA

The mentorship between Kristen and Cascandra began early in February 1998 and continued until the third week in March 1998. Kristen met with Cascandra once a week at lunch hour. Jan observed their sessions on February 5, 12, 19, March 12, and March 19. She interviewed Kristen four times, on February 12, 19, March 12, and March 19.

Kristen was a second-year student studying psychology and education at a Lutheran college. She came from a large family and was raised in small town in western Alberta. Kristen mentored Cascandra, an eight-year-old girl in grade 3 who was a new student in the school that year. Cascandra experienced the arrival of a first sibling during her mentorship with Kristen.

Cascandra had had a mentor in the fall term of that year, so Kristen was her second mentor. Cascandra had enjoyed a very satisfying relationship with her first mentor, who had been a female university student. Because of a number of conflicting demands and pressures in Kristen's life, she had to stop coming to the school a couple of weeks earlier than anticipated, and her last visit with Cascandra was on March 26.

Kristen did not begin the mentorship with a great deal of confidence about how she would establish a relationship with an eight-year-old girl. Cascandra, in turn, did not seem easy to get to know. Kristen focused on creating open, inviting spaces for comfortable conversation to support their getting to know each other. In Jan's presentation of this case study, we witness Kristen's challenges, efforts, and successes.

"I have a new mentor!"

On Thursday, February 5, I was walking down the school hallway and had just stopped to read children's poetry on the wall outside the grade 2/3 class when I felt an arm around my waist and heard a familiar child's voice. "Hi Jan! I want a hug." Cascandra was standing beside me, sporting a smile that stretched from ear to ear across her round, full face. "Hi, sweetie!! How are you?" I said. "Guess what!" she blurted out excitedly. "I have a new mentor." I said, "That's wonderful!! What's your mentor's name?" "Kristen, and she's in there," she said, pointing down the hall toward the mentor room. "She's waiting for me. I just had to get something from my cubby to show her." She ran off with a book under her arm. Then she stopped and asked: "Want to meet her? Come here. Come with me." She ran back toward me, grabbed my arm, and led me toward the mentor room. She opened the door, and still grasping my arm, said, "See, I told you! This is my mentor."

About Cascandra

This was Cascandra's first year at this school. She was an only child. Since I met her in October she had an ongoing preoccupation about a first sibling. All she ever talked about each time I saw her from October to December was the new baby that her mom was expecting after Christmas, sometime in February. She told the story this way. "I went to BC for the summer and stayed with my grandma. When I came back, Mom and Dad moved to a new building and Mom is pregnant. She is going to have a baby" (Oct. 8). Cascandra was very excited about the baby. When she told people about the baby, she had a habit of putting her hands up, shrugging her shoulders, and with a smile, saying, "I don't know, it might be the 16th, the 17th or the 18th. I don't know for sure, but around then." She was thrilled about having a sibling and longed for a sister: "I hope it's a girl!! I want a sister!! Oh, I hope it's a girl!! Do you think it's a baby girl?" (Oct. 15). During this year, Cascandra experienced many transitions—anticipating a first sibling, moving to a new school, a new apartment building, meeting new neighbors, new friends, new teachers and a principal, and now the second of two mentors.

About Kristen

Kristen grew up in a small town in western Alberta and moved to Edmonton after completing high school to enroll in postsecondary studies. Kristen was in her second year of college and living in the residence on campus. She looked forward to transferring into either the faculty of education or the faculty of arts at university the next year. Kristen was a serious student and very conscientious about her studies. She described living in residence as being "a disaster" for her.

> The girls stay out late and drink too much. When they get home, they are loud; so getting enough sleep is a real challenge. But I feel fine today because I stayed at my aunt's place last night because it is closer to here [this school]. (Feb. 5)

Kristen said that behavior such as "drinking and fooling about" is irresponsible.

Kristen's family was extremely important to her. She missed her siblings and parents very much and went home as often as possible. She was the second child in a tightly knit family of seven—two parents and five girls. At a young age she assumed a motherly role at home with her younger siblings.

> When I was little I knew I would have to help my mom with the babies. I was five years old when the twins came, and my older sister, who was six, we learned to change diapers and carry babies and bring them to my Mom, because she had her third C-section and was in a lot of pain. So right early on we learned to do all this kind of stuff. (Feb. 12)

Kristen spoke in detail about how her mother prepared her and her older sister for the birth of her younger siblings.

> But my Mom knew that she wasn't going to have a lot of time with Sara and I, just to spend one-on-one with us—Sara's my older sister—when the babies came. She prepared us for that; she talked to us and said, "There's two of them coming, and it's going to be hard," and she talked to us from day one when she got pregnant with them, explaining how there's going to be another baby, and there's not going to be time for us to watch *Little House on the Prairie* with her; we're not going to be able to sit on her lap as much. And she sat down and explained it to us and said, "They're going to sit on your lap, and you're going to hold them." And she kind of turned it back [to us] and said, "Now you're responsible for someone too," and "You've got to help me out here." (Feb. 12)

Kristen talked about the relationship she had with her little sisters and caring for her sisters during her childhood years.

> And I'm very close with my little sisters, and even when they were little, they weren't dolls; they were little babies that I had to take care of and I cared for more than anything. Dolls didn't mean anything to me anymore, because there were babies there. And I still remember thinking the absolute world of those kids. (Feb. 12)

Responsibility was something that Kristen learned and admired. She described her older sister's responsible behavior when Kristen was in a car accident.

> When I was in my car accident my mother was in the city with me for ten days, and my older sister was back home in her grade 12 year, and she was getting ready for the prom, buying her dress and things like that. And I got in the car accident and she put everything on hold, took care of the kids. She took that motherly position automatically, made sure they got where they were going, made sure they

had money, made sure that if they were going to go to their friend's house, they had a ride there, they were going to get back, she knew what time they were going to get back. Took care of everything, took that position like you wouldn't believe it; put her whole world on hold. (Feb. 19)

Preparing to Be a Mentor

Kristen anticipated an awkward phase in the beginning of this mentorship. She recalled her thoughts and concerns before starting the program.

> This is the first time I've been in a mentor program or anything like it. I just didn't know what to expect going into this and seeing that it might be a little grade 2 girl and thinking, "What am I going to talk to her about? How am I going to sit here for an hour? What are we going to do? What are we going to talk about? What am I going to tell her? What is she going to tell me? How is this going to work?" (Mar. 12)
> ...And I had to do a lot of thinking about it before I came here to work with her....I thought, if I'm going to do this, then I'm going to do it right, and I'm going to have fun with it, and I'm going to want her to have fun with it too. So I did think about it a lot. I did think about how to do this, how to go about it, how to be comfortable with her, how she's going to be comfortable with me, because I love her a lot. (Mar 12)

As part of her preparation, Kristen sought her mother's advice. Her mother was a teacher aide who works with "kids who have a lot of learning disorders and behavior problems." Repeating her mother's words, she said,

> If you want these kids to work, then you have got to be at a level with them where it's a relationship where they feel comfortable with you. If they're not comfortable with you, then they're not going to be able to do the work. They're not going to be able to trust you to say, "Can you help me?" (Mar. 12)

Kristen gained further confidence about becoming a mentor by baby-sitting her five-year-old cousin.

> Right before I started this program, I went back home, and I've got a little five-year-old cousin, and I baby-sat her for four days before this. I could sit there and talk to this little girl for an hour, and I was thinking, "If I can talk to a five-year-old for an hour, then I can talk to a grade twoer for an hour; it's just a matter of her knowing me."...So since I went and saw my little cousin, that's what really passed it over for me, gave me the confidence that I could sort this out and kind of gave me the idea of how I was going to do it and things, because with my five-year-old cousin, I sit down and I'll help her read and things like that, and she'll tell me stories, that kind of thing. So I thought, "That's what I'm going to have to do." So

that's how I related it;…I didn't know what to do, and then going back and seeing my little cousin did it. (Mar. 12)

Getting Past the Uncomfortable Stage

In spite of the time spent with her five-year-old cousin, Kristen still experienced an uncomfortable stage with Cascandra. It wasn't until their third visit, when Kristen began to tell Cascandra about herself, that Cascandra too started to open up.

> It was kind of a little bit hard [in the beginning], yes, because I didn't know what to say to her. And it's just because I didn't know what to expect….The first two times it was just kind of uncomfortable, the kind of stage when you ask her about herself. Then the third time is when I started talking to her about myself. And then this time was the time that she really started to bring out herself….So at first she was just kind of, you know, and I was uncomfortable too, because I'm not quite sure what we were going to do and not sure how it was all going to work out and everything, so we just kind of had to get past that. And then once we started to talk to each other more comfortably, and then she comes up and hugs me now and that kind of thing, once that started to happen, then things really smoothed out….She had to get used to me and I had to get used to her; that's what it was. But that worked out fine. (Mar. 12)

Kristen also elaborated on what it was like to tell Cascandra about herself.

> I'd tell her about when I was little and when I was in her grade, memories that I have,…then she'd come back and tell me stuff too. And then I told her what I was taking in school and how I was thinking of being a teacher, and she's really interested in that kind of thing. And now she has a big interest in me, just as I have got a big interest in her, and we just both know each other at that level. She can ask me questions about my family and when I grew up and where I came from; she can ask me who my second-grade teacher was and that kind of stuff, and that's more comfortable for her. And I remember all that stuff, so I can share that, so it's nice….Yes, it's nice, because we're very comfortable with each other now. (Mar. 12)
> And then I brought pictures of my family and my boyfriend and she got a big picture of her little sister, and I asked her what she was doing over spring break, and she's just like, "I don't know," kind of thing. But I find that she's much more willing to come out with things now. I'm going to miss her when I have to go; on my last day it's going to be hard to leave. I'm getting pretty attached to her. (Mar. 19)

Cascandra Testing the Water

Kristen seemed to find it very challenging to connect with Cascandra; not because Cascandra was distractible or overtly resistant, but rather because her consistently pleasant, happy manner seemed to mask over whatever might be on her mind. She seemed inscrutable. As Kristen put it, "At first she was a very friendly and very positive little girl, but she still did not want to tell me a lot about herself" (Mar. 12).

For a period of time, Cascandra was very tentative, exploratory, and testing in her relationship with Kristen. Kristen was very sensitive to and observant of the ways Cascandra made overtures and listened for feedback.

> Now, I noticed, she really watches my responses….She really kind of sits there, and she's not necessarily actually looking at me, but listening for each tone in my voice, I could just tell, when she tells me about things, just to find out what I think about it, whether it's good or bad or that kind of thing….She really does watch me and really listens to what I'm saying and how I'm saying it, and just trying to feel me out still, just kind of how I'm reacting to this. (Mar. 12)
>
> There was almost like one stage where she was getting comfortable but not completely kind of trusting me, I guess you could say. But there was that stage where she was really still unsure, but comfortable enough to sit down and talk to me, and that was actually quite an interesting stage, because she was very, very—wanted to tell me jokes, wanted to make me laugh, wanted to make me happy. That's what I found with her, and she was an absolute sweetheart there….And now she trusts me a little bit, tells me about her grandmother, tells me about her little sister and things like that. (Mar. 19)

Art, Talk, and Childhood Memories

Kristen wanted Cascandra to find it comfortable and inviting to talk to her. In her search for strategies to support this goal, she drew on her own childhood memories for ideas. She recalled how craft activities and special books facilitated spontaneous conversation and connection in her own home. Art or craft activities became a centerpiece in her mentorship sessions with Cascandra, and she read the favorite book her mother had read to her. In the following interview excerpt, Kristen shares her memories of doing art projects at home as a child.

> I remember, I was quite young, sitting at the table with my mother and older sister, who's a year older than me, and we were sitting there doing these little art projects, just sitting there with my mom, and the babies were all in bed, and my dad was at work, and it was just the three of us. And we were just sitting there doing these art projects and talking away, and now I'm really into art just because we

did so much when I was little.…It [art] always did [encourage conversation] with me and my mom, because you're sitting there and you're working with your hands and, "Okay, pass me that," and then you get into conversations, and then you can talk and work at the same time with that; whereas if you're reading, we're just reading a book and concentrating on the book. Reading is an excellent thing, but it doesn't give you that time to talk. (Mar. 12)

Kristen also described how she experienced doing art projects with Cascandra.

And I find when we do art projects and that, there's a lot more socializing, where you're sitting there and you're working and talking at the same time. But I think that's a good thing, because if we get into big conversations we can talk about something as simple as school. Today we were talking about the games that she plays at recess too, and we can talk about that or else we can talk about anything she wants, and those are the times that kids will really open up, and those are the times that they will remember too, because you remember sitting there talking to people. (Mar. 12)

In the following excerpt, Kristen reflects on reading Cascandra a book that her own mother read to her when she was a child.

There's this book, it's called *I Love You Forever* that's in the library, and my mom bought it just because she liked it; she ended up reading it to all of us girls when we were little, and I wasn't even that little at the time and I loved to sit there and listen to her read it. There's a little song in it and everything and we sat there and looked at the pictures in the book and how cute the book was, and I told her [Cascandra] about when I was little and I used to read the book. And that was nice because it was an interaction there [between me and Cascandra] when she was paying attention. (Mar. 19)

Kristen's stories revealed how important it was to her to connect with Cascandra and the concerted efforts she made to do so.

Finally—the Mentor Is a Safe Place

Eventually, Kristen's dedication and efforts gained her ground with Cascandra. The always positive but nondisclosing Cascandra finally confessed to Kristen that it bothered her "when people call me fat" (Mar. 12).

On another occasion, Kristen was surprised and concerned by another disclosure. Kristen had brought art materials to make Easter baskets and was teaching Cascandra how to do paper weaving. She cut off some strips and was showing the process. Cascandra asked, "How do we do this?" Kristen said,

"It's really easy to do; it's no big deal," and Cascandra replied, "I'm not a very fast learner." And I said to her, "Yes, you are." I said, "Don't say that! It's no big deal. I'll sit there; I'll help you out if you need help. But you're fine. You're really very good." I said, "You have nothing to be ashamed of. You should be proud of yourself. And you seem to be a very fast learner," and she says, "No, I'm not a very fast learner, so I'm going to need a lot of help." (Mar. 19)

And I just looked at her and I was like, I've never seen that in her before; never once has she said that to me, "I'm not a very fast learner!" Never once has she shown that lack of self-confidence! (Mar. 19)

While Kristen was concerned about Cascandra's self-doubts or troubles, she could recognize that Cascandra was showing more trust and comfort with her.

Unsayable Troubles

Finally, Cascandra experienced troubles that she didn't or couldn't articulate. The changes in her mood and behavior, and her sense of preoccupation, were very evident to Kristen.

She kind of seemed out of sorts today for some reason. She usually talks a lot and she didn't do a lot of that. And she usually helps me pick everything up and takes her books and goes and things like that. Today it was like she was in a big fluster when the bell rang, and I said, "Are you going to take your books?" and "Oh yes my books," and she takes her books and forgets her lunch bag, and I had to get her to come back and get her lunch bag. Usually she's very well thought out on what she's doing, but today she was just running in circles, it seemed. She just seemed in a frenzy almost. (Mar. 12)

Kristen was concerned about Cascandra and wondered if her preoccupation had to do with her grandma's pending departure. Her grandma had come to stay with them for a month after her baby sister was born. Cascandra was very attached to her grandma and not accustomed to losing her mother's attention to the new baby.

She [Cascandra] was always very involved in the interaction of the two of us. But today, she got pulled away very easily. And she was quite quiet. Usually she's talking to me all the time—constantly, but today it was more like me asking her questions and trying to get her to come out, so I don't know what's going on there, whether she's starting to [worry], about her grandma leaving. I'm not quite sure. But she just is a bit off today, so I picked up on that and I'm going to have to watch her next time and see her quite closely. (Mar. 12)

The next time Kristen saw Cascandra, she was even more concerned.

I picked up on that [Cascandra's mood and preoccupation] right when she came in, because she hugs me every day when she comes in. And we sit down and start talking, and she'll tell me about little things that are happening in school, things like that, but there's not really any of that today….She's a little bit off, not sitting and talking to me as usual. With Cascandra, she's very, very comfortable with—she'll touch my hand, and she's laughing and very, very caring, very physically caring and things like that, hugging me all the time….She seemed almost off somewhere else today. I had to kind of talk to her and bring things up with her, before she'd talk to me. Usually she rambles on, tells me about what she did at recess, tells me about her class, tells me about this, tells me about that; and today she was just really mellow. (Mar. 19)

When Kristen asked Cascandra how the baby was doing, Cascandra's response was not at all enthusiastic. She simply shrugged her shoulders and said, "Oh, good." Kristen explained that this response was not typical.

Usually she'll tell me how big she is and what she looks like and things like that, but now it's just—didn't really say much. And then she started telling me about her grandma and her grandma leaving, and I said, "Oh, that's too bad" and "So are you going to miss her a lot?" and she said "Oh, yes!" with emphasis, really meaning it. I remember having a big shock, a lack of time with my mother when my little sister was coming. I think she's going to feel it too. And her grandmother's leaving in a couple of days;…once her grandma's gone I think it's going to be quite the shock. (Mar. 19)

An Abrupt Ending

The last time Kristen was at the school she had to leave in a hurry after her session with Cascandra. She explained, "I have no time for an interview today because I have to get to my class. I have an exam. Here is my phone number—you can call me" (Mar. 26). I tried calling her many times. There was no answer and no answering machine to take a message. After that, there was a recording stating that the number was no longer in service. Kristen telephoned the school on three occasions and left messages for Cascandra. On two occasions, she explained that she was not coming because of final exams. On another occasion, she was unable to come because she was moving out of the college residence.

It was unfortunate that Kristen and Cascandra had their last session together without realizing that it would be their last session and having the chance to say good-bye. Other mentors came for another three weeks. Most mentors who were students attended university and had a later exam schedule. Cascandra joined another mentor pair but said that it wasn't the same. Although she received Kristen's phone messages, she said that she felt bad and missed her.

This mentorship program did not yet have funding for a program coordinator. One of the functions of a coordinator could well be to monitor mentorship pairs and to encourage mentors to plan for realistic program schedules. Similarly, orientation sessions and handouts for mentors could include reminders about the importance of a last visit or session dedicated to celebration, ritual, closure, and a "good leaving."

❧ Chapter Thirteen ☙

APPROPRIATED AS A GRANDMA:
CASE STUDY OF ELIZABETH AND NARISSA

The mentorship between Elizabeth and Narissa began in late January 1998 and continued until the end of April 1998. Elizabeth met with Narissa on Thursdays from 1:00 to 2:00 P.M. Jan interviewed Elizabeth eight times on the following dates: February 12, 19, March 12, 19, 26, April 9, April 16, 23.

Elizabeth, a grandmother and widow who lived in the school community, mentored Narissa, a seven-year-old girl in grade 2. Narissa's family had immigrated to Canada when she was three years old. Her parents did not speak English, and Narissa said she could only speak to her mom a little in their first language. Elizabeth was Narissa's first mentor. Narissa had not participated in the fall program because all the mentors had come at lunch hour and Narissa didn't spend lunch hour at the school.

Elizabeth began the mentorship program with a view to fulfilling a civic duty by helping a child learn to read and insisted that she didn't want to get too involved because she had already raised her own kids. Narissa, a shy little girl with everyone else, took Elizabeth as her own, hugging her around the legs each time they met or parted. While Elizabeth was never effusive or demonstrative with her affection, Jan's case study reveals how the two charmed each other and developed a significant and satisfying relationship.

Meeting Elizabeth and Narissa

There was a buzz in the air. This was the sound that I usually heard around 1:00 P.M. in the school hallway. A group of mentors stood together talking to one another, sharing the highlights of their mentoring session. I always hung around to hear what they had to say (Feb. 12).

It was then that I noticed a tall, mature-looking woman who I had never seen before walking toward the mentor room with a frail-looking little girl. A cream-colored canvas bag hung on the woman's shoulder. The little girl carried two books under her arm. They walked together silently and then entered the mentor room. Curious, I followed them into the room.

"Hi!" I smiled. "I'm Jan. Are you a mentor?" I asked the woman. She looked at me with a puzzled look on her face. "Yes," she said. I continued, "We haven't met before." She replied "No, we haven't, I'm Elizabeth Chapman. This is Narissa. I come at one o'clock, you know, for the mentor program they have here." "Yes, yes. Mind if I stay—if I sit in on your session?" There was an awkward silence. Then I heard, "Umm, umm." She was obviously uncomfortable with this request. I jumped in. "No, no. That's okay. Can we meet after your session? I just want to chat with you about the mentoring you are doing with Narissa." "Well, I don't see *that* as a problem," she said. "I'll come back at two o'clock? Is that okay?" "Okay," she agreed.

At two o'clock, I returned to the mentor room. Narissa was just getting up to leave. Elizabeth stood up as well and walked her back to class. I couldn't help but notice the contrast—how different they looked walking alongside one another. I wasn't sure if Elizabeth was unusually tall or if Narissa was particularly small, or if it was the age difference and the silence between them that was staggering. There seemed to be such a striking contrast.

Introducing Elizabeth

Elizabeth has lived in the school community for years. One day, when she drove past the school, she saw the sign that the principal put up to recruit mentors. She was curious and inquired about becoming a mentor. When she found out that mentoring involved engaging in reading with a child, she signed up because she values reading.

> If you can help a child—I love to read, and I can't imagine a child or a person not being able to read or to enjoy reading….I hope the program gets made much larger for other schools, because I think it's a great asset. They're our future generation, and when you hear the statistics of how many can't read and can't write—they were talking about that on the news today, that—I think it's a shame—they were saying the ones in the prisons even, most of them can't read or write. Terrible. And today you have such an opportunity to go to school. (Feb. 12)

Elizabeth lives alone. She has two grown children—one daughter and one son. She is retired and loves to golf. Although she was committed to mentoring Narissa one hour a week, and genuinely wanted to "help her improve in her reading and writing," she insisted that she did not want to be involved beyond that.

I have raised my own children and they are very successful. I'm happy to mentor Narissa, to help out. But I have already raised my children. I am happy to help out, to spend time mentoring a child, one day a week—but that's all. As long as I come to the school and do it, that's fine. I have my life. It's taken me a while—my husband died two years ago, you know, and it's taken me a while. But I am 76 years old, I have raised my children. (Feb. 19)

Although Elizabeth began mentoring Narissa because she felt that volunteering and helping others is the right thing to do, she did admit that she quite enjoys it.

Introducing Narissa

The first time I met Narissa was the day I saw her walking down the hall with Elizabeth. I hadn't run into her before because she went home for lunch every day except Thursday, when she had choir. Narissa's teacher commented that she was very quiet and kept to herself.

She's not like Michael and some of the other kids [that] you know—she doesn't go out of her way to talk to people [who] she doesn't know. Some kids see a new face in the school, doesn't matter if it's an adult, an older student, a baby, a workman, and they go up to them, "What's your name? What are you doing here? Are you a sub?" Not Narissa, she basically stays to herself, it's hard getting anything out of her. I think it's her family, her culture, you know. Nice girl, though. (Feb. 19)

Elizabeth pointed out that Narissa was well-behaved in school, that "she doesn't cause any problems for the teacher." Although she appeared shy, quiet, and timid with most people, she was more talkative with Elizabeth. According to Elizabeth, "She likes to chat, to talk. I think she likes the time spent [with her mentor]."

I was pleased to hear that because when I first met Narissa I couldn't get her to even look up at me, let alone make any verbal response. She hung her head low and clung to Elizabeth's arm. Her long, shiny, black hair covered most of her tiny face. I tried to be friendly and asked her about the books she held tightly under her arm. When she finally looked up at me, her big brown eyes didn't smile back. Instead, they appeared vacant. She spoke quietly, telling me the titles of her books. She kept fussing with the neckline of her T-shirt that kept sliding to her right shoulder. The short-sleeved shirt hung loosely on her, accenting her slight frame and her long, thin arms.

Narissa lived with her parents and siblings. Elizabeth initially told me that Narissa had three siblings; a younger brother in kindergarten and two older sisters in high school. She later told me that Narissa had five brothers and sisters in their country of origin. She also said that she had learned from Narissa that her parents didn't speak English at home and that Narissa described herself as being able to speak only a little bit of her parents' language with her mom (Mar. 12).

Elizabeth learned a lot about Narissa's background. As she said, each week when they were together, she spent some time "chatting about Narissa's family. She just rambles on and on." Elizabeth enjoyed this part of their sessions and felt that Narissa did as well. Elizabeth felt that "it helps me understand Narissa better if I know about her family."

A Shy Beginning

Narissa was quite shy in the beginning of the mentorship. Elizabeth shared memories and reflections about this first period in their mentorship.

> Yes, she was [shy at the beginning]. Yes, she was, and always talked sort of with her chin down—you know how kids do when they're shy. But she's got her head up now, and she looks at you more and so on. So she's coming out of her shell, which is good. Takes a while for a child to bond, and besides, I'm a lot older. I don't know. But no, I think she's come out of her shell a lot; I feel she has. (Mar. 19)

When asked what might have contributed to Narissa's increasing comfort, Elizabeth reflected,

> I think she just felt more comfortable with me; that's what I would say. I would think, for a child that age, that I'm tall and she's short; [and] they are told, "This is your mentor"; and you kind of intimidate them, I think, almost because she's so little; I don't think she weighs very much at all. So it would take a while to bond or to get used to me, so I just continue on the same way. (Mar. 19)

In a later interview, Elizabeth added,

> She was a little maybe shyer [in the beginning]. As I told you, I am tall, and there she is, this little girl standing down there, and her parents aren't tall or anything. I'm not that much taller, but I'm still taller, and I'm white, I guess. So she did whatever you said, but as I say, she didn't project any personality. It seems to me that her personality is coming out a bit more all the time, which is good. I'm glad she feels at ease. (Apr. 9)

When asked when Narissa became noticeably more at ease, Elizabeth replied:

> I guess about the third time. About the third time she really settled in, and then she'd begun to talk a lot more to me, and I'd say about the third one she started to

tell about her family, and I'd ask questions, and she'd tell me more about them. Yes, I'd say it took about three times. (Apr. 9)

Gifts, Praise and Thoughtfulness

In anticipation of mentoring Narissa, Elizabeth put together a collection of things to bring to their sessions. She brought them each time in her canvas mentor bag.

> I bought some crayons and I've bought a coloring book, and my daughter was clearing out her desk and she found these stickers, and some of them are "Looking Good, and "Good Going" and so on. Some of her pictures I was starting to put some of these stickers on, and the rest of them I'll just give to her and she can take them home and play with them. (Feb. 19)

Elizabeth explained how she approached giving gifts to Narissa.

> Every once in a while, and only for special occasions—I just thought it was kind of nice to give them something. I don't know whether they [Narissa's family] observe it or not. It's just something I give, certain days. Not a habit—of course with my daughter I could not give my grandkids something every time; I was not allowed to do that. You know how you see these grandparents, every time the kids come, it's a [big thing] and she wouldn't let me, just once in a while and things like that. And I guess the way I feel, just bring it for special occasions. Probably the year end I'll bring her some little thing. (Mar. 26)

Elizabeth discussed a gift she brought for Narissa from her vacation and described how she recognized special days such as Valentine's Day and Easter.

> Before Valentine's, I bought her some Valentine cookies, and when I came back from Hawaii—she loves stickers—I bought her some stickers and a little cuckoo-shell necklace. She was very pleased with it. She was pleased with the stickers because they are different than you buy here, and they were kind of fluorescent. She told me that she liked flowers and birds on stickers—this was when I first started with her. So that's what I was looking for. I found them hard to find over there. I probably wasn't looking in the right place, but they don't have the Dollar Store or the K-Mart; they're all these tourist stores. But anyway, she was very pleased with it. A nice little girl. (Apr. 16)

Elizabeth bought Narissa a decorated chocolate Easter egg. When I commented to Elizabeth that "Narissa looked so pleased," she said,

> Oh, yes, she was! "Oh," she says, "it's pretty. Now I'll have to get my sister to buy you something." I said, "No, no, no. I gave this to you." I don't know, she seems

to think that her sister has lots of money, but she only works at McDonald's, and she's going to school, so I don't think she has that much money. (Apr. 9)
I don't know how much English her sister speaks. I should ask her. (Mar. 26)

When I commented that it was nice of her to bring Narissa the Easter egg, she said, "I'm glad she enjoyed it; her face lit up. I said to her, did you eat your Easter egg? She says, 'Yeah!' So she didn't say whether she shared it with her brother or not, so more power to her. But she is a cute little kid, very polite, and she likes approval" (Apr. 16).

Elizabeth was very observant of Narissa's appreciation of praise for her work.

Just if I say, "You know, Narissa, you're reading really well," and she looks up and her face just beams. And when she did her math I said, "You did really well." So I said to her, "We'll have to put one of these [stickers] on. Which one do you want to choose?" So she chose that one and she just beamed. (Apr. 16)

Elizabeth also shared a story about teaching Narissa to tie her shoelaces.

You know, I noticed a little boy in the hallway with his shoes untied. I taught Narissa to tie her shoelaces. She didn't know how, you know. And I showed her. In my day, we made sure our kids could tie their shoes before they went to school. I showed her how to tie her shoes, you know. And the next time I saw her, she came up to me and reminded me, "I can tie my shoes all by myself, I remembered how you showed me." And she remembered that, you know. So I let her show me and she did it just like I showed her. There's a lot of little things that mentors do that are not reading and writing but that still help, you know, that help the child in other ways. (Apr. 9)

At one point, Narissa said to Elizabeth, "I'd like to know how to knit." Elizabeth replied: "I can knit. I'll teach you how to knit." Elizabeth discussed her plans for teaching Narissa to knit: "I think next week I will try and bring some wool and knitting needles and we can spend fifteen minutes and then I'll just put it away until she gets used to it, and then she can always take it home and practice with it" (Mar. 19).

Narissa's Affectionate Responses

In interviews, Elizabeth mentioned many of Narissa's expressions of affection and appreciation. These began with hugs and then verbal expressions.

At first she was very shy. She's come out of her shell a bit more with me. When she sees me she hugs me around the legs, and [says], "Hi, there." And when it was

Teachers' Convention [and the mentorship session had to be cancelled], she'll say, "I missed you." So she does show emotion, which is nice. (Mar. 12)

I asked her if the hugging was new, and Elizabeth replied, "No, no. I think from the third time I was here she did. She's so little, and then I feel this little hand come around; it's more just below the hips. Yes, she does. Yes, so, I'm glad, yes" (Mar. 12). Elizabeth also described poetry and drawings that Narissa gave to her:

She's a very nice little girl; I quite enjoy her. Before I went on my holiday she wrote and gave me the cutest little poem—*Roses are red, violets are blue*—and she's got a couple of sentences at the bottom [and then] *Love, Narissa.* And when I got that letter from the school last week [recognizing mentors], she had a drawing at the bottom. She had myself and herself, but I'm taller and she the shorter one, and she drew the table [that they work at], and she even had my [mentor] bag on it. She puts in great detail, and the book and the chairs, and wrote a few nice words at the bottom. So, yes, she is a delightful child. (Mar. 19)

The week after Elizabeth gave Narissa an Easter egg, Narissa made Elizabeth a special Easter card. Elizabeth shared it with me: "Look at the work she put into it." On the card, she had written, Thank you for the Easter egg. It was good. Happy Easter Mentor! I hope you have a great day. Sincerely, Narissa. I noticed something else written on the card: Happy Easter Beth! and a sticker beside it. And I asked her if Narissa had ever called her Beth before. She replied,

Isn't that cute, yes. No, no. But she asked me, and I said, "It's Elizabeth, but you can shorten it to Beth, B-e-t-h." And she drew the bunny. She says, "I'm not very good at drawing bunnies." And the heart. I think it's lovely. I told her I had the one she gave me before on my fridge, and I'll put this on my fridge. (Apr. 16)

On another occasion, at the end of their session, Narissa asked Elizabeth to play Hangman.

She said, "I'll just show you." And at the end she said, "No, you didn't get the words right." She said because I put **you** down," and then she puts [writes], *You are the best mentor.* Oh, she does, she often says that....So I try to help her and that, but I think she likes the time spent as much as anything. (Apr. 9)

Elizabeth came to acknowledge and value her positive relationship with Narissa.

I think that she looks forward to it [the sessions], I really do. I said to her, "I'll see you next Thursday, Narissa," and she says, "Yes," happily. So it's nice. I do think that I've bonded with Narissa. She always seems happy to see me and likes to tell me about things in the past week. (Apr. 16)

Helping Narissa with Reading and Math

Elizabeth noticed an improvement in Narissa's reading. When I asked her how working with Narissa was different from what it had been in the beginning, she explained:

> She's improved in her reading; I've got her to slow down, so she quit missing words. I think she thought she was supposed to impress me, and by impressing, she read fast. So I told her, "Narissa, you have to slow down. You're missing words. Later on when you have to learn grammar and form sentences that are correct, if you start missing all these little words, you'll have problems." So she doesn't miss words now, and she has slowed down. She has improved, even if I do say so myself. She has progressed, but I want to stay with it too; I don't want to just sit chatting and not staying with the reading. But I think she's doing very well, I don't know about what [her teacher] thinks, if she can see an improvement or not. (Mar. 12)

In subsequent interviews, Elizabeth again raised the topic of Narissa's progress with reading.

> She read well today, and a little louder, not sort of the whisper she'll get sometimes. (Apr. 16)
> But can I ever see a difference in her reading! She's reading with so much more confidence! Before she was very quiet when she was reading. But now she speaks out with a fair amount of authority, shall we say, when she's reading. You can hear it, you're not sort of having to watch her do the words to be sure if she's reading correctly. (Apr. 23)

Elizabeth also helped Narissa improve in math. At one point, Narissa's teacher told Elizabeth that Narissa was weak in math. The next time she saw Narissa she asked her, "'How are you in math?' She says, 'Not very good. I have trouble with it. I'll show you what I have trouble with'" (Mar. 26). Narissa proceeded to write down a group of three numbers, and then another three. Then she began to count on her fingers. Elizabeth was shocked, and commented,

> You can count on your fingers today? We got the ruler! They let you? Oh yes, probably, because she's having so much trouble. She's probably letting her take the easiest way out....I don't mind helping her in math, not at all. As long as it isn't the new math, I don't know the new math. (Mar. 26)

Realizing that it was basic facts that Narissa was having trouble with, I said, "But the basic facts?" She answered, "Oh, heavens, yes! Heavens! It wouldn't be any problem at all. I could easily make up some at home and then help her a bit with it. It's a long way to go to get through school, to get a career or whatever she plans [without knowing her basic facts]" (Mar. 26). When I asked how their session went on a later date, Elizabeth replied, "Very good, *very* good. She read well today. I gave her math questions and she got them" (Apr. 9). Whether it was reading, basic facts, or even tying shoelaces, Elizabeth was happy to help Narissa in areas where she experienced difficulty. She also witnessed Narissa's success in response to her help. Elizabeth felt that a mentor's main role is to help the child. She often said, "As long as I'm helping her, that's the main thing."

She received feedback from Narissa that she was helping her and making her happy. She also received feedback from her son. She telephoned her son after each session with Narissa. He reassured her that she was making a difference. She often reminded me, "He's a school principal, at the high school, you know. My son said, 'Mom, I'm sure you are having quite an impact on a little girl like that'" (Feb. 19). Elizabeth also hoped for feedback from Narissa's teacher. As she told me, "I was going to ask [her teacher] if she's seen any improvement in her reading and things like that" (Mar. 19). Encouragement is important to mentors just as it is to students. Some programs use communication booklets passed between teacher and mentor so that they can leave each other little notes about how things are going.

In June, the mentorship program was over for the year. On sunny days, Elizabeth was on the golf course. One rainy afternoon she called me on the telephone (June 11). She told me a story about a day she had visited the school to drop off her consent form for participation in the mentorship program research. She saw Narissa in the school playground, climbing on the monkey bars. Narissa saw her and called out to her, "Can I come out and give you a hug?" Elizabeth motioned for her to come down. Elizabeth's last comment to me about Narissa was, "She came from a student who was mediocre to a student who wanted to learn. So, I think it [the mentoring] helps."

⽂ Chapter Fourteen ⽁

UNLOCKING THE SECRET
TO MENTORSHIP RELATIONSHIPS

The previous four chapters presented case studies of four mentor pairs who enjoyed weekly one-hour visits in a two- or three-month literacy mentorship program at the children's school. From the research results reported in Chapter 4, we had reason to believe that mutually satisfying relationships developed between mentors and children in a mentorship program as short as eight weeks. In the case study research that followed the progress of four mentor pairs, we hoped to gain insight into the key dynamics of the successful development of such relationships. Each of the four mentor pairs and their relationships were unique, with different preoccupations, favored activities, routines, and dramatic moments. In this examination of the case studies we sought to learn how these relationships were the same in spite of their evident differences.

To examine the case studies we worked with key ideas about relationships that have been offered by Brendtro, Brokenleg, and Van Bockern (1990). Larry Brendtro and his colleagues have long been involved in efforts to reclaim children and youth in conflict with family, school, and community. As a framework for this reclaiming work, they use the Circle of Courage with its identification of children's four developmental needs—belonging, mastery, independence, and generosity, or *attachment, achievement, autonomy,* and *altruism.* In this conceptual organizer, attachment is understood to foster achievement, autonomy, and altruism. Their work is informed by Native American tribal wisdom (Brokenleg, 1998); Eric Fromm's *The Art of Loving;* Bowlby's (1973) research on separation, anger, and anxiety; other related research; and their own work with violent youth for over three decades (Brendtro & Long, 1995).

The Circle of Courage model is a promising one for this analysis, since it links children's achievement to their attachments to significant adults and emphasizes attachments to significant adults who are not the child's parents. In their elaboration of this model, Brendtro, Brokenleg, and Van Bockern (1990) have focused on how to put it into practice with children and youth who are already in conflict with family, school, and community. The more general ideas they offer can serve as a starting point or set of interpretive ideas for beginning a similar elaboration for primary prevention programs in which nonrelated adults mentor young children. Thus ideas from their model can be used to guide investigation of the case studies, and what is learned from the analysis can serve to provide further elaboration of these ideas. Since the purpose of this examination of the case studies is understanding relationship development, the ideas about attachment in the Circle of Courage will be the focus in the analysis.

Brendtro et al. (1990) have observed that the most potent behavioral influence an adult can have in the life of a child comes when an attachment has been formed. They have also argued that it is the quality of human relationships in schools and youth service programs that makes a difference and that the quality of relationships may be even more influential than the specific interventions or techniques that have been repeatedly tried and tested. They offered the following observations about recently renewed interest in the significance of attachments.

> Adults who work with youth have long been aware of the awesome power of relationships. This was a dominant theme of the early writings in education, counseling and youth work. However, as professional literature became more scientifically oriented, relationships were increasingly ignored. Now there are signs of a renewal of interest in the synergistic power of human relationships. (p. 58)

While asserting the potency of relationships, Brendtro et al. (1990) acknowledge that there remains an affective vagueness about this concept. They have, however, specified the following key ideas about relationships:

- Relationship is not simply a feeling but rather is something that results from action and this action involves giving.
- A strong sense of belonging or attachment makes young people more receptive to guidance from adults.
- Adults who are engaged in a helping role with young people must be able to offer warm and stable attachments.
- Eric Fromm's (1956) model of positive relationships shows the four common elements to be *caring, responsibility, respect* and *knowledge*.

These ideas about relationships are very global ones. Brendtro et al. acknowledge that there are not 10 easy steps to relationship building; there is no cookbook approach that can be thoughtlessly followed. One has to be fully present to build a relationship. By revisiting the case studies with these general ideas as lenses, this analysis will undertake to clarify the quality or character of the relationships and the ways in which they developed.

Relationship Results from Action and This Action Involves Giving

Over the course of the mentorships, expressions of giving were enacted in numerous ways. The different kinds of giving that occurred appeared to be related to the stage of the relationship, the child's characteristics, the mentor's characteristics, and the child/mentor combinations. Table 4 provides a categorization of the different forms of giving that were discernible in the four mentorship case studies. The relationships formed in very different and complex ways as a result of many influences and through many kinds of giving—giving that made sense for the mentor pairs involved. Revisiting the case studies through the framework of "forms of giving" highlights the uniqueness of each pair's relationship, illuminates the diversity among pairs, and attests to the boundless creativity of human care and connection.

Table 4: Mentors' Forms of Giving

Giving Concrete Gifts

- The giving of general age-appropriate treats (e.g., candy, cookies, stickers)
- The giving of personal gifts related to the child's interests (e.g., posters)
- The giving of working materials and craft materials

Giving Attention and Care

- Giving opportunities for the child to talk and to become increasingly comfortable talking to the mentor (taking time for this, showing interest in the child's talk, or planning activities that would provide the space for free-ranging talk)
- Giving recognition and praise for the child's work
- Giving parent-like or friend-like care in noticing and responding to the child's needs for support whether emotional or practical (a shoulder to cry on or learning to tie one's shoes)

Giving Opportunities for Common Ground and Empowerment

- Giving personal information about one's own life (photographs, sharing stories from the past and present)
- Giving the child the prerogative in determining the activities for the sessions
- Giving the effort to become knowledgeable about the child's interest areas and thereby creating conversation topics of common interest

While the various forms of giving may not appear surprising or unexpected, what is noteworthy is the degree to which some forms were more dominant in one pair than in another. Each pair was unique in terms of the expectations, life experience, and confidence that each person brought to the relationship. While the diversity among the pairs was considerable, giving in one form or another was prevalent.

Recognizing the importance of reciprocity in relationships, we also noted the giving that took place on the part of the children. Table 5 presents a categorization of the children's forms of giving.

Table 5: Children's Forms of Giving

Giving Affection, Attention, and Interest

- Giving expressions of affection or happiness to see their mentor (smiles, hugs, hand-made cards, or verbal statements of affection or admiration)
- Giving expressions of appreciation for mentor's gifts or efforts
- Making efforts to amuse, tease, or joke with the mentor
- Being interested in the mentor's news, life, and well-being

Making Sacrifices to Be with the Mentor

- Giving up other activities to be with the mentor (e.g., lunch time traffic patrol position)

Self-Disclosure

- Showing not only willingness but eagerness to tell the mentor their news
- Giving personal information about their lives and feelings
- Giving trust in revealing self-doubt, fears, or troubles

This discussion has highlighted the forms of giving that were easily identifiable in the case studies. Who the mentors were and who the children were at the time of the mentoring relationships appeared to have much bearing on what was given by each of the parties. In one form or another, however, giving can be seen to be a central, active dynamic in the development of the relationships that evolved. The mentors gave in ways that made sense to them based on their understanding of the child and children in general, their life experiences, and their life space at that particular time.

While this discussion has presented categorizations of observable acts of giving, it is appropriate to close with a reflection on Fromm's more phenomenologically expressed understanding of the nature of giving in mentoring relationships. This statement (presented in Chapter 1) reminds us of the vitality that was inherent within and beyond the easily describable acts of giving and receiving. What the mentors observably gave or did not give to the children varied considerably. Each of the mentors gave what he or she thought was important to give. Beyond their discernible expressions of giving, however, they gave their very presence, their aliveness, and all of their nuanced responses to the child's aliveness. By giving in this way to the child's life and having what they brought to life in the child reflected back, they also gave to themselves, enriching their own aliveness. It is through two lives coming together in this intentional and focused way that giving can occur spontaneously and even in spite of intentionality, and relationships or attachments can grow.

Children's Receptivity to Guidance and Modeling from Their Mentors

An adult who is liked and admired is also an effective role model. Youth who admire an adult will also attempt to imitate that adult's values and behaviors. In discussing the pivotal role of attachment in supporting the development of achievement, autonomy, and altruism, Brendtro et al. (1990) and Lee and Cramond (1999) reminded us of theories pertaining to social reinforcement and role models. If an adult has status in the child's eyes and has a positive healthy relationship with the child, the elements are in place for the adult's social reinforcement and modeling to be effective. The child will value the adult's approval and opinions. The child will also seek to imitate the values, attitudes, and behaviors of the adult. Thus, Brendtro et al. have argued that once a bond is firmly established between an adult and a younger person, the younger person more readily receives guidance from the adult. If significant attachments were formed in the mentor pairs in the four case studies, one would expect to find that the children became increasingly receptive to guidance from their mentors. One would also expect to observe examples of the children modeling the mentors' values and/or behaviors.

In general, children's receptivity to guidance from mentors showed itself as listening and responding to suggestions and advice of the mentors, asking mentors for help with schoolwork, and seeking help from the mentors with personal troubles. Examples of the children's receptivity are described below.

Tiara and Joel

Early in the mentorship between Tiara and Joel (the "soul mate" relationship with a grade 6 student), Tiara stated that Joel listened to her and did not argue or complain about doing schoolwork during mentoring sessions. She said that he complied when she suggested that they do something. For example, when she suggested that they sit in another place for a mentoring session, his response was, "Okay, yes, that's good." Tiara further commented, "He doesn't argue with me about anything."

Carey and Dustin

When Dustin, the grade 2 boy, told his mentor Carey that he was going to shoot gophers when he went to the farm, she expressed disapproval and told him that she did not want him to shoot gophers. She told him that when she was little, she didn't want to shoot animals and that she "used to just shoot tomatoes and just watched it all spurt out." Dustin thought this was funny. When Dustin returned from the farm, he volunteered that he did not shoot gophers, stating that he "just shot pop cans." This met with Carey's approval.

Kristen and Cascandra

Cascandra sought guidance from Kristen by asking her for help with the Easter basket weaving that Kristen had brought for them to do together. Referring to the weaving, Cascandra asked, "How do we do this?" adding, "I'm not a very fast learner." When Kristen expressed surprise with this comment and offered reassurance, Cascandra insisted, "No, I'm not a very fast learner. So I'm going to need a lot of help." Cascandra also sought guidance from Kristen when she was upset about her grandma's pending departure.

Elizabeth and Narissa

At Elizabeth's request, Narissa began to read more carefully. Elizabeth asked her to slow down, explaining that she would not skip words if she slowed down. Narissa asked Elizabeth for help with her math, showing her the type of questions she had difficulty with. Elizabeth showed her how to do them and then gave her a page of questions to practice, which Narissa then completed.

While it could be argued that a child might comply with the requests of an adult because of the adult's authority, a number of these examples show that the children also actively sought the guidance, opinion, or approval of their mentors.

Modeling can take very subtle forms and, of course, children have a number of role models. Consequently, attributing children's behavior to modeling of their mentors involves considerable speculation. However, in revisiting the case studies with the question of modeling in view, it was interesting to note and consider the following examples as possible manifestations of modeling.

Tiara and Joel

Tiara, a student teacher, and Joel, a grade 6 boy, were both children of divorced parents. They connected quickly and were inclined to spend a great deal of time visiting. In the beginning of this mentorship, Tiara took responsibility for getting them back to their task. Over time, it was Joel who began to remind Tiara that they had to get back on track after a period of chatting. Mimicking her very words, he often reminded Tiara, "Okay, we've got to get back to reading."

Carey and Dustin

Early in their mentorship, Carey, a student teacher, learned that Dustin, a grade 2 boy, did not enjoy writing tasks. Nevertheless, Carey continued to try to engage Dustin in writing because she wanted to help him improve in this area. Dustin was not responsive to writing tasks in the beginning of the mentorship. Later in the mentorship, he surprised Carey by actually initiating writing activities himself.

Kristen and Cascandra

In the mentorship between Kristen, a college student, and Cascandra, a grade 3 girl, it was not until Kristen shared stories with Cascandra about her family, her boyfriend, and her childhood experiences, including her experience of the arrival of new siblings, that Cascandra began to share related stories about her family life with Kristen.

Elizabeth and Narissa

During the initial stage of the mentorship between Elizabeth, a retired grandmother, and Narissa, a grade 2 girl with non-English-speaking immigrant parents, Elizabeth read aloud to Narissa. Elizabeth read with expression. As time passed in the mentorship, Narissa "came out of her shell" and "read with authority." Not only had Narissa's confidence increased, but she also appeared to model Elizabeth's reading style.

Since the behaviors described above tended to occur in the later stages of the mentoring relationships, it is conceivable that they do in fact represent instances of the children modeling the mentors' behaviors and values. The examples of the children modeling the mentors' behaviors and being receptive to their guidance suggest that the mentors in these case studies had become effective role models who were liked and admired by the children they were paired with.

Mentors' Warmth

In discussing the development of relationships, Brendtro et al. (1990) have emphasized the importance of warmth and stability on the part of the adult in the helping role. Adults who can offer warmth and stability can more effectively cultivate intimacy and provide safety for such intimacy. We examined the mentorship relationships with the purpose of exploring how the notions of warmth and stability can extend understanding of the case studies and how the case studies can inform understanding of warmth and stability on the part of the nonrelated adults working with young children.

In psychological terms, warmth can be understood as a state or a trait. In everyday understanding of the term, one hears the expressions: "So-and-so is a very warm person" or "She greeted us warmly." For the purpose of examining the case studies it is perhaps most useful to think of warmth as a state and as a person's communication of an "I-like-you" feeling.

Much of the expression of warmth is nonverbal, and the intended recipient is the judge of its authenticity. Thus while observations of mentors' words, actions, and reflections may be of interest, the responses of the children to mentors are perhaps of greatest interest in determining whether mentors' warmth was experienced by the children. Thus, in examining the case studies we reviewed whether and how mentors experienced and acted on an "I-like-you" feeling toward the children and also highlighted indications that children experienced warmth from their mentors. We also identified children's observable expressions of warmth toward their mentors.

Although warmth is very much a feeling and much of its expression may be nonverbal, the case studies reveal a number of mentors' efforts and actions that are consistent with or can communicate an "I-like-you" feeling. These efforts or actions took a number of forms:

- actions taken specifically to befriend the child
- being physically close to the child
- "talking, joking and stuff" with the child
- efforts made to make the child comfortable
- careful planning of activities for the child
- reflections or statements revealing positive feelings toward the child

Below we give examples of mentors expressing warmth in each of the case studies.

Tiara and Joel

Tiara, a third-year university student in a teacher education program, thought carefully about how to put Joel at ease. Before meeting him, she asked herself questions that, in her words, "might be going through a grade 6 boy's head" upon meeting her. From the beginning, she said, "I let him into my life by sharing my life with him" and "He [Joel] is my little friend." She also stated that she was not "an authority figure"; instead, she was someone Joel could "go to with his problems." Telling Joel that she considered not going to Quebec to study French because she did not want to interrupt the rhythm of their relationship and telling him that she would miss him when they were apart also told him that he was important to her. Interview statements made by Tiara such as "I love him already. Our time together is special," and "We don't have a teacher-student relationship, we just have a friendship," gave further indications of the warmth that she felt toward Joel.

Carey and Dustin

In the beginning of the mentorship between Carey and Dustin, expressions of "I-like-you" were manifested by Carey, when she followed Dustin's interests and allowed the sessions to become whatever Dustin wanted to do even though it meant abandoning the plans she had prepared. During the second stage of their mentorship, chatting, giggling, teasing, and sitting close together rather than across the table from one another became the norm. At a later stage Carey used the word friendship to describe her relationship with Dustin. She explained, "As I got to know him, I see that he's not this genius boy; he's average, he's nice, and he's fun." Carey's warmth toward Dustin was accepted and returned with warm gestures. Describing how Dustin greeted her each week, Carey stated, "He's skipping, he's happy and I love him. I really enjoy it." Friendship was the result of giving warmth and inspiring its reciprocation.

Kristen and Cascandra

Before the mentorship between Kristen and Cascandra, Kristen, a second-year college student, thought carefully about how to be a mentor to a grade 2 child. Kristen returned to her hometown and sought advice from her mother, a teacher aide. She also spent a weekend with her young niece in an attempt to see what it would be like to spend time with a six-year-old. Initial planning for mentorship sessions included deliberate efforts to put Cascandra at ease as well. Kristen told Cascandra about her life when she was Cascandra's age, the school she attended, and her grade 2 teacher. Relying on her fondest childhood memories to guide the mentorship with Cascandra, she read Cascandra her favorite book, *I Love You Forever*—one her mother had read to her when she was Cascandra's age. She engaged in crafts with Cascandra, something else she had done as a child with her mother. Such activities created the space for spontaneous, relaxed chatting, which she thought was important for Cascandra. Kristen revealed her feelings toward Cascandra, stating, "I love her a lot," "I'm going to miss her when I have to go. I'm getting pretty attached to her," and "I really like her; I really do. She's a sweetheart."

Elizabeth and Narissa

At the beginning of her mentorship with Narissa, Elizabeth, a retired grandma, insisted that she had raised her children and was not looking for an emotional investment. She did, however, believe that literacy was important for a child's education and future and she said that she was in the program to make a contribution to the community. She often stated that she wanted to help Narissa. Although Elizabeth was never demonstrative with her affection, she did bring treats and always asked Narissa about her life outside of school. Narissa's parents did not speak English and Narissa did not speak her parents' language. Narissa's grandparents did not live in Canada. Elizabeth's simple, reliable presence each week seemed to be enough to make Narissa believe that Elizabeth liked her. Early in the mentorship, Narissa always hugged Elizabeth around the legs as soon as she saw her. Elizabeth's acceptance of Narissa's physical affection was the main observable physical manifestation of Elizabeth's warmth. In interviews, however, Elizabeth stated: "Narissa is a nice little girl," "a delightful child," and "I quite enjoy it [mentoring]." Such statements revealed an "I-like-you" feeling on Elizabeth's part.

These case studies, and the few examples taken from them here, illustrate diverse ways that warmth can be acted on and communicated by mentors in this kind of program. While the more intimate nonverbal expressions of warmth are more difficult to adequately report in words, it is evident from the examples reviewed here that warmth gives direction to action and spontaneously reveals itself in mentors' conversations with other adults.

Children's Response to Mentors' Warmth

In their own ways, each of the children came to show that they believed that their mentors liked them. Intimacy was possible. The mentors were safe people to tell things to. They could be themselves with their mentors in a more unguarded and spontaneous way.

Tiara and Joel

In the mentorship between Tiara and Joel, the bond was strong from the beginning because of their similarities in background. Joel was comfortable telling Tiara about the divorce of his parents when he was very young, and about his relationship with his father. His willingness to share such personal details of his life with Tiara showed that he viewed Tiara as safe and accepting.

Carey and Dustin

Carey initially experienced Dustin, a grade 2 student, as seeming older than his years. Over a number of sessions they became increasingly comfortable together and Dustin began to trust Carey. Admitting that he did not have fun at the farm because "these big boys were chasing us" meant that he felt safe enough to tell her that he was afraid of the big boys, despite his cool, older-than-his-years self-presentation.

Kristen and Cascandra

At the beginning of their mentorship, Kristen worked hard to get to know Cascandra. During this time Cascandra always appeared happy. Later in the mentorship, if Cascandra was not happy, she did not pretend to be. Over time, Cascandra also trusted Kristen enough to tell her secrets such as, "I'm not a very fast learner," and "It bugs me when people call me fat."

Elizabeth and Narissa

Elizabeth experienced Narissa as very quiet and withdrawn in the initial stage of the mentorship. Eight weeks into the mentorship, Narissa made another card for Elizabeth and for the first time, addressed it to "Beth," a nickname Narissa had given her. This represented a shift for Narissa.

The children's expressions and actions toward their mentors show that they felt safe and comfortable enough to take risks required for further intimacy, such as using a nickname, sharing personal details of their lives, or admitting fears and insecurities.

Each of the children in the case studies observably expressed warmth to their mentors. They gave their mentors personal compliments, greeted them enthusiastically or affectionately when they arrived, and expressed affection toward them physically. These expressions of warmth on the part of the children can be understood as reciprocation of the warmth they had experienced from their mentors.

In a letter to Tiara, Joel wrote, "I hope you can be my mentor next year." During the second stage of their mentorship, Dustin always looked happy to see Carey. As she put it, "He doesn't ignore me. He comes running out, beaming, bursting with news to tell me." Kristen noted that Cascandra was "always very physical." Cascandra sat close beside Kristen, held her hand, and gave her lots of hugs. As of their third session together, Narissa always greeted Elizabeth with a hug and did the same when they parted. In a handmade card that Narissa made for Elizabeth, she wrote "Roses are red, Honey is sweet and I love you." Also, when Narissa showed Elizabeth how to play Hangman, the message Narissa wrote to Elizabeth was, "You are the best mentor."

Warmth itself may be a gift given, a way of interacting, or a state of being that resists definition. The preceding discussion has explored warmth on the part of the mentors by identifying some of the mentors' "I-like-you" actions and statements. These efforts or thoughts by mentors can be seen to be congruent with warmth or even as extended expressions of the same. Parents are sometimes advised to keep warmth in their relationships with their children by prefacing any command or request with a term of endearment, as in "Sweetie, please put your things away." The mentors' specific "I-like-you" actions and efforts outlined in the first part of this discussion may function as metaphoric terms of endearment prefacing later requests for cooperation with academic tasks.

The Mentors' Stability

In examining the form and function of stability on the part of the mentors in the case studies, one can begin to appreciate why mentors can be so different from each other and yet all be effective in establishing relationships with the children they work with.

Stability on the part of the mentor would mean that he or she is consistent, reliable, and predictable. Each of the four mentors was consistent and reliable in coming at the same time each week and interacting with the children in the same way each week. This was sometimes challenging for mentors in the early sessions, as the children didn't tend to give mentors a lot of feedback at first. Each of the mentors, however, stayed on the track she had initially set in spite of any uncertainties. Although each mentor emphasized different activities or forms of giving, as discussed in the beginning of this chapter, each was consistent in whatever she did or emphasized. Thus while the mentors' preferred activities or ways of proceeding were different, each mentor's consistency had the same effect. Each child could experience his/her mentor as safe, reliable, and predictable. This stability encouraged trust, and the children responded by telling their mentor secrets and by going to them for help. The following paragraphs highlight aspects of the case studies that pertained to the mentors' stability.

Tiara and Joel

Tiara brought Joel something each week such as M & Ms, Skittles, cookies she had baked, a poster, and so forth. She always shared what had transpired in her life during the week when they were apart. She consistently read books with him and helped him with his math and other assignments. When Tiara returned from her trip to Quebec, she and Joel picked up where they left off. Tiara stated that nothing had changed between them. Tiara continued to mentor

Joel until the end of the school year rather than stopping when the university term ended in April. Even after the school year, she remained a presence in Joel's life through telephone calls and occasional recreational visits.

Carey and Dustin

Carey arrived at the same time on the same day of each week. Despite the uncertainty and the lack of feedback she experienced in the beginning of the mentorship, she related to Dustin the same way each time she saw him. Although she often wondered if she was "doing it right" or if Dustin was enjoying the sessions, she continued to follow Dustin's lead and to follow his interests. Carey witnessed other mentors bringing their students treats and engaging them in crafts. Although she was uncertain about what to bring Dustin, she didn't give up and buy him an age-appropriate general treat or try to engage him in craft-like activities that she didn't believe he would enjoy. By keeping to her convictions about personalizing gifts and activities, she manifested a reliable and predictable way of relating to Dustin. And Dustin was able to become accustomed to Carey's way of being.

Kristen and Cascandra

Like Tiara, Kristen came at the same time and on the same day each week. She consistently shared stories about her family, her boyfriend, and college. She always brought appropriate supplies each week so that they could engage in craft-like activities together. Cascandra came to enjoy such activities and even began to expect Kristen to bring a craft with her. The expectation of a craft activity seemed to give continuity to the weekly sessions.

When Cascandra became preoccupied and mellow following the birth of her younger sibling, Kristen consciously made efforts to keep relating to and interacting with her in the same ways she always had. Because Kristen's good will toward Cascandra was reliable in spite of Cascandra's mood changes, Cascandra could experience Kristen as a safe, reliable person who could be trusted.

Elizabeth and Narissa

Like the other mentors, Elizabeth, a retired grandma, was predictable for Narissa by arriving on her scheduled day and time each week. She was consistent in terms of bringing Narissa treats and presents for special occasions. In the beginning of the mentorship, Elizabeth said that Narissa was shy and withdrawn and that her response was to remain the same, or as she put it, "I just carry on." In response to Elizabeth's simple, clear, reliable presence and activities, Narissa did "come out of her shell" and began greeting Elizabeth with a hug by the third session.

There are perhaps more mysteries than there are answers to questions about relationships. To what is the child actually responding when s/he gives trust and affection to a nonrelated adult? Perhaps there are no words that can in fact capture the answer to that question. And perhaps it is in fact only the joy and relief of one adult paying positive attention just to that child, repeatedly, week after week. Certainly, there was considerable diversity among the mentors in the case studies. What was common was that all the mentors were consistent in whatever they were doing or whoever they were being. If one hopes that children will connect with mentors whom they see for one hour once a week, it seems reasonable that it must be easier for them to zero in on and connect with a stationary rather than a moving target. Thus stability on the part of mentors as it has been explored in this discussion may be a very key support for the development of relationships in mentorship programs.

Caring, Responsibility, Respect, and Knowledge

Drawing on Eric Fromm's work in *The Art of Loving*, Brendtro et al. (1990) have identified *caring, responsibility, respect*, and *knowledge* as four elements that are common to positive relationships. This section revisits the case studies with a view to examining them for the manifestations of these elements in the relationships. It makes sense that positive relationships should be characterized by these elements. In this examination of the case studies, we ask what these elements look like within the constraints and opportunities of once-a-week mentorship sessions between adults and young children. We also remain alert to interrelationships among these four elements.

Caring

Brendtro et al. (1990) defined caring as "concern for the life and growth of the person in the relationship." Simply by coming to serve as mentors in this program, the adults in these case studies showed their willingness to care about the life and growth of another person. As reviewed in the first section of this chapter, the mentors gave to the children in a number of observable ways that could support the children's comfort, responsiveness, and sense of worth. In interviews, the mentors also discussed their concern about the children's lives beyond the mentorship sessions themselves, thus revealing the caring that provided direction for their activities in the mentorship sessions.

Tiara's comments in interviews showed her concern for Joel's life, growth, and road ahead. She was concerned about the future of Joel's education. Joel was to enter junior high the following September. At the time of the mentorship he was in a split-literacy class, a special class for grade 6 students who were below grade level in reading and language. Tiara said it bothered her that Joel was in a special literacy class and that she felt he should have had help a long time ago. Tiara cared very much about what would happen to Joel and what his life would be like.

Carey perceived that it was important to Dustin's life and growth to have a person who was there especially for him—someone he could talk to about what whatever was on his mind. Dustin was the grade 2 boy who seemed older than his years, wore beer logo T-shirts, was interested in Prowlers, Hummers, and hockey, and was excited about the prospect of shooting gophers. Carey came from a very religious background. Perhaps she intuited that she had to join him where he was in conversation and show interest in what was meaningful to him in order to support his continuing growth through her attention and their dialogue. This appeared to be happening as he took pleasure in reassuring her that he had shot pop cans and not gophers when he went to the farm.

Eight weeks after the mentorship with Kristen began, Cascandra's usual happy demeanor evaporated. Her grandmother, who had come out to visit after the birth of her baby sister, was leaving. Kristen was very concerned about Cascandra's sense of loss. In interviews, Kristen talked at length about how her own mother had carefully prepared her for the arrival of new siblings in her family. She remembered how she felt when her baby sisters were born and the effect that it had on her time with her mother. Kristen wanted to support Cascandra through these transitions. She said that it bothered her to see Cascandra upset. She described Cascandra as being "just really mellow."

Over the course of the mentorship with Elizabeth, Narissa began to show progress in reading. Once Elizabeth saw results from her support, she wanted to continue in order to increase Narissa's achievement even further. As she stated, "She has improved....She has progressed....But I want to stay with it too; I don't want to just sit chatting and not staying with the reading." Elizabeth's focus on helping Narissa improve in schoolwork may also have been related to her awareness that Narissa's parents didn't speak English. Elizabeth once said, "You know, I probably talk to her more than anyone. Her mom can't speak English and she doesn't speak her mom's language." When Elizabeth learned that Narissa had difficulty with basic facts in math, she offered to help her learn them.

A willingness to care brought each of the mentors to the door of this program. Once they knew the children better, their caring became very focused on what they perceived to be the most pressing needs for the life and growth of the children they worked with. Tiara cared about Joel's chances of success in later grades and was still continuing her relationship with him after the school year ended. Carey saw that Dustin needed another significant adult to talk to, and she worked hard at learning about hockey, Hummers, and Prowlers in order to be an engaging conversation partner for him. Kristen was concerned about the sadness in Cascandra's life as she adjusted to having a newborn sibling, and she worked hard to support her in having a happy time in their sessions. Elizabeth was concerned about Narissa's future if there was no help with academics at home, and so she focused on schoolwork rather than just sitting and chatting. In each of the relationships, the focus of the caring gave direction to the use of time in the sessions.

Responsibility

Brendtro et al. (1990, p. 62) defined responsibility as being "ready to act to meet the needs, expressed or unexpressed, of another human being." Thus, being responsible, in this sense, means both being capable of responding in an appropriate or helpful manner and being able to discern the needs of the other person. Below, the case studies are revisited to highlight ways in which mentors appeared to manifest responsibility of this kind.

Tiara and Joel

According to Tiara, Joel did not have to express his needs to her; she had an intuitive way of knowing what these were. As she stated, "We just understand each other. We don't talk about our parents being divorced. We talk about sports and doing things. But we just understand each other." Tiara knew what to do and what not to do without being told. She and Joel had a way of knowing, a way of being responsive to one another. On another occasion Tiara said, "I know what he likes and he knows what I like, and I know what he doesn't like and [I] stay away from things he doesn't like." In terms of topics for reading or just everyday conversation, she said, "I know what kinds of things he doesn't like to read, and even in subject areas, talking about things."

Tiara thought it was important to be available to talk to Joel because she recognized that teachers do not have the time to be there for children on a one-on-one basis all the time. As she said, "Sometimes you just need an extra person around that's not your parent or your aunts or your uncles, just somebody you can talk to....So we just talk, not just about school things, about life. I'm more like a big sister, I feel, to him." After the school year ended, Tiara continued to see Joel to go swimming and do other recreational activities. Perhaps, even in this, she was responding to his need to not have an important person leave his life at this time.

Carey and Dustin

When Carey met Dustin, she was taken aback by the differences in their life experiences. She wasn't knowledgeable about his experience and interest areas. She even wondered out loud, "I wonder if I'm meeting his needs." But Carey perceived Dustin's need to have a significant adult to talk to, so she set about equipping herself with the background knowledge that could make her a more satisfying conversation partner for this boy.

Carey thought that Dustin came across as older than his years, more cool or sophisticated. Consequently, she purposefully refrained from offering the age-appropriate treats and craft activities that the other mentors used with their children in the program.

Carey was also responsive to Dustin's expressed needs or wishes. When Dustin asked Carey if she had any books on dirt bikes, automotives, and so forth, she sought out these materials for him. She was also flexible with her plan for the mentoring sessions. For example, one day Carey had planned a writing activity and just as they started it Dustin said, "Why don't we just read and stuff?" Carey complied. On another occasion, Carey said, "Would you like to read?" and Dustin answered, "No, I would rather do this." Again, Carey complied.

Kristen and Cascandra

Kristen believed that Cascandra would need to feel safe and comfortable talking to her if she was ever going to talk about anything that was important to her. Consequently, Kristen consistently planned and prepared for craft activities that would provide the space for comfortable free-ranging talk. Kristen explained that it was when they engaged in art projects that they got into, in her words, "big conversations." She said that while she recognized the value of reading with Cascandra, spending time talking was also important. "Today we were talking about games that she plays at recess too, and we can talk about that or we can talk about anything she wants, and those are the times that kids will really open up, and those are the times that they will remember too." Kristen sensed that Cascandra might need to "open up" to someone sometimes. As time passed, Cascandra did open up when she asked for Kristen's help with making the Easter basket and described herself as not being a "fast learner." Cascandra also confided her distress about other children saying that she was fat, and about her grandmother leaving. As a general support to Cascandra, Kristen complimented her for work she had done well, saying, "Good Job!" and "I'm proud of you."

Kristen also responded to Cascandra's explicit wishes about how their time would be spent together. Kristen explained, "Sometimes I'll read to her and sometimes she'll read to me, but it depends on what she wants to do. So I ask her, 'What do you want to do?' instead of saying, 'Okay, today we are going to do this.'"

Elizabeth and Narissa

Aside from a focus on Narissa's academic work, Elizabeth, a 76-year-old retired grandma, did not discuss Narissa's needs at length. In fact, Elizabeth expressed a reluctance to become emotionally invested given that she had already raised her own family. She did, however, observe that when she said to Narissa, "You know, Narissa, you are reading really well," that Narissa "just beamed" with happiness. Elizabeth offered approval because she genuinely recognized the quality of Narissa's work.

Given Elizabeth's somewhat undemonstrative manner, it was a poignant moment in the research when she decided to teach Narissa how to tie her shoelaces. And after Narissa had given Elizabeth a handmade card, Elizabeth remembered to tell Narissa that she had put the card on the fridge. By saying this, Elizabeth was telling Narissa that she valued the card, that the card and Narissa meant something to her. Although Elizabeth did not consciously set forth to be responsive to a wide range of Narissa's expressed and unexpressed needs, her actions or responses were satisfying for Narissa.

In their own wonderful ways, each of the mentors showed the magic of the responsiveness and play between two people as they read each other's intentions, signals, and needs. The examples in these case studies suggest how counterproductive it could be to rigidly prescribe how time should be spent by two people in a one-on-one mentoring situation.

Respect

Using Fromm's model, Brendtro et al. (1990, p. 62) defined respect as having the ability to see an individual as s/he is and allowing that person to develop without exploitation. Each of the mentors in the case studies spontaneously offered their own observations about the ways they recognized and respected the children's limits or comfort zones. In the paragraphs below we highlight examples of such observations from each of the mentors.

In interviews, Tiara had made the following statements when discussing her relationship with Joel: "And I respect him. Respect is probably more important than anything.…I respect his differences; I respect his difficulties; I respect his limits, what he can and can't do; and I build on that." Tiara explained how she worked with Joel on content he found challenging. Tiara stated, "We'll do things that if I know it's hard for him, I'll push him, but I won't push him too much."

Carey waited for Dustin to ask her for help on skills and areas that he knew he needed to work on. Carey was aware of Dustin's weaknesses and his limitations in writing, but she did not push him. She waited until he was ready to request help from her. It was at a much later stage in the relationship that Dustin asked Carey for help. When he did, Carey was there to help him.

At the beginning of their mentorship, Kristen observed, "At first Cascandra was a very friendly and very positive little girl, but she did not want to tell me a lot about herself. So, okay, no problem." Kristen allowed the relationship to develop without putting any pressure on Cascandra. She gave Cascandra the space she needed and waited until Cascandra was comfortable with her. She later said of Cascandra, "She is willing to open up to me more."

Elizabeth respected Narissa's initial display of shyness. She recognized that it could take a while for Narissa to get used to her. Elizabeth stated that it could be intimidating for a child to be told, "This is your mentor." In response to Narissa's shyness and possible feelings of intimidation, Elizabeth said, "So, I just continue on the same way." She respected the limits of what Narissa was able to contribute in the initial stage of the mentorship.

In each of these relationships, the mentors' respect entailed perceiving the child's limits, accepting the child's boundaries, and preserving the child's comfort. It often took the form of waiting and displaying acceptance of boundaries. Mentors were very self-conscious about refraining from prying, pushing too hard, offering unwanted help or advice, or causing embarrassment. Each of the mentors was very able to articulate these sensibilities and each spontaneously talked about this aspect of mentorship in the interviews.

Knowledge

Brendtro et al. (1990, p. 62) explained that, as a key element of positive relationships, knowledge "is not a superficial awareness but genuine understanding of the other's feelings, even if they are not readily apparent." The paragraphs below highlight examples of how each of the mentors demonstrated knowledge of her child by understanding the child's feelings.

Tiara learned a lot about Joel during their first session when they discussed their commonalities in family history. She continued to deepen her knowledge of him throughout their time together and this showed in the way she discussed how she worked with him. For example, she showed her ability to read Joel's feelings when she commented, "I know that he's reached his limit in reading; he doesn't have to say, 'I don't want to read anymore' and I don't have to say, 'Do you want to read anymore?' I say, 'Oh, okay, let's go on to something else.'"

Carey had to work hard to become more able to understand Dustin and his feelings. She had to become knowledgeable about his passions—Hummers, Prowlers, dirt bikes, and hockey. Carey in fact developed a genuine interest in hockey. Once they shared this enthusiasm, Dustin began to let his guard down and became more self-disclosing. For example, he told Carey about being afraid of the big boys who were chasing him and his friend at the farm. After Carey had worked to share his interests, Dustin became more willing to share his fears with her. Then Carey was finally able to say of Dustin, "He's not so different after all."

Kristen, a second-year college student, intentionally used craft activities to create opportunities for relaxed conversations so that she could get to know Cascandra. At the beginning of the mentorship she felt awkward with Cascandra and sensed that Cascandra also felt awkward with her. Thus the getting-to-know-you conversations were important. Until Cascandra began to open up, Kristen tried to make her comfortable by talking about her own family and sharing stories about what her life was like when she was in grade 2. When Cascandra's grandmother was leaving, soon after the birth of her baby sister, Kristen noticed her mood changes and could understand how she felt about these changes in her life. Both in interviews and with Cascandra, Kristen talked about her own experience of losing time with her mother when her baby sisters were born. Kristen also offered reassurance, encouragement, and praise when Cascandra described herself as not being "a very fast learner" or complained about other students calling her fat.

Elizabeth was interested in knowing about Narissa's family. As she said, "It helps me understand Narissa better if I know about her family." This showed Elizabeth's desire to try to make sense of Narissa. Elizabeth showed awareness of Narissa's feelings when she commented on her shyness at the beginning and later noted that Narissa was liking the time they spent together and was beginning to feel at ease with her. Elizabeth also showed understanding of what made Narissa feel happy when she talked about how Narissa experienced praise for work well done and how appreciative Narissa was of anything special that Elizabeth did for her.

In revisiting the case studies with the idea of "knowledge" or "the understanding of the other's feelings" as a lens, it becomes more apparent just how important it was to mentors to feel that they did understand the feelings of the children. It seemed that they realized that without such knowledge they couldn't proceed in an intelligent way—in a way that made any sense. Tiara's statements about knowing how Joel was feeling about reading at any given time without asking him showed how pervasive this kind of knowledge is in guiding the action of the mentor. Carey's statement, "He's not so different after all," perhaps expressed her relief that she could expect to understand Dustin's feelings. In revisiting the interview transcripts it becomes clear that it is difficult for the mentors to talk about the children at all without also talking about their perceptions of the children's feelings. Mentors are the initiators of the action in the sessions and they are always "reading" the children to determine whether their actions are welcome, appropriate, or helpful. Carey and Kristen showed us the efforts mentors can make when the children they are working with are difficult or confusing to "read."

The Dynamics of Mentorship Relationships

In this analysis of case studies of four mentorship pairs of nonrelated adults and children, Brendtro et al.'s (1990) key ideas about relationships were used both to gain insight about what happened in the relationships and to provide elaboration of the meaning of these key ideas in programs such as this one. The key ideas were as follows.

- A relationship is not a feeling, but results from action, and the action or process entails some form of giving.
- If helping adults are liked and admired by young people, the young people will be more receptive to the adults' guidance, will seek their approval, and will be inclined to imitate their behaviors and attitudes.
- Helping adults must be able to bring warmth and stability to their attachments.
- Common elements of positive relationships are caring, respect, responsibility, and knowledge.

Using the key ideas served as a strategy for looking at each case study or each relationship in terms of its parts. Seeing the parts more clearly also provides the opportunity to better understand the whole. In other words, by having the opportunity to discern any relationships among the parts, one can better speculate about the workings of the whole.

Some of the analyses served to highlight the diversity among the four mentorship relationships. For example, there were considerable differences among mentors in terms of what each one observably *gave* to the child, and there was great variation in their "I-like-you" behaviors and actions that were identified in the section on *warmth*. All four of the mentors were shown to be characterized by *stability* in that each one came at the scheduled time and showed consistency in their approach to their child and way of proceeding in each session. Each of the children showed that they experienced their mentors as *role models* by seeking their approval, being receptive to their guidance, and imitating some behavior of the mentor. And each of the mentors were shown to *respect* the limits of the children they worked with.

The remaining key ideas of **caring, knowledge,** and **responsibility** seemed to be the ones that inspired and gave direction to all of the mentors' actions and efforts that were described in the sections on "giving," "warmth," "stability," and "respect." These key ideas also clarify why it makes sense that each of the mentors could do very different things with children and yet each could be equally successful in forming a positive relationship with the child. Each of the mentors cared about the life and growth of the child (caring) and each responded in some helpful way to the needs of the child (responsibility)—if the feelings and needs of the child were known. This caring and responsibility gave direction to the way time was spent and what the mentors chose to give to the children.

If, however, the mentor could not read the child's feelings (knowledge) and did not have knowledge of the child's life and growth needs (the focus of caring), the focus of their efforts and activities became the acquisition of such knowledge. This emphasis was evident in the case studies of Kristen and Cascandra and Carey and Dustin. Both of these mentors made concerted efforts to get to the point where they could more confidently read the child's feelings (knowledge). Without being able to read children's feelings, mentors cannot make sense of what they are doing with the children; in other words, anything they are doing with the children is "nonsense."

Thus, without being told, mentors' first priority is to become able to understand what the child is feeling (knowledge). Mentors come to a program because of their willingness to care about the growth and life of a child. Thus they remain alert to or constantly seek out knowledge about the life and growth needs of the child to give specificity to their caring. The knowledge of the child's needs and the ability to read the child's feelings constantly inform the mentor's activities and ways of proceeding. To a large extent, this may explain much of the consistency shown by each mentor, the difference among mentors in terms of what they were doing, and the fact that each child responded positively to whatever his or her own mentor was doing.

These findings have very important implications for program structure. It is imperative that mentors' activities not be prescribed. Mentors must have the opportunity to spend session time in whatever ways they need to until they can "read" the child and the child's responses to activities. What mentors may do to support the child's comfort, spontaneity, and engagement will vary greatly.

Once they can better discern the child's interests, needs, and responses, they also need the opportunity to follow through with activities that they perceive to be both helpful and engaging for the child.

❧ Part Two ☙

PEER SUPPORT AND STUDENT LEADERSHIP PROGRAMS

ಬ Chapter Fifteen ಔ

DESCRIPTIONS OF FIVE PEER
SUPPORT PROGRAMS K–12

This chapter provides descriptions of five successful peer support programs—two in elementary schools, one in junior high, and two in secondary schools. Together they illustrate a variety of program models that can be used or adapted to meet students' needs and accommodate school and community characteristics. Peer support programs provide the organizational support and structure for students to:

- help other students individually or in small groups
- provide support in a variety of ways for the entire student population
- improve the spirit and climate of the school for students and staff
- enhance their own capabilities and self-esteem

The programs described in this chapter are sequenced as listed below.

Elementary
- A K–1 Program in a Multilingual School in Ontario
- Wes Hosford School

Junior High
- Fort Saskatchewan Junior High School

High School
- Bev Facey Composite High School
- Someone to Talk To: Peer Helping in High School

A K–1 Program in a Multilingual School in Ontario

Dr. Linda Cameron and Ms. Jacqueline Karsemeyer (1998) of OISE/UT (Ontario Institute for Studies in Education of the University of Toronto) have reported on their action research project, which entailed having five grade 1 children serve as "language play partners" for kindergarten children who share the same first language. The grade 1 children who volunteered to participate and had parent approval were trained to help the younger children learn English while playing with them. For three months, these grade 1 children spent one morning a week with their partners in the kindergarten classroom. The researchers used videotaping, observation, and interviews to study the weekly sessions for three months.

Background

This action research project was part of a larger early intervention research program in an urban multicultural school in Ontario. The class of 19 junior kindergarten students were predominantly immigrant and refugee children who spoke 13 different languages and represented many cultures. The children tended to be silent and mainly engaged in solitary play at the manipulative stage of development. It appeared that the kindergarten children could benefit from regular interaction with partners who knew how to speak English and who knew how to play.

Volunteers for the language play partner program were sought from the corresponding first language and ethnic groups in the grade 1 class. This program idea appeared promising, since some of the children's cultural backgrounds made them more accustomed to learning from peers than from adults. Further, the use of language play partnering applies Vygotsky's concept of scaffolding to peer interactions in an English immersion environment. In future programs, the researchers noted that they want to give more attention to matching in terms of interests, learning styles, personality types, and gender rather than only by language and culture.

Purpose

While this intervention was generally aimed at supporting young ESL students in learning English and accessing the curriculum, it was also prompted by the researchers' concerns about enabling the children to:

- experience belonging in a community of learners
- establish and maintain their identities
- have opportunities to play and develop sociodrama skills
- understand what to do, what is going on, and how to reach the teacher
- have the opportunity to play, communicate, and learn

Benefits

This project supported the social, language, and literacy development of the kindergarten children. They experienced having a special friend who gave care and attention, thus supporting a sense of self-worth. The grade 1 partner became someone to look up to, besides being a model for language and play. They gained cognitively from the direct teaching of the grade 1 partner. They learned how to use classroom materials and resources and engaged in sociodramatic play. Social skills were further developed as the grade 1 partner monitored and modeled these.

The grade 1 children who served as mentors also experienced having a special friend. In caring for someone else they acquired a sense of their own worth and importance. They further developed their own communication skills, understanding of others, and understanding of materials and processes as they endeavored to teach their kindergarten partners. The experience also gave them the opportunity to play themselves.

Wes Hosford School

Lynda Ward, the counselor at Wes Hosford School, an elementary school in Sherwood Park, Alberta, has been operating a peer support program for over eight years. This peer support program places an emphasis on helping rather than counseling. Students who are members of peer support learn to listen to and support the growth of fellow students. The peer support program includes four teams. These are called Playground Pals, Cross-Age Tutors, Buddies, and Service. Students rotate across these teams during the year in order to have a broad range of experiences.

Selection and Training

In this program all of the grade 6 students in the school receive the training to be peer support members and all are invited to participate in the peer support teams. The training is provided as part of their health class and is supplemented by lunch hour sessions in which programs are evaluated and modified. The training topics include identifying feelings, reflective listening, role playing, qualities of a helper, verbal and nonverbal communication, assertiveness, problem-solving strategies, open questioning, and confidentiality. The training sessions culminate in a four-hour roundup, at which time group-building exercises continue and the peer helpers brainstorm the kinds of things they can do to make the school a better place.

Playground Pals

When students work as Playground Pals, they sign up for either morning or afternoon responsibilities. Any student who is serving as a Playground Pal wears a brightly colored vest to be easily identified on the playground. This is experienced as a high-status position. As Playground Pals, students' duties are the following:

- to help organize noncompetitive activities for interested students
- to help shy or withdrawn students engage with others
- to officiate games such as soccer or basketball if necessary
- to play with students
- to be positive role models
- to promote a safe environment
- to assist the adult supervisors if requested to do so (for example, to escort a sick or injured child to the principal's office)

The emphasis for Playground Pals is to be proactive rather than reactive. They are not responsible for discipline. Instead, if Playground Pals notice that groups of children are inclined to start fighting or arguing when trying to play games, they would make a plan to help organize those games in a better way. For example, they would pick each of the teams to make them more fair. They would officiate. They would play with the children to model fair play, turn taking, and sportsmanship.

Cross-Age Tutoring

Members of this team work as study buddies to help younger children with reading or other tasks. When working as a Cross-Age Tutor, a Peer Support team member is partnered with a child and works with him or her at recess or lunch once or twice a week for six weeks. The grades 1 and 2 teachers have commented on "what a difference" this has made for their students' work.

Buddies

Buddies are matched with children who are isolated or shy for any of a variety of reasons. A Buddy will help a student to meet other children and to develop appropriate skills and strategies for friendships. To help a child in this way, a Buddy might initiate a low-organization game with him or her. Other students seeing the game would want to join in and would begin interacting with the shy child very naturally. The Buddy would slide out of the situation as she or he saw the shy child beginning to interact comfortably with the other students. Children in need of a Buddy can self-identify by putting their name on a teddy-bear-shaped piece of paper and putting it in a designated place. Others can also nominate a child for getting a Buddy.

Service

The Service team undertakes projects that promote school spirit or provide help or assistance to the community in some way. They also assist other classes with a variety of special projects.

Fort Saskatchewan Junior High School

> It makes me feel very important realizing that we're representing our entire home-rooms....We want the other students' opinions. All their opinions are valid. We're the reps from the classes. What we do is not just what we think is good. We start bringing ideas from the home room to whole-school projects.
>
> —a Peer Support Team member

For three years, Karen Baxter, a full-time aide with a nursing background, facilitated a peer support program at Fort Saskatchewan Junior High School in Fort Saskatchewan. At the commencement of the program, the school administrator expressed the hope that the activities of the peer support program would improve school spirit. The Peer Support Team conducted a large number of highly successful activities. Just a few examples include raising $800 in a penny drive for the SPCA; becoming a peace site and making paper cranes; raising $6,500 in a 30-hour fast for famine relief; monthly food bank contributions by the school; special theme staff appreciation lunches; a number of Special Days for improving spirit in the school, and more.

Program Structure

In September, each homeroom was invited to elect a class representative to be a member of the peer support team. Students were encouraged to choose individuals who were approachable, good listeners, and dependable, rather than perceiving this as a popularity contest. In the second year of the program a number of members wanted to continue their participation. They were allowed to continue, and each homeroom still had the opportunity to elect a representative. Following successful events, other students often express interest in joining the Peer Support Team. Sometimes some of the previous year's team members wish to come back and work on a particular event that they especially enjoyed organizing the year before. Mrs. Baxter suggests an open structure that permits various kinds of joining in.

Members of the peer support program were given a training program in an overnight-retreat format using AADAC (Alberta Alcohol and Drug Abuse Commission) training materials. They then attended weekly planning meetings during Monday lunch hours. Anyone who missed three meetings without excused absences was expelled from the peer support team.

The entire student body was invited to complete questionnaires to offer suggestions for peer support projects and to vote for their most preferred activities of all those suggested. In general, the kinds of activities included:

- community service and fund raisers
- organizing special days
- staff appreciation
- teaching organizational skills to peers
- peer tutoring prior to exams

When Mrs. Baxter had the opportunity to have another adult work with her to cofacilitate the Peer Support Team, she found this to be very beneficial. Between the two of them it was easier to inspire and motivate students by modeling their own energy and "off-the-wall" ideas.

Students "Buying In"

In a junior high school, there is typically concern about whether grade 9 classes will participate enthusiastically in school projects coordinated by a peer support program. In the Fort Saskatchewan Junior High program, incentives supported a friendly, competitive spirit for participation. The procedures for food bank contributions illustrated this well. One day each month was designated as Hat and Food Day. Students brought in food items for the food bank and placed them in a communal shopping cart in the foyer. Once they had their hands stamped and were checked off the class lists, they were able to wear a hat for the day. A tally chart was updated monthly and hung in the foyer. At the end of June prizes were awarded to the top three contributing classes. First prize was a half day off for a fun activity such as an afternoon movie, bowling, or swimming. Second and third prizes were class party packs of donuts. Over the course of one year, the students collected over 2,500 items for the local food bank.

Views of Peer Support Team Members

In a group interview with the Peer Support Team, students were asked to talk about their experience in response to a number of questions. Results of this interview are reported in Chapter 16.

Advice and Ideas from the Program Coordinator

We had three interviews with the coordinator, Karen Baxter, to learn all the advice she could offer on the basis of her three-year experience with this program. Listed below are a number of the key ideas and suggestions she shared.

- Students' ownership of ideas for projects they work on is imperative.
- Trust the students. Give the responsibility to the students and let them run with it.
- Establish guidelines and then let them take a task from there while touching base with the Coordinator regularly.
- Keep activity ideas coming from the student body as a whole. Some students who don't want to be members have great ideas.
- In a new program, where older students have not had related program experience, figure out who the leaders are and who the reliable workers are and play to these strengths.
- Try to ensure that a new program or a new year begins with an activity that is a school-wide success. This will inspire the group and bring in more participants.
- Remind students to keep activities simple.
- Remind students that some good activities can be short. (For example, in Lucky Days, a PA announcement invites all students wearing the color orange to come to the office to receive prizes—vouchers from community fast food and movie outlets.)
- Exercise caution with previously successful events that may have become tired.
- Conduct a group evaluation of each event.
- Once an event idea is chosen, keep students involved with posters, PA announcements, and other "off-the-wall" lead-ups to keep students fired up about the event idea.
- Consider developing an inventory of the interest and talent areas of all students in the school. This list can provide ideas for both resources and high interest events.
- Consider using retreat-type events such as the 30-hour fast early in the school year. Well-chosen feature activities at the "retreat" can draw in groups of students from different subcultures in the school. Once there, energizers and icebreakers can support bonding in a diverse student population.

Bev Facey Composite High School

The Peer Support Team is requesting your assistance in nominating students who you feel would be suitable Peer Support students. We are looking for students who

take the time to talk with students, help with their personal concerns and generally provide support when needed. These students tend to be the ones that others turn to when they have a problem or just need to talk.
Please list at least five students who you feel would do a great job if they chose to join Peer Support.

—from a survey form that invites students to nominate other students
for the Peer Support Team at Bev Facey

Nina Hoffman, counselor at Bev Facey Composite High School, has facilitated a Peer Support Program for the last seven years. The school has approximately 1,100 students. The Peer Support Team typically includes 12 to 20 students. This is a good number to work with, as it makes program facilitation and coordination manageable. The Bev Facey program history demonstrates that a Peer Support Team makes a real difference to the school experience for everyone.

Benefits

The activities of the Peer Support Team provide many benefits for individual students in the school, the entire student population, and wider community projects. These benefits are discussed in the description of Roles and Services provided below. There are also many benefits for the Peer Support Team members themselves. They commonly report improved relationships with peers and family. Some join the team as a way to give themselves a supportive environment during a time of need. Many clarify their career goals through this program experience and choose counseling, social work, or psychology as future directions in their education.

Recruitment

The size of the Peer Support Team ranges from 12 to 20 students from year to year and tends to include more female than male students. Efforts are made to ensure that the team is a good representation of a wide cross-section of the school population. In particular, Mrs. Hoffman always makes certain that there is representation from special needs students in the school. The overall recruitment effort is very important to secure the team that is formed each year. Recruiting entails the following components.

- An information table staffed by Peer Support Team members is in place when grade 9 students from feeder schools tour the school in the spring.
- The spring Open House is another opportunity that is used to bring the program to the attention of students.

- In the spring, teachers and students are surveyed to invite their nominations of students with the skills and interests to be good additions to the Peer Support Team for the following year. Mrs. Hoffman follows up on these nominations with one-on-one contact.
- In the fall, at the first information meeting for the whole school, the program is brought to the students' attention and posters are displayed throughout the school.
- An information meeting is scheduled for students who may be interested in becoming members of the Peer Support Team. At this meeting, students from the previous year's team are present to share their experience and enthusiasm.

Organization and Structure

Beginning. Interested students are provided with an information letter about the program and are asked to complete an application form in which they identify their interests, expectations, and strengths. Parents of team members receive a letter indicating that their son/daughter has elected to participate in the program, outlining what some of the activities may be, and asking for their support for the student's participation in after-school preparation for events. Students are asked to sign a contract, which emphasizes the importance of confidentiality and their awareness of their limitations and the importance of referring problems beyond their scope. Commitment is stressed and the concept of a team with each person carrying his or her weight is emphasized.

Support for Peer Support Team Members. Team members all have their own mailboxes to facilitate ongoing communication and coordination. Within the group they have "secret pals" to ensure that all the caregivers are also always experiencing some care. Mrs. Hoffman suggests that it is also important to plan celebration times throughout the year to ensure that all of their time together isn't only work.

Training. Because some of the students must take the bus home when school ends, regular meetings are scheduled during a lunch period each week. Since this limits the amount of training that can be conducted weekly, a retreat is held in the fall to provide the opportunity for training activities. Mrs. Hoffman notes that since students come with good skills, a natural empathy, and sometimes previous peer support program experience, training can be quite minimal. Examples of training activities are described in the last section below. Students may also choose to attend out-of-school conferences on topics such as suicide prevention to extend their peer support background and training.

Planning Events. At the beginning of the planning for an event or activity, Mrs. Hoffman facilitates the whole team's initial brainstorming. Once component activities are identified, smaller groups of students take responsibility for these. The student facilitator of each small group completes an "activity planning sheet" and reviews its contents with Mrs. Hoffman. For one of the annual activities, "Student of the Week Display Board," Mrs. Hoffman has found a classified staff member to serve as the cofacilitator. Finding more staff facilitators for individual events or activities would make this program more manageable.

Coordinating with Students' Council. The Students' Council in the school holds major responsibility for school spirit events. Typically, one of the members of the Peer Support Team is also a member of Students' Council and this facilitates coordination and communication. Usually, the Peer Support Team will organize fund-raising activities such as "ghost-o-grams" at Halloween or "candy-grams" at Valentine's Day. Students' Council, in turn, will sometimes ask for a Peer Support person to help staff coat check at a dance and so forth.

Roles and Services

Support to Individual Students. Peer Support Team members offer informal support to other students who are obviously upset or in need of someone to talk to. They use whatever skills, strategies, or opportunities they have to do this. It may be just a friendly quip to show the student that someone cares, notices, or is "on their team." If the Peer Support member is shy, he/she may enlist another team member to help the student in need or may ask Mrs. Hoffman to offer support.

As formal support to individual students, Peer Support Team members are sometimes matched with students in need of a buddy. This can be a short-term arrangement, such as for the first two days of a new student's arrival at the school. It can also be a long-term arrangement such as a regularly scheduled visit for half of a lunch period each week. The latter arrangement might be used for a special needs student or a student who is struggling socially or academically. Matching is done carefully. Steps are taken to prevent or stop dependency.

Assistance to All Students. Peer Support students participate in the orientation offered to new students to the school. They also provide a great deal of service to students during Career Week to help them use the career resources center and decision-making computer software. During that week they also serve as hosts and chairs for sessions conducted by guest speakers.

School Spirit. The Peer Support Team facilitates activities that help all students to express care and interest in each other. Examples of such activities include a Birthday Board, ghost-o-grams, love-a-grams, and so forth. The Birthday Board lists the names of students with a birthday that day. These students also receive a cupcake. The Student of the Week Display Board recognizes a student for a random act of kindness or doing something beyond the call of duty. It provides a biography and indicates why the student was nominated. The student also receives fries and a pop at lunch.

Community Service. The Peer Support Team typically chooses a community project to contribute to. Examples of such contributions have been the Christmas Hamper Program, selling daffodils for cancer month, and participating in the Safe Place Community Run.

Providing Information and Learning Experiences. The Peer Support Team chooses issues or topics for school-wide educational experiences. Examples of topics chosen have been relationship abuse, substance abuse awareness and Students Against Drunk Driving. Mrs. Hoffman assists them in accessing school or community resources for these projects. The students have generated and implemented many creative and dramatic ideas for these one-week educational campaigns.

Promoting Peer Support

Throughout the year, posters are used to identify team members and invite new people to join. There is a display case to feature the team members, and they are also included in a section of the yearbook. Each year they design a T-shirt, which they wear when doing peer support work at functions.

Training Activities

Mrs. Hoffman uses AADAC training materials and a number of other resources in her work with this program. Listed below are some examples of activities she has found to work well in training sessions.

Communication Activities. Name and Color Game. People introduce themselves by saying their name, a color that best represents them, and why that color says something about them. Each person has to say both the name and the color of the people who have already introduced themselves.

Nursery Rhyme Game (Nonverbal Communication). Using a simple nursery rhyme such as "Mary Had a Little Lamb," each person recites the rhyme in a way that expresses a different underlying emotion.

Specific and Immediate Feedback. Each person writes specific, positive feedback on pieces of paper worn on the backs of people in the group.

Fish Bowl (Active Listening). Two people role play being engaged in resolving a conflict. Others in the group watch, and when asked offer suggestions or help.

Group Work Activities. *Balls in the Air (Group Dynamics).* Standing in a circle, the group is given a number of balls of various sizes and shapes. First they establish a routine that involves three people keeping each ball in motion (Team work). Next they are asked to reverse the routine for each ball (Response to change). Next two people are taken out of the group without notice (Loss of team). Later two people are added to the group in different spots (Including new members).

Group Problem Solving. The group is given a novel task such as figuring out how to get a series of objects from one spot to another without touching a particular obstacle (e.g., an electric wire fence or pond full of alligators). Afterwards they analyze their process. Alternately, the same problem is attempted by a number of smaller groups, who then compare their processes.

Someone to Talk To: Peer Helping in High School

> You don't say I've been through that, I know how
> you feel. They need to say how they feel.
> You need someone your own age to talk to.
> Listening is really big—just having someone to listen
> to you, that's one of the things that really helps.
> A lot of people feel they have nowhere to turn; peer
> helping shows them they do have someone to go to.
> Not every problem is a crisis; sometimes just being
> there is enough, especially for the youngest kids in
> the school.
>
> —Voices of Peer Helpers

An NFB video entitled *Someone to Talk To: Peer Helping in High School* (Rodriguez, 1996) documents Peer Helping programs in two high schools in the Ottawa area. These programs are intended to extend counseling support to students throughout the school.

Program Rationale

In the high school context, school counselors cannot even know what all of the students' needs are, let alone hope to address all these needs. For students with troubles, the counselor's office is typically the last stop rather than the first place they turn. With Peer Helpers, there is no guidance form to complete and the feeling is less structured and more laid-back. A number of topics of concern to students are not ones they would like to discuss with adults.

Program Structure

Emphasis is given to ensuring good representation of the student population on the Peer Helping team. The more Peer Helpers reflect their school, the more they can connect with students when parents and friends can't. Students who have had problems themselves are welcome to be Peer Helpers. This opportunity has in fact motivated some students to pull their situations together in order to make a successful application.

Each morning, the guidance counselors and the Peer Helpers get together for a few minutes. This gives the guidance counselors an opportunity to plan their training. It also serves as a daily reminder to Peer Helpers that they have support.

Peer Helpers' Activities

Peer Helpers will approach students who are obviously upset and offer an opportunity to talk. Students, even those who don't know them, also approach them and ask to talk. When Peer Helpers become concerned about a common or recurring problem, they will sometimes plan a presentation on the topic for the school assembly. They will also visit junior high schools to teach conflict resolution skills to grade 9 students.

࠮ Chapter Sixteen ࠯

DESCRIPTIONS OF TWO
STUDENT LEADERSHIP PROGRAMS

his chapter presents descriptions of two student leadership programs. Both of them were in K–9 rural schools. Each program was developed by a teacher or administrator who saw a need worked creatively to meet it, and in so doing transformed the school experience for all students.

Clive School

> To me T.E.A.M.S. is a valuable option in which you can learn leadership and social skills. We plan dances and school activities that everybody can participate in. We try and help out students and be there for them to talk to. I think I can learn valuable skills in T.E.A.M.S. that will come into use in my future. I think I can learn how to deal with people and try to help them in every way possible.
> —A T.E.A.M.S. student

At the time of this study, Brent Galloway, the assistant principal at Clive School, an ECS–9 rural school of 300 students in Clive, Alberta, had been operating a complementary junior high course called "T.E.A.M.S.—Together Everyone Achieves More Success." Students in grades 7, 8, and 9 were able to choose the T.E.A.M.S. course as a complementary course. In fact, it was partly because there was space for one more complementary course at those grade levels that Mr. Galloway initiated it.

Rationale
In developing T.E.A.M.S., Mr. Galloway intended to:

- improve the former Student Council approach to student leadership
- increase accountability for student leaders
- provide more training in leadership
- have more work at the school being done by students rather than staff

- increase student involvement in school-wide decisions
- increase opportunities for student leadership

Structure

T.E.A.M.S. assumed responsibility for:

- functions of the former Student Council
- the school-wide Social Skills Program
- the School Recognition Program

The T.E.A.M.S. course included training in leadership skills and a required Service Learning component. Mr. Galloway made good use of many commercially available training activities and packages in this leadership course.

T.E.A.M.S. Responsibilities

In the second year of the program, the mandate of T.E.A.M.S. was articulated in the following way.

1. School-Wide Social Skills Program
   - social skills training (e.g., conflict resolution)
   - social skills assemblies (script writing and performing)
2. Student Council Activities
   - monthly meetings
   - social activities (e.g., dances, initiation, theme days, TEAMS Zone, campout)
   - sporting activities (e.g., hiking trip, ski trip, hockey game)
   - fund-raising activities (e.g., bake sales, magazines, candy-o-grams, ticket packs, raffles, etc.)
3. Service Learning
   - Remembrance Day Service
   - Project Christmas Child
   - Baby-sitting
   - Bowl for Kids
   - Terry Fox Run
   - School beautification
   - Peer tutoring
   - Student newspaper
   - Intramurals refereeing
   - Conflict management team

4. School Planning
   - school calendar/school planners
   - school policies (e.g., dance, late arrivals, student recognition)

The schedule for 1997/98 showed each month to include a fund-raiser, a theme day, a sports activity, a social activity, and a recognition rally. Additional services and projects were ongoing as a result of the Service Learning component. The T.E.A.M.S. course provided for ongoing training, planning, accountability, and evaluation.

Students' Voices

During the first year of the program, students were asked to write about their experience in the T.E.A.M.S. course. The following is an excerpt from one student's written reflections. This one and the others were analyzed and reported in Chapter 17 to clarify the meaning of this program for the participating students.

> T.E.A.M.S. has helped Clive School by uniting the students of Clive Junior High. It brings all the members of grades 7, 8, and 9 together. T.E.A.M.S. always encourages the participation of everyone. T.E.A.M.S. has enabled me to become a strong leader. I have the opportunity to talk in front of large groups of people, including adults, my peers, and younger children. I can also debate subjects and see both sides of the argument, not just the side I am on. Through T.E.A.M.S. I have also learned to respect younger students, because often the younger students—and even older ones—look up to me. I have to treat everyone fairly because that is what makes a strong group of leaders like T.E.A.M.S. I feel that T.E.A.M.S. has influenced me to become a stronger person. I now not only think of myself, I think of other people and what I can do to benefit others....The weakness we have been working very hard on as the leaders of Clive School is getting along within our group. Although we are leaders, we don't always see things the same way. So, before we can become better leaders, we must respect others and realize that they have their own opinions and should get a chance to share. In order to be effective as leaders, T.E.A.M.S. must work together as a whole; we must look out for the group and not just ourselves. I feel we have done this very well, and by the end of the year T.E.A.M.S. will have produced an amazing group of strong leaders.

Fultonvale Elementary Junior High School

> It seems that in giving things up you get even more back. Like it seems that the more responsibility I give to students, the more they will give back to me in terms of personal loyalty, in terms of willingness to help, and willingness to do things I value and think are important. Not only do we not lose but we gain. But sometimes it's hard to see that in the short term.
>
> —James Taylor, Fultonvale Elementary Junior High School

At the time of this study, James Taylor had been a teacher at Fultonvale for 22 years. The school had approximately 450 students, with about 220 of these being in grades 7, 8, and 9. This rural school is a 15-minute drive south of Sherwood Park, a city of about 45,000 just outside of Edmonton, Alberta. This section provides an overview of the peer support, student leadership, and student service programs and practices that James Taylor had been facilitating at the school for the previous seven years.

How It Began

In describing the interrelated collection of leadership programs and practices, Mr. Taylor emphasized the philosophy of beginning with the students' needs rather than school program needs. Thus they didn't begin, for example, with the idea that the school needed to have a students' council. Instead they began with the recognition that the grade 7 students didn't bond quickly when they came from three feeder schools in the district, as well as from other districts. Thus, a key organizing structure became a September Friendship Camp for all grade 7 students, and other programs and practices were built on the base of that event. This report describes the operation and benefits of:

- Friendship Camp
- Students' Council
- School and Community Services Option

Friendship Camp

For the previous seven years, the grade 7 students at Fultonvale had spent the third week of September in a Friendship Camp. This typically involves 75 grade 7 students and seven counselors who are grade 9 students. Most years, Mr. Taylor was the only adult facilitator. There were a couple of years when two parents or two other teachers also attended. Mr. Taylor observed, however, that adults tend to step in and do things for students that they could do for themselves. The students spend the week doing friendship activities and leadership development activities such as group problem solving with novel tasks. The students also do all the cooking, cleaning, and setting up of tents. The camp takes place in St. Paul, Alberta, at Bellevue Lake. The Legion there has a well furnished campsite including a pavilion and heated huts with refrigerators. They also had a mandate to support youth, and thus made the site available for a small honorarium. The grade 7 students love the Friendship Camp experience. It's fun. They bond. And at the end of grade 9 they wish they could have another week like that for closure to their experience at the school.

Counselors. The grade 9 students who serve as counselors for Friendship Camp plan the menus and activities for the week. They have experienced the camp when they were in grade 7 and have strong ideas about the importance of the camp and ways to make it work well. They love the responsibility and do an excellent job. The care and interest that the counselors develop with the grade 7 students during the camp carries over into the school and helps to break down the pecking order between grade 9 and 7 students.

The selection of counselors is conducted with great care. In March, all grade 8 students are invited to apply for the counselor positions for the coming September. Typically, about half of the grade 8 students apply. They complete formal written applications, which include letters from external references. The current year's grade 9 counselors serve as the selection committee. As the first step in the selection process, names are removed from the applications and all the applications are ranked. Then the names are replaced and the ranking is discussed further. Next all applicants are interviewed using a standard format. School administrators provide training in the interviewing process. Finally, in a simulation exercise, applicants are observed in group problem solving with novel problems. Mr. Taylor has observed that the selection committee members will sometimes sacrifice friendships in order to choose the best people for the counselor positions.

Through the foundation of the Friendship Camp experience, the counselors learned to care for each other, care for the school program, and work well with Mr. Taylor. Whenever anything was needed in the school, the counselors could be counted on to help out. When there was no one to coach the junior girls basketball team, two of the counselors worked with one parent volunteer to do it. When a custodian reported vandalism in the washrooms, Mr. Taylor was able to ask five counselors to supervise washrooms until the vandalism stopped. Students who serve as counselors for the camp have later reported that this was the most significant experience of their time at the school. They know how to organize projects and carry responsibility. They are typically instrumental with initiatives in the secondary schools they later attend. Some graduates report that they did not have another opportunity for such responsibility until after they turned 20.

Students' Council

The seven counselors of the current year form the core of the Students' Council. Among the grades 7, 8, and 9 classes, one in six students are on Students' Council. Students submit applications to be on Students' Council. They are not elected, but rather selected by a team of students and teachers. An effort is made to ensure representation from all student groups. When possible, an effort is made to select all students who apply. Application and selection is completed in the spring, with the new grade 7 students completing their process in the fall.

After Friendship Camp in September, the Students' Council has a full day and night retreat to plan the year's activities. As outlined below, the council is organized into three committees of 7 to 10 students to take responsibility for service, dances, and special days. Each committee has two teachers to work with. Teachers choose committees after learning which students are on each of the committees. Each committee has a combination of grades 7, 8, and 9 students. This facilitates participatory learning. It also means that the supervising teachers can change from year to year, but the knowledge of the committee's work is always perpetuated within the group of students. The two teachers are very important supportive partners for whichever two students on a committee are currently carrying the larger responsibility for conducting meetings or organizing events. First-time leadership positions can feel isolating and frightening for students.

School and Community Services Committee. A major responsibility of this committee is to organize and conduct the school assemblies for the year. This was found to work much better than having administrators and teachers conduct the assemblies and deal with students acting badly at these. This committee collects for a child in Colombia. They plant flowers in front of the school and help with a variety of functions in the school and community.

Dance Committee. This committee organizes sock hops and dances for the year. Funds raised through sock hops pay for DJs for larger dances. The students use other funds raised to pay for the fall retreat and to buy items such as sound equipment they want the school to have.

Special Events Committee. This committee organizes special days such as Hat Days and Wacky Olympics. They also typically work with the parent advisory council to organize a staff appreciation lunch: securing gifts from the community, planning draws for prizes, having an emcee, decorations, and a fun theme.

School and Community Services Option

This is a half-year option that was developed for the grade 9 students. At the beginning of the course, students write resumes, assess their skills and attitudes, and consider their life direction and future jobs. The course requires them to secure volunteer or paid work for 20 hours of time. The work must be evaluated in an ongoing manner by "employers." Students can quit or be fired from these "jobs." The students also write about what they are or are not learning in a weekly journal. Teachers in the school post classified ads to advertise work they have to offer. Students apply and are interviewed for these jobs. Students may also choose jobs at home or in the community.

Given that students typically hope that options will be "fun," Mr. Taylor has been very surprised at the strong appeal this course has for many students. He observed that many students want to be of real service and to have their work appreciated and valued. This is evident in the way they will come in at lunch or stay late in order to complete pieces of work that are needed by others.

Thoughts on Empowerment

Through the collection of programs and practices Mr. Taylor has facilitated, students have been repeatedly presented with problems and provided with the space to deal with these challenges or tasks relatively autonomously. They become accustomed to taking initiative when something is not working well. While students may be very nice and very polite in their manner of expressing their ideas, teachers can experience such initiative in the classroom as "pushing." To avoid a "them" vs. "us" experience, Mr. Taylor recommends that teachers identify shared goals and values with students and talk together with them about proceeding toward those goals. He also observes that it is valuable for facilitators of student activities to communicate a great deal with school staff, but that splitting time between student contact and staff contact can be very difficult.

❧ Chapter Seventeen ☙

STUDENTS' PERSPECTIVES ON PEER SUPPORT AND STUDENT LEADERSHIP PROGRAMS

Chapters 15 and 16 presented descriptions of several peer support and student leadership programs. In research with students from two of these programs we had the opportunity to learn how they experienced their participation. In this chapter we highlight students' perceptions of the benefits of participating in the peer support program at Fort Saskatchewan Junior High in Fort Saskatchewan, Alberta, and the student leadership complementary course at Clive School, Clive, Alberta.

A Peer Support Program

From 1996 to 1998, Karen Baxter, a full-time aide at Fort Saskatchewan Junior High in Fort Saskatchewan, Alberta, coordinated a peer support program. This program was described in Chapter 15. We met the students who were peer support team members in February of 1998 and endeavored to learn about their experience of participating in this program. Our discussion with the students was audiotaped and transcribed. To initiate discussions, we used the following questions as prompts.

1. At the September retreat, what did you learn about communication?
2. At your September retreat, what did you learn about conflict mediation?
3. How has it felt to accomplish things in your community service projects?
4. What was it like to help fellow students with their organizational skills?
5. What was it like to do peer tutoring?
6. Can you imagine your school without the kinds of activities you've made happen? What would it be like? How would you be different?

In analyzing the transcripts of the discussions we identified a number of benefits for the students in peer support and the school as a whole. These benefits, with illustrative comments excerpted from the transcripts, are listed below.

- Students had acquired skills and knowledge related to communication.

  Eye contact makes people feel that what they are saying is important.
  Listening well helps people realize that what they have to say is important.
  Communication helps us to get to know each other better.
  We learned that stereotypes are roadblocks.
  We learned that rumors are roadblocks. We won't say things that hurt another person. Rumors aren't good. If you don't know for sure, then don't say anything.
  To help someone solve a problem, you have to ask the right questions. You have to ask questions without hurting their feelings. Your questions have to be open-ended instead of yes-no questions.

- Students had acquired skills and knowledge related to conflict mediation.

  If the problem is too big, don't try to solve it yourself. Get a teacher to help.
  To help someone solve a problem, it's a good idea to give choices or ideas instead of telling someone what to do.
  If someone is fighting with someone or just not getting along with them, you can help them by being a sounding board, acting like a mirror. Just try to reflect their ideas when they talk out loud to you.
  Give hints. Don't go straight out and tell someone what to do. It can backfire if it doesn't work. They're not you. Just give them ideas, but don't tell them what to do.

- Their successful projects motivated them to do more and they believed they would continue with such initiatives after they left school.

  It's motivating when you have an opportunity to make something happen. Even when I leave school, I believe now that I can make things happen in the community.
  We are so proud of what we can do and accomplish. It makes us want to do more.

- They experienced and valued the strength of a team.

  It makes us a team. We get closer and stronger together. It makes you realize that as an individual, just yourself, you can't make a big difference, but you can working in a team.
  We make a commitment to the group and to ourselves to do the work.

- Helping others and getting others to join in the helping made them feel good.

  It feels good to know you're helping other people and getting others to join in this helping.
  You feel good because you're helping someone else.
  When you help someone else, you feel so good.

- They perceived benefits from their activities for individual students, the entire student body, and the community beyond the school.

  Kids know that they can talk to you without being afraid that you will put them down.
  All the students feel more comfortable. They feel like they have input in the school.
  Helping the community revitalizes the community.
  When we worked on the famine relief and participated in the 30-hour fast to help raise money for Third World countries, we got a lot of donations, as much as we could, to help these countries. This expanded all the students' horizons.
  When we organize special days like Hawaii Day, everyone in this school is happier. We get to be funny. We get to see everyone look funny. It's not like the normal, everyday, hard-work feeling.
  The activities we did gave more spirit to the school.
  When we made special days, it was more relaxed. Everyone knows it's going to be a fun day. It's fun and exciting. There are judges and prizes. There's more excitement.

- They experienced a number of personal benefits such as increased self-esteem, self-confidence, responsibility, approachability, more friends, and a feeling of involvement in the school.

  Working in peer support gave me more self-confidence and self-esteem.
  We're more approachable because of this experience.
  We get lots of friends at school.
  I feel more involved in the school.
  It makes me feel more important realizing that we're representing our entire home rooms.
  This experience helps us manage our time better.
  We've become more responsible and committed.

Through their comments, students demonstrated the knowledge they had gained from peer support participation; their awareness of increased skills, confidence, and peer friendships; their belief in the value of service and community initiatives; and their awareness of the ways they had supported individual students and the student body as a whole. The students came to believe in themselves and what they could accomplish. They made the school a friendlier, more supportive place for all. They felt worthwhile because of their responsibilities and approachability to other students. And they expressed commitment to service and community projects in the future.

A Student Leadership Program

In the fall of 1996, Brent Galloway, the assistant principal at Clive School, a K–9 rural school of 300 students in Clive, Alberta, initiated a complementary junior high course called T.E.A.M.S.—Together Everyone Achieves More Success. T.E.A.M.S. assumed responsibility for: the functions of the former Student Council; the school-wide Social Skills Program; and the School Recognition Program. The T.E.A.M.S. course included training in leadership skills and a required Service Learning component.

To learn the perspectives of the T.E.A.M.S. students themselves, Brent Galloway asked them to write personal accounts of their views about T.E.A.M.S. toward the end of its first year of operation. Our analysis of the written accounts revealed that leadership was a salient topic for them, and they perceived many benefits for the school as a whole and for themselves personally.

The following excerpt is an example of the way students explained T.E.A.M.S.

> To me T.E.A.M.S. is a valuable option in which you can learn leadership and social skills. We plan dances and school activities that everybody can participate in. We try and help out students and be there for them to talk to.

Below we have listed the three thematic topics of leadership, personal benefits, and school benefits with illustrative excerpts from the students' writing.

- Students made many comments about the meaning of leadership both in their own growth and as a process within the course itself.

> T.E.A.M.S. has helped me a lot in being a leader in Clive School. T.E.A.M.S. shows me that being a big leader in the school isn't as easy as it looks; you have to first of all earn that leadership to the students so they will look up to you, and then you have to set up a lot of activities to make the school a fun place for the students. T.E.A.M.S. is about sharing ideas to make a good school even better. It also teaches how to be better leaders, not just for the school surroundings, but in other social groups too....T.E.A.M.S. has helped me, as a leader, by building up my

confidence to speak to large crowds. It's helped me make more friends and talk about matters that have affected my classmates and myself.

T.E.A.M.S. has helped me as a "leader" to not be shy and stick up for what is right—and be a leader. ... I think all Junior High should be taking it [T.E.A.M.S.], so we can all learn valuable skills to be a leader.

To be part of T.E.A.M.S. you have to be able to speak your feelings, hold your own, and participate in school-wide activities. ... I believe T.E.A.M.S. has changed me to speak out more and learn that I can make things happen. This kind of leadership lets everyone have a chance to be heard even if you're not a member of our school government. In this leadership class we have a lot of strong leaders that are heard more often than others, so we do have heavy debates, but in the end we work them out.

T.E.A.M.S. has given me the courage to speak out in front of people and this makes it easier to be a leader and to argue (not too loud) and express my feelings towards something a whole lot better. T.E.A.M.S. has helped me because now I know what goes on in meetings and it helped me to become more vocal than I've been in the past.

- Students identified a number of personal benefits from participation in T.E.A.M.S.

T.E.A.M.S. has helped me a lot. It has helped my reputation in the school, and it has put the opportunity in my hands to make the school a fun place for all the students.

I think I can learn valuable skills in T.E.A.M.S. that will come into use in my future. I think I can learn how to deal with people and try to help them in every way possible.

I am new to this school and have never heard of this program, but it makes me feel very welcome.

I feel that T.E.A.M.S. has influenced me to become a stronger person. I now not only think of myself, I think of other people and what I can do to benefit others.

- Students perceived the student body and school as a whole to benefit from their activities. Such benefits included making school more fun; encouraging the participation of all students in activities; providing service to the school; and teaching all students to talk in a nice way to others.

I think T.E.A.M.S. has done a lot for the other students in school, and in their everyday lifestyle too, because it has helped them to learn in a fun way, and T.E.A.M.S. has helped the students talk in a nice way to others.

T.E.A.M.S. helps the students of Clive School forget the stress that a classroom sometimes brings.

T.E.A.M.S. also helps good causes in fund-raising, and volunteers to do some work like baby-sitting and working in concession. We are recognized school-wide for our cheerful, helpful way of working out problems.

This year I think all the students of Clive School have felt welcome. Also every member of T.E.A.M.S. tries their hardest to encourage the participation of everyone. The only effect that T.E.A.M.S. has had on our school is a good influence. We make school fun and make everyone want to be there.

The students were very aware of their own growth in leadership skills and general social skills. They knew that their service was helpful. They were proud that they helped all students learn to talk to each other in a nicer way. And as a support to everyone in the school, they "made school more fun and made everyone want to be there."

As shown by the views of students in both of these programs, students themselves are an extremely valuable resource in the school. Student leadership and peer support programs can provide the training and structure for students to enhance their own capabilities and sense of belonging while contributing to a more positive school experience for the entire student body.

❧ Chapter Eighteen ❦

CLOSING THOUGHTS:
SOMEONE TO TALK TO

The chapters in this book have been full of stories about ways that children and youth have been given "someone to talk to" through the organizational structures of mentorship programs, peer support programs, and student leadership programs. All children and adolescents want to learn and want to accomplish things, and they are more available to those undertakings once they have had the pleasure, relief, comfort, or stimulation of having someone to talk to.

When kindergarten children in an inner-city school—children who were silent in the classroom—got mentors, they talked to them nonstop after either the first 20 minutes or the first session. Most children in grades 1, 2, and 3 took until the third session to become comfortable with their mentors. Once that happened, they always met their mentors, beaming and bursting with news to tell them. Once the mentorship sessions progressed and the children had enjoyed lots of visiting time, it was often the students themselves who were heard to say, "Okay, we have to get back to reading now."

In the after-school recreational program for grades 4 and 5 boys with single-parent moms, the boys said of the men rotating as mentors through their program, "They all became our friends." The boys in the program also started to talk to each other in the school hallways about each week's anticipated event. The boys drew on the male mentors' support to improve both their academic work and their sports skills.

In the secondary school mentorship program, one boy said of his mentor, "She always made me laugh." One of the girls said that all of the students and staff in the program became "more people for her to talk to and get ideas from." Another girl said that her special memory of her mentor was "that you actually listened to me talk about horses, 'cause I couldn't find nobody else who would."

Similarly, the peer support and student leadership programs gave more students someone to talk to. In the elementary peer support program, three of the four teams—Playground Pals, Buddies, and Cross-Age Tutors—did this very directly. In the junior high peer support program, many activities gave all students in the school something positive or fun to talk to each other about. Special events included "ice breakers" and other opportunities for bonding among different groups of students at the school. Additionally, peer support members themselves learned how to be good listeners and helpful people with conflict resolution. In both secondary school peer support programs, students experiencing difficulties sometimes joined these teams as a way to give themselves a support group. They also learned how to extend support to others who were upset or needed someone to talk to.

Both student leadership programs had a focus on improving the social climate for all students. In one program, grade 9 counselors (students) worked with all grade 7 students at a one-week fun camp to support bonding among all grade 7 students and nurturing relationships between the grade 9 students and the grade 7 students. In the other student leadership program, T.E.A.M.S., the T.E.A.M.S. class conducted skits at school assemblies to teach all students how to talk to each other in a nicer way. The class members themselves were happy that through their work in the program they "got more friends" and students in the school generally found them more approachable.

Anyone who has traveled or attended conferences has likely noticed the great comfort there is in having "someone to talk to" there—someone who is not a stranger, but a familiar, trusted friend. Students, leaving the intimacy of their homes, may very well experience new or large schools the way adults can experience travel or conferences. As adults, if we were left at our new destinations or conferences for a long period of time, we would work to cultivate friendships. Young students may sometimes lack the social skills to do this, and some may need more opportunities to develop better skills in oral language, conversation, and narration.

Some students have troubles in their lives that are long-term. Such troubles can become preoccupations that are carried heavily all day long. Without relief, students may exhibit withdrawal or "acting-out behavior." Their performance on schoolwork then becomes less than they are fully capable of. Having a sympathetic person to simply tell one's troubles to brings great relief and comfort and frees the student to get on with his or her day and become available for constructivity (Ellis, Hart, & Small-McGinley, 1998). The sympathetic listener can be a teacher, classmate, other peer, or mentor. The programs described and discussed in this book can help to ensure that targeted students or all students can have more access to social support that contributes to their well-being and their growth.

The emphasis on social support in this closing discussion is not intended to undervalue the educational dimensions of the programs studied in our work. Learning and relationships were inseparable in the mentorship programs. As we learned from the mentors in the research on the mentors' pedagogy, "the friendship was rooted in learning and the learning was rooted in friendship." Similarly, we learned in the research on how mentors developed their relationships with students that once relationships were established, the students willingly asked the mentors for help with both intended mentorship activities such as reading and writing as well as other schoolwork such as math. Even in the grade 5 Writing Partners Program, students began to ask the seniors to read other writing they had completed outside of the mentorship sessions. The research with students in peer support and student leadership programs also clarified the nature of communication, organizational, and leadership skills they were developing through their participation. The students also provided or organized tutoring support for other students in their schools.

It is very clear that the programs we have studied have facilitated powerful learning experiences for students. Learning with someone who likes you, focuses on your interests, focuses on your learning needs, makes it fun, and brings you treats is difficult to match. There are, however, a great many other supports for learning in schools that students should also be able to benefit from. Our point in emphasizing the importance of "someone to talk to" is that social support, through one means or another, may be a prerequisite for many students to be able to get the most out of all of the learning experiences provided in schools.

ᚥ Appendices ᚦ

❧ Appendix A ☙

RECRUITMENT POSTERS AND LETTERS FOR ELEMENTARY SCHOOL LITERACY MENTORSHIP PROGRAMS

❧ Appendix A1 ❧

POSTER FOR SCHOOL-WIDE LITERACY MENTORSHIP PROGRAM

Be a Mentor and Make a Difference!

At: [School name]
                                [School address]

Principal: [Principal's name]

Program Coordinator: [Coordinator's name]

Telephone: [Telephone number]

Fax: [Fax number]

Do you have one hour a week to work as a volunteer in a school?

Would you like the opportunity to make a difference in a child's learning and success?

Would you enjoy sharing books, playing games, and visiting with a child for one hour a week?

[School name] has a Volunteer Mentorship Program and is seeking interested adults to participate in this program. Please contact the school principal or program coordinator if you are able to be a volunteer mentor.

❧ Appendix A2 ❧

POSTER FOR A CLASSROOM LITERACY MENTORSHIP PROGRAM

VOLUNTEERS NEEDED
Your Gift of Time

Where: [School name]
                    [School address]

When: [Time and day]

Why: To befriend an elementary student who needs help
                    reading

Job Description: To listen to these Grade [ ] students read and to read
                    to them for 1¼ hours per week

Interested?   Call [name of teacher, name of school] [telephone
                    number] [hours]

❧ Appendix A3 ☙

LETTER TO PARENTS FOR SENIOR/STUDENT WRITING PARTNERS PROGRAM IN GRADE 5

[School Letterhead]

Dear Parents:

This year we would like to begin a pilot project for writing skills. This project involves seniors and students working together on writing projects. We would like to invite senior citizens from the community to work with students in teams on the writing projects. This project will be called the

"Student/Senior Write On Club!"

This pilot project will provide many opportunities for our students:

1. Improve writing skills with one-to-one attention and assistance.
2. Develop a friendship with a senior.
3. Become involved in the community.

We are requesting names of seniors who might be interested in this program. If your child has a grandparent or great-grandparent, etc., who would be interested in coming in and being your child's partner, please fill out the bottom portion of this sheet and return it to the school. We would prefer that partners be senior citizens (65 or over). We will also be contacting some senior organizations in our city to find participants for this program.

Please inform us of names and telephone numbers of anyone you feel might be interested in participating in this program. The program will run [days] from [time] to [time] in [location] at the school.

Please feel free to contact [teacher's name] at [telephone number] if you have any questions about this project.

Student Name	Senior Name and Phone #	Relationship

Sincerely,

[Teacher's name]

❧ Appendix B ❧

SUPPORT MATERIALS FOR MENTORS IN A LITERACY MENTORSHIP PROGRAM FOR K–3

❧ Appendix B1 ☙

SHARING A BOOK WITH A CHILD

Sharing a Book with a Child

Children seek meaning in all parts of their world. The *way* we share books with children can help them to develop strategies for finding the meaning in books. The following is a collection of specific things one can do while sharing a book with a child.

Invite the child to use the *picture on the cover* of the book to *predict* what the book will be about.

Allow the child to *leaf through the whole book* before you begin reading it to her.

Begin by *reading the title* on the cover of the book.

As you read through the book, stop to offer *explanations or comments* along the way. (You may find that on the third reading of the book the child may start to interject these same explanations or comments.)

When *new characters* are introduced in the story, ask the child to *identify pictures* of these characters.

Invite the child to make inferences from the pictures by asking *"why" questions* that can be answered by looking at the pictures.

Ask the child for *suggestions* about how to *solve a character's dilemma*. Then have her decide if that is in fact what happens in the book. (The child's ideas will be logically based on her own experience and knowledge.)

Have the child "read" the book by *using the pictures to explain* what the book is about.

After reading the book:

- have the child tell the *favorite part* and perhaps draw a picture about it.
- invite the child to use puppets, dolls, or figures to *act out* something from the book.
- ask the child *if she liked the book* and why.
- have the child discuss *related experiences* she has had.
- ask the child how some of the *characters might feel* about what happened.

෨ Appendix B2 ෬

IDEAS FOR READING ACTIVITIES

Ideas for Reading Activities

1. Bring three or four books on a theme such as pets and show them to the child. Ask her to pick one for you to read and read her the story. Ask her what she liked about the story and what she didn't. Get her to show you her favorite part. Have a conversation with her about the book.

2. Do a read-along with your child. A read-along is a supportive technique that is used to increase the fluency of those who read individual words and letters instead of reading for meaning. It changes the focus so that the child reads in chunks of meaning and hence increases her comprehension. You read orally in chunks of meaning, using proper intonation and emphasizing meaningful words. You maintain a normal reading rate and ask the child to read along with you.

3. Bring two or three books by the same author, and read them with or to the child. Ask the child what might make him think that these two books were written by the same person. Early readers might just notice the illustrations. For young children you might pick books that are illustrated by the same person too. With an older student you could ask him about the author and ask if he sees any patterns or similarities among the books.

4. Read poetry with your child and ask him what he likes about poetry. Bring several different kinds of poetry (e.g., shape poems or haiku), and find out what he knows about poetry. Play a song on tape and do a read-along with the words on chart paper (so you can both see them), and ask him how he thinks that songs are like poetry.

5. Brainstorm with your child about what kinds of things she is interested in. Select some nonfiction material on that topic. Try to find a range of genres (e.g., books, magazines, brochures) and read them with your child. You might try each reading portions and then asking her about reading these kinds of materials.

6. Take advantage of Valentine's Day and find poems and valentines to read together. Write a valentine for your child, personalize it in some way, and have her read it. Bring colored paper and pens and have her make a valentine for someone special. Watch and record what and how she constructs what she wants to say. Ask her to read the card back to you.

7. Go the library with your child with the purpose of having him pick something he wants to read. Observe where he goes in the school library, what he knows about how the library is organized, what kinds of books or magazines he picks up to browse, and what he does when he looks at books. Once he has picked something, ask him why he picked this book, what caught his attention, how he generally picks books, and what he normally looks for.

8. Read a predictable book with your child. Stop several times at suspenseful points and have her try to predict what she thinks is going to happen next. Try having the child write the ending and read it back to you or act as a scribe yourself to write the ending for her.

9. Write a letter to your child about something you are doing together. You may read it together (supportive reading) and then have him read it.

10. Write a story together on chart paper. You will be the scribe, but make sure it is the child's language. Have the child read it back to you. How does this reading compare to the telling? Have her read it again and note how that compares.

11. Try supportive reading with your child. It involves reading and reading together from a script and could be in the form of a chant, a song, a choral reading, or a dramatic reading.

12. Try book writing and book making with your child. Have the student write something either individually or with you. You might even model it from another predictable book. Go through the process of making a book with him. This process will include producing and illustrating the story as well as the mechanics of layout and bookbinding. Have him read it back to you and take it home to read or take it to his class to read.

ࠏ Appendix B3 ࠎ

"GETTING TO KNOW YOU" CONVERSATIONS AND ACTIVITIES

"Getting to Know You" Conversations and Activities

1. Spend the first session making "All About Me" posters or booklets. These will include pictures of each of you engaging in your favorite activities. When these are complete, use them to initiate conversation. Ask the student questions about the poster. For example: I see skates and a hockey stick. Do you watch hockey games on TV? What is your favorite team? Do you skate? Have a hockey stick? Play hockey? etc.

2. Find out what the child likes to do in her spare time. If a child tells you she likes to watch television, ask about favorite shows.

3. Ask the child about her family: How many brothers and sisters does the student have? If the student is an only child, ask about cousins, friends, grandparents, aunts, uncles, etc. At a second session have the student draw a picture of her family. You do the same.

4. Ask the child about her favorite foods. For example: Do you like pizza? What do you like on your pizza? If you could make your own pizza, what would you put on it? Draw your special pizza for me.

5. Ask the child if he has a pet, and if so, to tell you about it. If he doesn't have a pet, have him talk about the kind he'd like to have.

6. Find out about the child's age: How old are you? When is your birthday?

7. Seasons: What is your favorite season? Why? What do you like to do most in the winter, spring, summer, and fall?

8. Bring a puppet. Take turns playing with the puppet. Students who are shy sometimes feel more at ease playing pretend.

9. Display a sense of humor. Laugh with the child. Tell a couple of age-appropriate jokes. This is always a good icebreaker.

10. Be a good listener. Give the child a chance to talk. This makes a student feel important, thereby building self-esteem.

11. Ask the student to take you on a tour of the school. The student will feel proud to be able to share her space and be the expert.

12. Be flexible. There may be times when a lesson is doomed to fail. If you sense that the child is not interested in the activity or reading, it is wise to abandon your plan and move on to something else. Sometimes simply talking with the child or playing a game will be the most effective use of your time.

13. If you come at lunch time, always bring your lunch and eat with the child. You may want to bring an extra cookie and share it with the child. Talk about your lunch, the child's lunch. For example: What did you bring for lunch today? What is your favorite lunch? Do you help make your lunch?

14. Bring a bag of tricks. You may need to have a supply of activities to use on those days when the child is off task, distracted, or simply not interested in the plan you prepared. Activities might include cards, puzzles, matching games, etc.

15. Ask the child to share five things about herself. You do the same. Play a memory game. Take turns telling one another as many things about each other as can be remembered.

16. Be calm. Fear, anger, excitement, and frustration are contagious. A calm mentor will have a calm student.

17. Follow the child's lead. Allow the child to lead the conversation. If he wants to tell you a story about what happened in the morning or the night before, show interest and listen attentively. The student will know that you care about what he has to say.

18. Be sensitive to the child's needs. If the child is quiet, shy, or withdrawn and does not offer much about herself, tell about yourself. Tell the student a funny story that happened to you when you were in school or when you were in grade 1.

19. Relationships take time to develop. Allow time for this to happen naturally. With each visit, the child will feel more connected to you.

20. Remember something the child told you from each visit so that you can ask her about it the next visit. For example, if the child told you that her grandmother was coming to visit, then ask about the time spent with grandmother. Or if the child told you that she was going bowling with her big sister, ask about the trip to the bowling alley. This demonstrates that you are interested in the child's life and that you care about what she does away from school. This may mean that when you leave

the school, you immediately write down a couple of things the child told you. It is easy to forget!

21. Location is important. Select a place to work with the child. Make that your special place and go there each week. Consistency is important to your student. Plus, the child will select a place where he is comfortable.

22. Follow the child's interest when choosing books. If the child tells you she likes books about horses, bring two books about horses. Let the child decide which book to read first.

23. Give the child something special from you on the first day. This may be a picture of yourself or your dog, a bookmark, a pencil, etc. Or share something of yours with the child early in the relationship. Let the student use your markers or your pen. This makes the child feel that you trust him with your belongings.

24. Teach the child a short song, chant, tongue twister, or clapping game. This is fun and students will laugh as they try to follow you. This may become a ritual that you do each time you meet.

25. Dress comfortably. Your student may wish to sit in a corner on the floor or outside on the grass in the spring.

26. Bring along a package of stickers. At the end of each session, let your student select one.

27. Everyone likes a compliment. Comment positively on the child's pretty pink outfit, flashy hiking boots, hairstyle, or sweater.

28. Play tic tac toe. Let the student win two out of three games.

29. Bring one of your favorite books to share. Students love pop-up books, Curious George, Dr. Seuss. The possibilities are endless.

30. Plan for continuity of the "story" of the mentorship sessions. There are many different activities that can be introduced and continued to help make the sessions feel connected, like an ongoing story. The following are just a few examples:

- Make a sock puppet together and let it become the main character in a story the child writes and keeps adding to over the course of the sessions (virtual pet concept).

- Make a scrapbook that can contain something you do or make together each week.

- Make a three-dimensional construction of a "monster" house from scrap materials (preferably natural ones)—keep adding to it each week.

- Bring the same distinctive-looking "craft box" each week with something special in it for a craft or a game (or just carry general back-up supplies in it like stickers and colored construction paper or a spare picture book in case plans don't work that week).

- Start a journal that the two of you write in at the end of each session to record the child's description and thoughts about what the two of you did that day.

❧ Appendix C ☙

SUPPORT MATERIALS FOR A SECONDARY SCHOOL MENTORSHIP PROGRAM ENLISTING SCHOOL STAFF AS MENTORS

❧ Appendix C1 ❧

INVITING SCHOOL STAFF PARTICIPATION

Memorandum (Version A)

To: All Caring and Concerned [Name of School] Staff Members
From: The Stay-in-School Steering Committee
Re: Stay-in-School Initiative Mentorship Program

Like many of you, the Stay-in-School Steering Committee is concerned about students dropping out of school. As we are all aware, dropping out has significant social and economic consequences. One prevention strategy that has been successfully implemented in a number of schools throughout Alberta and Canada is the Mentorship Program. This proactive initiative involves enlisting the many natural mentors already existing within a given community and matching each with an identified student; [name of school] professional and support staff are recognized throughout the city as ranking "tops in the caring department." Given this inherent collective quality of our staff, we would like to introduce a Mentorship Program on a pilot basis to cut the risk of students dropping out. We would therefore encourage all staff to read the following proposal, as well as the attached brochure, and to give careful consideration to participating in the Mentorship Program. More information and an opportunity for questions will be provided at the June Staff Meeting. Please plan to attend; [principal's name] assures us that this item will appear first on the agenda to allow support staff to leave early.

Proposal

It is proposed that our school implement a Mentorship Program for "at-risk" incoming grade 10 students on a pilot basis for the ['XX–'XX] school year.

Background

Research has shown that matching caring, concerned adults with a student in need of wise counsel and emotional support can have a powerful impact on the future of that young person. Many youths need additional adults in their lives to provide them with opportunities for growth in academic achievement, building self-esteem, motivation, goal setting, and personal responsibility. Ultimately, mentors can increase the likelihood that young people will benefit from educational services, thus reducing the school dropout and unemployment rate. This process is already occurring naturally because we are all mentors to some of our students. Unfortunately, there are a number of "high-risk" students who do not spontaneously find informal mentors, and as a consequence, their feelings of alienation and hopelessness continue or even intensify in the new secondary school setting. It is important to meet the needs of these potential dropouts by implementing preventative and proactive measures.

One such strategy known to be surprisingly effective in meeting these objectives is the Mentorship Program. Mentoring is a relationship that encourages personal growth and development in both individuals. It is not role modeling, which says "Be me." The mentor must be prepared to listen, prod, and provoke to help the young person "be the best they can be." One of the key findings from the literature on dropouts is the fact that few students discuss their decision to drop out with teachers, peers, or parents. An effective mentoring program can reduce the likelihood of a student dropping out by ensuring that the three R's are increasingly met and by providing opportunities to speak with a concerned adult.

Brochure
Stay-in-School Initiative Mentorship Program
Purpose/Program Goals

- Provide a systematic approach for identifying at-risk students and matching them with adult volunteers.
- Help ease the transition from junior to senior high; cope better with high school expectations/pressures.
- Give high-risk students an opportunity to encounter a positive school-related experience.
- Improve student attitude toward self, school, and learning.
- Ensure that student knows where to turn for help; mentor/advocate assists student in securing appropriate resources.
- Ensure ongoing contact to monitor progress toward specific goals.
- Use strategies to propel student forward academically (teach how to learn—resources will be provided).
- Promote self-confidence, greater participation in school community; improve grades/attendance.
- Reduce the number of school dropouts by enhancing student self-esteem and improving school climate.

Implementation of Staff-Student Mentorships

At-risk incoming grade 10 students will be identified prior to school opening and during the first few weeks in September. Criteria for student selection will include prior attendance patterns, grades, how the student applies him/herself in class (including an inability to concentrate or a propensity to disrupt), other factors interfering with performance in school, and a willingness to participate in the program. Each volunteer staff member will be matched with one student. Whenever possible, pairings will be based on gender, background, interests, and personal preferences (e.g., student enrolled in mentor's class).

Volunteer mentors are asked to make regular contact with their student partners (at least once a week for 15 minutes—the time and place to be determined by mentor and student). The meetings should primarily focus on getting to know the student as a person, monitoring academic progress, and providing strategies to help the student move forward academically. For staff who choose to accept this challenge, training and ongoing support will be arranged. An orientation to the program will be conducted in September; three luncheon in-services/support sessions have been planned throughout the year (topics will include suggestions for connecting activities, limits of the relationship, confidentiality, personal problems, successes).

Enter the Mentor

We believe that with your active support and cooperation we can make a difference to improve school climate and to reduce the dropout rate at [name of school]. If you might like to become involved and learn more about the program, there will be a short noon-hour session occurring on [date and place] for all those who are interested. Please complete the attached application form and submit it to [Program Coordinator] before [date].

On behalf of the [name of school] Stay-in-School Steering Committee, I would like to thank you for taking the time to read this proposal and to consider your potential participation. Please feel free to contact any member of the committee [names of committee members] should you have any questions or concerns.

Mentor Application Form

[Name of School] Mentorship Program [20XX/XX]
To: All Professional and Classified Staff
Date: [Date]
From: [Name of Program Coordinator]
Re: Staff Volunteer Mentors

Due to the success of this "stay-in-school initiative" in other secondary school settings, we are preparing to offer a mentoring program to our incoming grade 10 students. Consequently, we are inviting all staff to consider participating in this very worthwhile, rewarding program. Please read and complete the application form below and return to me by [date]. Feel free to see me if you have any questions. Many thanks for your anticipated cooperation.

[Name of High School]

Mentor Volunteer Information Form

Please indicate your preference by checking one of the following responses:
A)   ___   Yes, I would like to become involved as a mentor this year.
B)   ___   Yes, I would like to become involved in one semester only (circle 1 or 2).
C)   ___   No, I don't think I can become involved at this time, thank you.

Name: _____
Department/Positions: _____

If you have selected either option A or B above, please complete the remaining section:
1)   Would you prefer to be matched with a male __ or female __ student? __either?
2)   Would you prefer to be matched with a student in one of your classes? Yes __ No __
3)   Please list any interests or hobbies you have:

_____
_____

Thank you for your assistance. Please return this form to [Program Coordinator] by [date].

Memorandum (Version B)

Student Mentoring Program

To: New Staff [20XX/XX] school year
Date: [20XX/XX]
From: [Name of Program Coordinator]

Over the past year we have implemented a very successful mentoring program (please see attached [year] evaluation summary), and we hope to offer it once again this year. New staff are most welcome to participate in the [20XX/XX] school term. An overview of the program is provided below. Please see [Program Coordinator] if you would like more information. We hope you will consider the benefits of the personal gratification that comes with being involved in this extremely worthwhile program.

Mentorship Program

WHAT: Matching a caring, concerned staff member to a freshman in need of wise counsel and emotional support to foster personal growth and development
WHO:
STUDENTS: selected from incoming grade 10 (based upon grades, attendance, attitude, untapped potential, willingness to participate)
MENTORS: staff volunteers; all personalities and areas of interest, 15 min./wk., orientation sessions and social activities provided

Responsibilities:

- to act as a friend rather than an authority figure
- to provide friendship and motivation to an incoming grade 10 student
- to listen without judging
- to act as a role model and advisory figure
- to be available (initially 10 to 15 minutes a week) to listen
- to encourage and to facilitate learning how to make decisions and how to take responsibility for them
- to be willing to share your thoughts, feelings, experiences, and ideas with your student partner
- to participate in social events with your mentor partner (fall, Christmas, year-end)

Do I Need Special Training?

Your personal qualities are ample "tools" for the job; however, a variety of support materials are also available. In the near future I'll be creating a list of what resources are available. I'll be offering an inservice on how these materials might be used with your student.

How?

Please read and complete the attached application form and return to [Program Coordinator] before [date]. Thank you again for your willingness to consider stepping out of your personal comfort zone to get involved with the mentorship challenge. I'm confident that as well as benefiting the new student, you will also have a rewarding experience.

❧ Appendix C2 ❧

PROGRAM DESCRIPTION

[Name of School] Mentorship Program

Thank you for your interest regarding this exciting new stay-in-school initiative. We are very encouraged by the positive response we have received to date from both classified and professional staff.

Program Benefits

- provides a systematic approach for identifying "at-risk" students and matching them with volunteer staff
- helps ease the transition from junior to senior high; students cope better with high school expectations/pressures
- gives "high-risk" students an opportunity to encounter a positive school-related experience
- improves student attitude toward self and school
- student knows where to turn for help; mentor/advocate assists student in securing appropriate resources
- ensures ongoing contact to monitor progress
- uses strategies to propel student forward academically (teaches how to learn; resources will be provided)
- promotes self-confidence, greater participation in the school community; improves grades/attendance
- reduces the number of school dropouts by enhancing student self-esteem and improving school climate

Implementation

Identifying and Selecting "At-Risk" Students
WHO:
- start with incoming grade 10 students
- meet with all feeder-school counselors in June for potential candidates

- meet with Basic Core and Learning Assistance students at feeder schools to promote program
- discuss this opportunity at individual registrations for IOP (Integrated Occupational Program) students and their parents
- show video *Borderline High* to potential participants
- administer inventory to each student on the combined "at-risk" list
- after scoring inventory, conduct individual interview (Sept.), targeting those with highest scores
- focus of interview centers around rapport building, program description, expectations
- students who indicate a willingness to participate in the program will be selected
- throughout the year take referrals from teachers/administrators/counselors/parents/students

HOW:

- have participants complete general information form to facilitate match of interests/values
- use student-mentor contract to reinforce expectations/level of commitment
- send follow-up letter and consent form to parents/guardians

Matching

- one-to-one ratio (recognizing limited personnel resources)
- match according to interests/gender/background recorded on the application form
- teacher may request a partner in one of his/her classes
- student may state teacher preference (though incoming 10 may not be aware of staff/selection)
- possible contract for both parties of the mentorship relationship
- in dissolution of match (circumstances could change for either member of the pair), consider rematch?

Procedures Following Successful Match

MENTORS:

- conduct a separate orientation/training session early in the fall
- training topics to include brainstorming definition of mentoring; program description/goals; limits of the relationship; problems; confidentiality; generating ideas for connecting activities

- provide print package (includes student application, timetable, mentor/partner list, overview)
- annotated resource list, orientation

BOTH:
- social gathering with refreshments/activities to facilitate rapport building (group photo)

Maintenance
MENTORS:
- provide copies of report cards for each term
- periodic group and individual support sessions to discuss problems, successes, novel ideas, etc.
- provide some release time for mentor to meet with student (student permission slips)
- maintain a student file by recording each meeting time/date/activity
- acknowledge efforts/show appreciation through written feedback, lova-grams, etc.

STUDENTS:
- group counseling for some, individual and group sessions for all
- possible participation in achievement incentive Youth P.R.I.D.E. Program
- goal setting for attendance, issue awards when goals consistently met

BOTH:
- semester/year-end celebration (tangible reward for completing, group photo, symbolic gifts)
- informal and formal evaluation
- community/business sponsorship for tickets to sporting/cultural events
- free products (Crunchie bars) and some monies available for refreshments

Organizational/Structure

Coordinator Responsibilities
- promote program to students and potential mentor volunteers
- identify and interview students; follow-up letters to parents
- gather application forms from mentors/students and arrange appropriate match

- arrange and present workshops for mentors/students/pairs
- prepare supplementary written materials/correspondence and disseminate accordingly
- provide opportunities for ongoing support, feedback from mentors/partners
- ensure regular opportunities for recognition
- liaise with personnel from complementary programs: Engage, Study Buddy, Youth P.R.I.D.E.
- general troubleshooter for mentors and partners
- assist mentor in accessing appropriate school service or community agency when required
- conduct formal and informal evaluation and final report
- maintain publicity (ongoing staff awareness, newsletter, news column, daily bulletin, etc.)
- remain available to allow mentors release time (coordinate substitutes?)

Please feel free to see me if you have any questions or require clarification; I'd be only too happy to respond. If you feel you would like to participate in this program next year, please complete and submit the mentor application form (I have extra copies) to [Program Coordinator] by [date].
THANK YOU!

❧ Appendix C3 ☙

STUDENT SURVEY

Student Survey

Name _____ Date_____
Current School_____
School Next Year_____

Please take a few moments to read each of the following questions; then respond by placing a check in the appropriate box.

Yes   No
☐   ☐   Do you feel it is important to choose classes on the basis of how well they relate to the "real world"?
☐   ☐   Do you like to know how well you did on an assignment/test right away?
☐   ☐   Do you prefer **doing** rather than **reading** about things?
☐   ☐   Do you consider yourself to be a knowledgeable person?
☐   ☐   Would you say that real learning begins when you leave school?
☐   ☐   Did you ever feel like just leaving your books in your locker, walking out, and never coming back?
☐   ☐   Do you sometimes feel powerless to make changes in school?
☐   ☐   Do you think that, for the most part, school is boring?
☐   ☐   Does school sometimes make you feel confused about who you are?
☐   ☐   Do you live in a rural or isolated area?
☐   ☐   Have you ever repeated a grade?
☐   ☐   Do you believe that teachers and their methods could be significantly improved?
☐   ☐   Do you tend to skip class or be absent from school mostly on Fridays and Mondays?
☐   ☐   Do you think of yourself as being of at least average intelligence?
☐   ☐   Do you have relatives or friends who have dropped out of school?

☐   ☐ Have you transferred schools more than three times in the last six years?

☐   ☐ Do you feel you are seldom understood at school and at home?

☐   ☐ Was junior high school your first true experience of disliking school?

☐   ☐ Are teachers generally not interested in your individual progress and welfare?

☐   ☐ Do your parents generally give you minimal support and encouragement?

☐   ☐ Do you wish there were more extracurricular activities at school?

☐   ☐ Do you tend to avoid seeing a counselor or believe counseling services are inadequate?

Thank you for taking the time to complete this questionnaire. We recognize that making the transition from junior high to high school is sometimes difficult. To assist our incoming students with making a successful start to their high school years, we have implemented a mentorship program. You will be given an opportunity to participate in this exciting new program. Please indicate your preference by checking one of the following responses:

_____   Yes, I would like to become involved in this program next year.
_____   I would like to learn more about this program before deciding.
_____   No, I do not wish to become involved at this time, thank you.

We look forward to working with you this fall.

⁊๏ Appendix C4 ᚳᛟ

STUDENT CONTRACT

[Name of School] Mentorship Program

Name: _____ Grade: _____ Date of Birth: _____
Phone: _____ Address: _____

Favorite Subjects:
_____

Career Interests:
_____

What do you like to do with your time?
_____
_____

How would people describe you?
_____

What would you like to get out of this program?
_____
_____

What qualities would you like your mentor to have? _____

Would you prefer to be matched with a male? _____ Female? _____
Subject Teacher? _____(Yes/No)

Mentoring Partner Agreement Contract

I understand that if I am selected as a mentoring partner, I have made a commitment to:

- attend and participate in the initial orientation activity (mid-September)
- meet one-on-one with my mentoring volunteer every week or biweekly
- report to the program coordinator any problems or issues that arise that may be adversely affecting my mentoring relationship
- attend program follow-up meetings, events, and celebrations
- give feedback to the program coordinator that will be used to build a better program

Signed: _____ Date: _____

Witnessed: _____ Date: _____

* A follow-up letter informing your parents about the nature of the program and your involvement will be sent home. They and you are encouraged to contact [the program coordinator] with any questions or concerns.

Thank you for your interest and willingness to become involved.

❧ Appendix C5 ☙

LETTER TO PARENTS

[School Letterhead]

[Date]
[Name of parent]
[Address of parent]

Dear [Parent's name]:

[Name of student] has been given an opportunity to participate in our mentorship program. The purpose of the program is to help ease the often difficult transition from junior to senior high and to increase the success rate from one grade level to the next. In other schools where this program has been offered, student and staff evaluation and feedback have been extremely positive. Improved attendance and student achievement served as additional testimony in support of this initiative.

With the size of our school and everyone's busy lifestyle, it is sometimes difficult for students to know where to look for help or direction. Therefore, one staff volunteer is matched with each student partner. The mentor will be available to answer questions and to help with difficulties when they occur. There will be weekly meetings between the mentor and student to keep the lines of communication open. We are hoping that this initiative will help students to cope better with the pressures of high school and, ultimately, to increase their chance of success.

I have met with your son/daughter to discuss the nature and objective of the program. [Name of student] has expressed an interest in becoming involved. To ensure an appropriate match and to understand the expectations and commitment to the program, each student has completed the attached form. The information garnered from this form enabled us to pair [name of student] with [name of teacher], who is a/an [subject] teacher at [school].

Our initial activity, "Mentor Mingle Pizza Party," occurred during the noon hour on [date]. This event provided an opportunity for the staff mentors and the student partners to meet for the first time.

We are excited about this project and confident that it will benefit many students. Should you have any questions or concerns, please feel free to call me at the school [phone number].

Thank you for your anticipated support.

Your Partner in Education,

[Name and title of program coordinator]

ɜ Appendix C6 ɞ

INVITATION TO
FIRST MEETING WITH STUDENTS

Invitation to "Mentor Mingle" (Version A)
[Name of School] Mentorship Program

TO:
FROM: [Program Coordinator]
DATE:

Thank you for your willingness to participate in the Mentoring Program. I am pleased to announce that a total of [XX] staff members will be involved this year.

I will now begin interviewing the incoming 10s as potential "partners" in the program. To date, I have compiled a master list of potential candidates by merging information from the feeder schools with specific student and parent requests. I have assigned each student to a category and ranked them according to priority. Over the course of the next few days, I will contact each student individually to discuss the program, to reassess their willingness to participate in the program, and to learn about their interests, hobbies, etc.

On the basis of this interview, I will match mentors and students and provide each mentor with a package that will include the following: student information/agreement sheet, student timetable, suggestions for conversation/activities, and an invitation to the "Mentor Mingle Pizza Party." Tentatively, we are looking at having all mentors and partners gather for the initial introductions and pizza party during the noon hour on [date]. Please let me know if you can or cannot attend by completing the survey below and returning the memo to me ASAP. HAVE A GREAT WEEK—YOU DESERVE IT!

_____   YES, I will be available for the luncheon mingle on [date].
_____   NO, it's impossible for me to attend on [date], but [alternate date] is OK.

Invitation to "Mentor Mingle" (Version B)
[Name of School] Mentorship Program

TO: [Mentor's Name]
FROM: [Program Coordinator]
RE: Your Student Partner, _____
DATE:

I have just completed the very enjoyable exercise of meeting with several of our new grade 10 students to discuss the mentorship program. Their response to the invitation to become involved in this project was very positive. Over the course of this past week, I interviewed 19 students with a wide range of interests, personalities, and educational needs. Every student who chose to become involved in the program was asked to complete an application and an agreement contract to facilitate an appropriate match and to ensure commitment to the program (please see the attached personal information on your student partner). If a student is enrolled in a special program, it was recorded above their grade. Two students requested to sign up for Semester 1 only and then to review the need to continue in Semester 2. This request has been noted on their forms. All students have consented to releasing this information to you, including their home phone number, should you need to contact them at home. I have also enclosed a copy of their schedule (for ease in locating them during the school day) and a copy of the letter that will be mailed to their parents/guardians. In addition, within the next few days I will be preparing a master list of all the mentors/student partners and distributing it to all staff. I will also be sending a copy of this master list to our feeder schools, who consented to meet with me before the summer vacation and advance names of the incoming students who could benefit from the program.

Please find enclosed your personal invitation to the Mentor Mingle scheduled for [time, date, place]. The purpose of this gathering is to provide you with an opportunity to meet the student whom you'll read about on the attached pages. Not only will there be ample food (pizza, vegetables, cake, and juice), but we'll also have a few nonthreatening icebreakers and getting-to-know-you activities. Hopefully, the casual, festive atmosphere will put the students (and staff) at ease. This event will enable you and your student partner to discuss the best time and place for future one-on-one meetings. RSVP ASAP to [name], or advise me ASAP if you are unable to attend.

Thank you again for your willingness to step out of your comfort zone to get involved with the mentorship challenge. I'm confident that, as well as benefiting the student, you will also have a rewarding experience. I'm looking forward to our gathering—see you there!

Mentoring Program Description/Responsibilities

I am including within this student information package a summary of the information that will be helpful for mentors. The following is an outline of the mentoring-volunteer job description and details of responsibilities.

The overall goal of the program is to select members of the school staff community who will each serve as a friend and mentor to an "at-risk" youth.

Responsibilities:

- to act as a friend rather than an authority figure
- to provide friendship and motivation to a child or youth
- to listen without judging
- to act as a role model and advisory figure
- to be available to listen (initially to meet 10 to 15 minutes a week; frequency often decreases in the second semester)
- to encourage and to facilitate learning how to make decisions and how to take responsibility for them
- to be willing to share your thoughts, feelings, experiences, and ideas with your student partner

What Do I Do First?

Your first encounter with the student may be uncomfortable for both you and the student. Try to put the student at ease by indicating that you are available to the student for support, advice, or just someone to talk with. Fairly early in the year you should discuss with the student what your relationship will be in order to avoid confusion or unrealistic expectations. The meetings should focus primarily on academic progress, although it is likely that some mention of personal problems will surface. Do not avoid them, but do not dwell on them either (suggest a referral to counseling if one is warranted).

Suggestions for comfortable meeting places: Student Services Library or Conference Room, cafeteria, outdoor stands or picnic table, walk around the grounds—be creative. Your partner may have a preference.

Suggestions for initial discussion topics: how "survived" first two weeks of classes—had any tests or assignments returned, achievement goals for the semester, using the school agenda (potential prizes), perfect-attendance benefits, comparison between junior and senior high, summer vacation, favorite classes, intention to join extracurricular activities in school/community, career goals at this point, possible meeting times and places, specific time and place of next contact, etc.

What If It Doesn't Seem to Be Working Out?

Although I attempt to consider all possible factors before matching a student to a mentor, certain variables are impossible to predict. Therefore, not every mentor/student relationship is going to work out. If you are experiencing some difficulties and no solution is achieved during an open discussion between the two of you, please let me know immediately, and hopefully we can assess the situation and resolve it to everyone's satisfaction.

What About Confidentiality?

Your relationship with your student is based on trust. If something is told to you in confidence, it is important not to repeat it so that the bond of trust remains intact. Please arrange to speak with the appropriate counselor (Gr. 10—[name]; Gr. 11—[name]; Gr. 12—[name]) if your student is involved in something that could be unsafe or illegal.

❧ Appendix C7 ❧

ICEBREAKERS FOR "MENTOR MINGLE"

Matching Game

Mentors and students "discover" the partner they've been assigned to by finding the person with the word that pairs with their word.

Word Pairs

1. Ham   Eggs
2. Romeo   Juliet
3. Jack   Jill
4. Salt   Pepper
5. Batman   Robin
6. Ice cream   Cake
7. Ken   Barbie
8. Toast   Jam
9. Black   White
10. Day   Night
11. Fish   Chips
12. Boys   Girls
13. Dogs   Cats
14. Hot   Cold

Mentor Mingle
Be Aware Bingo

Can you or your partner answer YES?

Does your birthday fall on a month ending in an "r"?	Can you play a musical instrument?	Are you wearing something with a pattern on it?	Can you hold your breath for 90 seconds?	Were you born in a place outside of Canada?	Do you know the names of 3 or more people here?	Is the letter "s" in your name?
Do you like working with computers?	Do you own a bicycle?	Do you get daily exercise?	Do you mind getting blood tests?	Do you have more than 3 brothers/sisters?	Are you able to speak another language?	Do you like broccoli?
Are you wearing blue jeans today?	Do you like eating eggs?	Do you sing in the shower?	Do you live outside of [name of town]?	Have you ever run a race and won?	Are you a [name of sports team] fan?	Do you own a CD player?
Did you walk to school today?	Can you skate?	Are you taller than 5'6"?	Do you own a pet?	Did you eat a piece of cake?	Have you ever attended a soccer game?	Did you eat breakfast today?
Have you ever ridden a ski-doo?	Are you a [school sports team] fan?	Do you own a pair of skis?	Did you bring a pencil with you?	Have you read 2 or more books this summer?	Do you read comic books?	Have you written a letter this week?
Can you pat your head and rub your belly at the same time?	Do you have a first and second name that begins with a vowel?	Do you have naturally curly hair?	Did you eat 3 or more pieces of pizza?	Can you name 3 [name of sports team] players?	Can you yodel?	Are you 15 years old or younger?
Do you wear hats?	Are you wearing a watch?	Do you wear glasses or contact lenses?	Can you stand on 1 foot for more than 2 minutes?	Do you own a pair of boxer shorts?	Do you enjoy country music?	Have you decided where and when you will meet next time?

Appendix C8

COMMUNICATION TO STAFF
ABOUT MENTOR PAIRS

[Name of School]
MEMORANDUM

TO: All Staff
FROM: [Program Coordinator]
DATE:
RE: The Mentorship Program
         Student/Staff Partners

In light of everyone's prior responsibilities, I have been amazed by staff response to this initiative. Please refer to the master student/mentor list copied on the reverse side of this memo. In addition, the following staff members have indicated their willingness to "adopt a student" in Semester 2:
    [names of staff members]
    Therefore, throughout this semester, please forward names of any other students that you feel could benefit from this program.
    Letters explaining the purpose and nature of this program have been mailed home to the parents or guardians of each student partner. We have launched this year's program with a fun-filled noon hour "Mentor Mingle Pizza Party," which provided an opportunity for the staff mentor and student partner to meet for the first time.
    Throughout Semester 1 each pair will meet, usually for 10 to 15 minutes, at a mutually convenient time and place. In most instances these sessions will occur outside of class time; however, there may be occasions when a mentor will request permission from you to see the student during class time. Your anticipated cooperation is greatly appreciated to ensure continued success of this worthwhile program. As the mentors will be tracking and encouraging student progress, please don't hesitate to inform them of successes and/or attendance/effort/achievement concerns.

Many thanks to all staff, for each and every one has a vital role in ensuring the continued success of the mentorship program.

[Program Coordinator]

Appendix C9

MENTOR EVALUATION FORM

[Name of School]
Mentorship Program Evaluation: Staff

I am inviting all staff mentors to please take a few moments to complete this questionnaire. Your valuable feedback will assist me in planning for improvement in next year's offering.

1. How often have you met with your student partner each semester? (It is expected that contact gradually declined in Semester 2.) Please circle.

<table>
<tr><td><u>Semester 1</u></td><td><u>Semester 2</u></td></tr>
<tr><td>a) rarely</td><td>a) rarely</td></tr>
<tr><td>b) once in a while (once a month)</td><td>b) once in a while (once a month)</td></tr>
<tr><td>c) regularly (once a week)</td><td>c) regularly (once a week)</td></tr>
</table>

2. If contact (especially in Semester 1) was limited, what reason(s) do you feel contributed to difficulty in meeting?

_____

_____

3. Please indicate which support materials were helpful by checking the appropriate space with comments.

<table>
<tr><td></td><td></td><td colspan="2"><u>Helpful</u></td><td></td></tr>
<tr><td></td><td></td><td><u>Yes</u></td><td><u>No</u></td><td><u>Comments</u></td></tr>
<tr><td>a)</td><td>mentor program description</td><td>____</td><td>____</td><td></td></tr>
<tr><td>b)</td><td>student information/contract</td><td>____</td><td>____</td><td></td></tr>
<tr><td>c)</td><td>mentor/student pairing list</td><td>____</td><td>____</td><td></td></tr>
<tr><td>d)</td><td>study skills package</td><td>____</td><td>____</td><td></td></tr>
<tr><td>e)</td><td>goal setting/marks record form</td><td>____</td><td>____</td><td></td></tr>
</table>

f) Progress Report Form   ____ ____
g) report cards   ____ ____
h) magazines related to working with youth ____ ____
i) Hire-a-Student information   ____ ____

4. Please indicate which activities you found to be useful.

   a) Mentor Mingle Pizza Party (Sept.)   ____ ____
   b) Christmas Gathering (Dec.)   ____ ____
   c) Mentor Mingle Windup (June)   ____ ____
   d) Treat packages (Thanksgiving,   ____ ____
      Valentine's, Easter)   ____ ____
5. Do you have any suggestions for change in selection/matching/organiza-
   tion?

   _____

   _____

6. Do you have any ideas for improvement?

   _____

   _____

7. Would you consider becoming a mentor once again next year with a new
   student? (Circle, please)   Yes   No

   Comment

   _____

Name (Optional): _____
Thank you for taking the time to complete this form. Please submit to [Pro-
gram Coordinator] by [date]. I will include these results with other data and
prepare an evaluation summary to distribute to all staff by next [day].

❧ Appendix C10 ❧

STUDENT EVALUATION FORM

[Name of School]
Mentorship Evaluation: Student

Please take a few moments to complete this questionnaire.

1. How often have you talked with your teacher/mentor this year? (circle)
   a) rarely
   b) once in a while (once a month)
   c) regularly (once a week)

2. If you circled (a), why do you think you didn't talk very often?
   _____
   _____

3. If you had any problems, would you go to talk with your mentor?
   Yes _____   No _____
   If no, why not?
   _____

4. Did you have any problems this year?
   Yes _____   No _____

5. Did your mentor help you with any of these problems?
   Yes _____   No _____

6. If you could choose your mentor, would it be (please check):
   _____ a teacher
   _____ a senior student

7. If you were given a choice to have a mentor again, would you want one? Please explain why or why not?

_____

_____

_____

_____

8. General comments:

_____

_____

_____

_____

Thank you for taking the time to complete this questionnaire.

Name:

Date:

❧ Appendix C11 ❧

SUPPORT MATERIALS FOR MENTORS

THE ABC's OF EFFICIENT STUDYING

A. HOW SHALL I PREPARE?

1. Have you got the right attitude? Without this, you're sunk!
Confidence: Studying is work; anybody can work; you can work!
Concentration: Nobody—not even you—can combine study, rest, and relaxation.
Habit: There was a time when tying shoelaces was a tough job; now you just do it. Habits help with homework and especially with studying.
Purpose: Set a goal for marks or time on task or "ways to make it easier" or ways to make it more understandable or enjoyable.

2. Have you set out a regular time and enough time? The amount you will need will depend on your grades, your grade level, how efficiently you study, etc.

3. Do you have a good place to study/do homework? Is this place relatively quiet, free from distractions, with good lighting and reasonable comfort?

4. Are you organized before you start? All equipment is there? Textbooks? Dictionary? Cold water?...

B. WHAT SHALL I STUDY?

1. Work on the day's assignments first.

2. Leave at least half an hour each evening for systematic review/study.

3. Go quickly over the new material for the day.

4. Have a plan by which you go over large sections of work previously taken.

5. Some general "rules":

- Plan your time for each subject before you start.
- Do your hardest work first. (But see rule below.)
- Don't spend too much time on one thing. When you slow down, switch to another item.
- Put most of your effort into the subjects or ideas that are giving you some trouble.

C. HOW SHALL I STUDY?

1. Always work your fastest; this improves understanding, limits day-dreaming, and, of course, gets more done.

2. Underline key statements; numbering points or making extra marginal notes in your notebook helps understanding, memory, and review.

3. Many people find that results are best when they use a notebook to jot down key ideas and questions as they read.

4. Read with flexibility. Reading a story, a social studies text, or a mathematics problem at the same slow speed puts understanding in a "strait-jacket" and wastes time.

5. If you have to memorize something, use several short periods of study spaced apart instead of one long period of time.

STUDY AND ORGANIZATION SKILLS (SOS)
GOAL SETTING

Name _____   Date _____

	Subject	1st RC Mark	2nd RC Goal Mark	Final RC Goal Mark
1.				
2.				
3.				
4.				
5.				
6.				

Directions:

List all of the subjects that you are taking this semester. Record the mark for each from the first reporting period. Think about the mark you will work to achieve in the next reporting period and place it under the "goal" column.

List four things you could do to ensure that you will meet your goals:

1. _____

2. _____

3. _____

4. _____

Record your actual mark for Term 2, and set a goal for the final.

GOOD LUCK WITH YOUR PLAN!

WATCH YOUR MARKS IMPROVE

❧ References ☙

Adler, A. (1939). *Social interest: A challenge to mankind.* New York: Putnam.

Alberta Teachers' Association. (1999). *Volunteer mentorship programs* (Video Program). Edmonton: Alberta Teachers' Association. (Website for ATA's Safe and Caring Schools Project: http://www.teachers.ab.ca./projects/safe.html)

Alexander, K. L., & Entwistle, D. R. (1988). Achievement in the first two years of school: Patterns and processes. *Monographs of the Society for Research in Child Development, 53*(20, serial No. 218).

Bandura, A. (1977). *Social learning theory.* Englewood Cliffs, NJ: Prentice Hall.

Barr, R. D., & Parrett, W. H. (1995). *Hope at last for at-risk youth.* Toronto, ON: Allyn and Bacon.

Benson, P. L. (1997). *All kids are our kids: What communities must do to raise caring and responsible children and adolescents.* San Francisco: Jossey-Bass.

Bettelheim, B. (1994). Seeking a rightful place. *The NAMTA Journal, 19*(2), 101–118.

Big Brothers, Big Sisters of Canada. (1995). *The in-school mentoring program.* Burlington, ON: BBBS.

Blum, D. J., & Jones, L. A. (1993). Academic growth group and mentoring program for potential dropouts. *The School Counselor, 40*(3), 207–217.

Bowlby, J. (1973). *Separation: Anxiety and anger.* New York: Basic Books.

Brandt, R. (1992–1993). Overview: Yes, children are still at risk. *Educational Leadership, 50*(4), 3.

Brendtro, L., Brokenleg, M., & Van Bockern, S. (1990). *Reclaiming youth at risk: Our hope for the future.* Bloomington, IN: National Education Service.

Brendtro, L., & Long, N. (1995). Breaking the cycle of conflict. *Educational Leadership, 52*(5), 52–56.

Brodkin, A. M., & Coleman, M. (1996). He's trouble with a capital T. *Instructor,* 105(7), 18–21.

Brokenleg, M. (1998). Native wisdom on belonging. *Reclaiming Children and Youth, 7*(3), Fall, 130–132.

Brown, R. S. (1995). *Mentoring at-risk students: Challenges and potential,* No. 217. Toronto, ON: Toronto Board of Education. (ERIC Document Reproduction Service No. ED 391 138)

Brown, R. S. (1996). Challenges and potential of mentoring at-risk students: A literature review. *ERS Spectrum, 14*(2), 17–28.

Cameron, L., & Karsemeyer, J. (1998, June). Language play partners: An interventionist strategy in a multilingual kindergarten. Paper presented at the Canadian Society for Studies in Education, Ottawa.

Ellis, J., Hart, S., & Small-McGinley, J. (1998). "Difficult" students' perspectives on belonging and inclusion in the classroom. *Reclaiming Children and Youth: Journal of Emotional and Behavioral Problems, 7*(3), 142–146.

Ellis, J., & Small-McGinley, J. (1999). *Volunteer mentorship programs: A practical handbook.* Edmonton: Alberta Teachers' Association. (Website for ATA's Safe and Caring Schools Project: http://www.teachers.ab.ca/projects/safe.html)

Flaxman, E., & Ascher, C. (1992). *Mentoring in action: The efforts of programs in New York City.* New York: Inst. for Urban and Minority Education, Columbia Univ. (ERIC Document Reproduction Service No. ED 354 291)

Ford, D. H., & Ford, M. E. (1987). *Humans as self-constructing living systems.* Hillsdale, NJ: Erlbaum.

Franklin, U. M. (1990). *The real world of technology (Rev. ed.).* Toronto, ON: House of Anansi Press.

Fromm, E. (1956). *The art of loving.* Toronto, ON: Bantam Books.

Glasser, W. (1986). *Control theory in the classroom.* New York: Harper & Row.

Green, J. A. (1913). *The life and work of Pestalozzi.* London: University Tutorial Press.

Kelly, F. J., Veldman, D. J., & McGuire, C. (1964). Multiple discriminant prediction of delinquency and school dropouts. *Educational and Psychological Measurement, 24*, 535–544.

Kennedy, M. M., Birman, B. F., & Demaline, R. (1986). *The effectiveness of Chapter 1 services.* Washington, DC: U.S. Department of Education.

Lee, J., & Cramond, B. (1999). The positive effects of mentoring economically disadvantaged students. *Professional School Counseling, 2*(3), 172–178.

Lefkowitz, B. (1986). *Tough change: Growing up on your own in America.* New York: Free Press.

Lloyd, D. N. (1978). Prediction of school failure from third-grade data. *Educational and Psychological Measurement, 38*, 1193–1200.

MacIntyre, A. (1981). *After virtue: A study in moral theory.* South Bend, IN: University of Notre Dame Press.

Maslow, A. (1971). *The further reaches of human nature.* New York: Viking.

Mighty Motion Pictures. (1997). *Listen Up! Kids talk about good teaching* (Videotape). Calgary, AB: Mighty Motion Pictures. Telephone: 800–471–5628. Fax: 780–439–4051.

Pianta, R. C., & Walsh, D. J. (1996). *High-risk children in school: Constructing sustaining relationships.* New York: Routledge.

Rodriguez, P. (1996). *Someone to talk to: Peer helping in high school* (Videotape). Montreal: National Film Board of Canada.

Slavin, R. E. (1994). Preventing early school failure: The challenge and the opportunity. In R. E Slavin, N. L. Karweit, and B. A. Wasik (Eds.), *Preventing early school failure: Research, policy and practice* (pp. 1–12). Toronto, ON: Allyn and Bacon.

Slavin, R. E., Karweit, N. L., & Wasik, B. A. (1992–93). Preventing early school failure: What works? *Educational Leadership, 50*(4), 10–18.

Slicker, E. K., & Palmer, D. J. (1993). Mentoring at-risk high school students: Evaluation of a school-based program. *The School Counselor, 40*(5), 327–334.

Smink, J. (1990). *Mentoring programs for at-risk youth: A dropout prevention research report.* Clemson, SC: National Dropout Prevention Center. (ERIC Document Reproduction Service No. ED 318 931)

Smith, D. G. (1996). Curriculum theory course outline. Lethbridge, AB: University of Lethbridge.

Staudt, D. (1995). *A school-university partnership that is making a difference.* Paper presented at the Texas University/School Research Collaborative, College Station, TX. (ERIC Document Reproduction Service No. ED 395 083)

Tully, F. G., & Brendtro, L. K. (1998). Reaching angry and unattached kids. *Reclaiming Children and Youth, 7*(3), 147–154.

Walter, K. (1995). *Excellent beginnings: An early childhood initiative.* Mount Kisco, NY: Plan for Social Excellence. (ERIC Document Reproduction Service No. ED 394 641)

Wasik, B., & Slavin, R. E. (1993). Preventing early reading failure with one-to-one tutoring: A review of five programs. *Reading Research Quarterly, 28*(2), 178–200.

Werner, E., & Smith, R. (1989). *Vulnerable but invincible: A longitudinal study of resilient children and youth.* New York: Adams, Bannister and Cox.

Yamamoto, K. (1988). To see life grow: The meaning of mentorship. *Theory into Practice, 27*(3), 183–189.

Studies in the Postmodern Theory of Education

General Editors
Joe L. Kincheloe & Shirley R. Steinberg

Counterpoints publishes the most compelling and imaginative books being written in education today. Grounded on the theoretical advances in criticalism, feminism, and postmodernism in the last two decades of the twentieth century, Counterpoints engages the meaning of these innovations in various forms of educational expression. Committed to the proposition that theoretical literature should be accessible to a variety of audiences, the series insists that its authors avoid esoteric and jargonistic languages that transform educational scholarship into an elite discourse for the initiated. Scholarly work matters only to the degree it affects consciousness and practice at multiple sites. Counterpoints' editorial policy is based on these principles and the ability of scholars to break new ground, to open new conversations, to go where educators have never gone before.

For additional information about this series or for the submission of manuscripts, please contact:

Joe L. Kincheloe & Shirley R. Steinberg
c/o Peter Lang Publishing, Inc.
275 Seventh Avenue, 28th floor
New York, New York 10001

To order other books in this series, please contact our Customer Service Department:

(800) 770-LANG (within the U.S.)
(212) 647-7706 (outside the U.S.)
(212) 647-7707 FAX

Or browse online by series:

www.peterlangusa.com